Lady Byron & her Daughters

Lady Byron & her Daughters

Julia Markus

W. W. NORTON & COMPANY

Independent Publishers Since 1923

NEW YORK · LONDON

For information about permission to reproduce selections from this book,
write to Permissions, W. W. Norton & Company, Inc.,
500 Fifth Avenue, New York, NY 10110

For information about special discounts for bulk purchases, please contact
W. W. Norton Special Sales at specialsales@wwnorton.com or 800-233-4830

Manufacturing by RR Donnelley Harrisonburg
Book design by Fearn Cutler de Vicq
Production manager: Devon Zahn

ISBN: 978-0-393-08268-5

W. W. Norton & Company, Inc.
500 Fifth Avenue, New York, N.Y. 10110
www.wwnorton.com

W. W. Norton & Company Ltd.
Castle House, 75/76 Wells Street, London W1T 3QT

1 2 3 4 5 6 7 8 9 0

To all those women,
young or old, rich or poor,
who know what it takes
to make a new life for themselves.

CONTENTS

Contents

FOREWORD

❧⁓☙

Anne Isabella Milbanke, always called Annabella, came to London in 1812 at the age of nineteen for the social season. An extremely pretty girl of high intellect, who would one day be an heiress, she had a swarm of suitors attending her. In that same year, twenty-four-year-old Lord Byron woke up to find himself famous, having just published his book-length poem *Childe Harold's Pilgrimage*. Overnight he became the toast of Regency society, sought after by everyone who was anyone in London. Annabella, a poet in a minor key, wrote "Byronmania," satirizing the women, including her cousin Caroline Lamb, who "aped" Byron, hoping to attract his attention at the London waltz they all attended. That was where Annabella first saw the handsome, dark, mysterious poet, whose sneering upper lip and lameness did nothing to diminish his celebrity.

Annabella was from the north country. She was actually more highborn than Byron, as he would later brag, and intellectually she was his equal. This "princess of parallelograms" as Byron called her lovingly during his courtship and snidely in his poetry after she would not return to his control, was a gifted mathematician. She believed that science gave humanity the tools for coming as close to the secrets of creation as possible. She was educated at home at Seaham by tutors from Cambridge, studied Euclid in the original, was a linguist devoted to literature, and was the only child of parents who adored her. From her earliest years, learning from her aristocratic parents' concern for their tenants and from their liberal politics, she had a desire to do good in the world—to live somehow for the service of others.

Her idealism was not uncommon among girls of high intelligence who had to be educated at home and knew of life mainly through books. The vicissitudes of life knocked that idealism out of Jane Welsh Carlyle, but not out of Annabella. In fact, the more life hit her in the face, the more she was "saved" as she wrote, through helping others.

Two years after having refused him, Annabella married Lord Byron. For all her earlier protestations, she was madly in love. She had no idea her aunt, Lady Melbourne, and Byron's half sister Augusta Leigh had prodded him into this marriage. His incestuous love of half sister Augusta was causing society to whisper, particularly after the birth of their child Medora. Freewheeling Regency high society had only one rule: Do what ever you wish—discreetly. However, incest was considered monstrous. The disclosure that Augusta and Byron had a child together would cast them both beyond the pale, and in the case of married Augusta, she and her children would be ruined.

From the moment Annabella entered the carriage that was to take the couple off to their honeymoon, the cruelty of Byron's verbal abuse was such that Annabella thought her new husband must be testing her love or was mentally unhinged. She thought he loved her? he chided. He'd show her. In Part One of this biography he certainly does. After a year, Annabella left their London home with their newly born daughter as Lord Byron had instructed her to do in writing.

The cycle and spiraling of marital abuse is something we understand two centuries after Byron's cruelty forced Annabella and her three-week-old daughter from the house of the man she loved. What is less understood today is a second focus of the first part of this biography: The legal difficulties a woman had, even of Annabella's class, in gaining a Decree of Separation from an abusive husband. Married women had essentially no legal rights—to their own money, to their own bodies, to their children. A child's "body" belonged to the father.

Enter Dr. Stephen Lushington, one of the important legal minds of the time, another devout liberal who would become a lifelong friend of Annabella. The image of a cold and unforgiving wife that Byron portrayed in his later poetry and his followers and later critics took to heart stem from the protocol this young woman had to follow in order not to be forced to return to her husband. After telling her to leave, Byron wanted her back under his control. She still loved him, but she refused to be his "victim." She had too strong a sense of self, and knew, as she put it, he had hurt her too much to forgive her. She feared for her child; she feared for her life.

Annabella learned a lot about the law in the first months of 1816. Still, with all the expert legal advice she received, it was only the clever way Lushington held his cards aided by a last minute stroke of luck that saved her from Byron's control.

LADY BYRON's life after love has never been fairly explored. In the second part of this biography, such an exploration is attempted. Hardly anyone is aware that after she separated, Lady Byron in her twenties founded the first Infant School in England and in her forties the first Co-Operative School, thus bringing progressive educational ideas from Switzerland and Scotland to her own shores for the benefit of the working poor. She was also an early advocate of the allotment system, and at her schools the children of workers were not only educated, but assigned plots on which to grow healthy produce for home use or for selling back to the school for its use. What's now being attempted in the White House garden and the roofs of Brooklyn, Lady Byron popularized in England in the early nineteenth century.

Harriet Beecher Stowe wrote that Lady Byron had with her silent philanthropy done more for England than any other one person of her time. The good she did, however, lies interred under the barrage of Lord Byron's brilliant poetic spite and later critics' overwhelming devotion to male genius. Particularly in the late twentieth century, for many, the poet was the only god who hadn't yet failed. The male poet, that is, though one wished one didn't have to emphasize the obvious.

The feminist defense of Lady Byron is left to Harriet Beecher Stowe in the third part of the biography.

FOR ALL THE GOOD Lady Byron did for the working poor and for agricultural reform in England, she was not a modern woman finding fulfillment outside her home (or in her case outside of her estates). She was a child of the Regency, and her lasting regret was that she had been torn from her proper role of being Lord Byron's "Wife." She knew her husband did not love her once they were married and he ruthlessly pulled the scales from her eyes, but through the marriage and through her life she believed herself to be Lord Byron's "best friend." Later in her life, she believed that if one person less had been in the world—his sister Augusta Leigh whom she both loved and hated—the marriage would have lasted come what may.

The French have a saying that a woman is either a lover or a mother. The first years after the separation, Lady Byron's infant daughter could not compensate Annabella for her loss of love. Annabella at twenty-four was an imperfect single mother and she knew it. Lord Byron, on the other hand, was a perfect father. As soon as he boarded the ship to leave England in the spring of 1816, he began to write of his enduring love for the infant he abandoned and once called his "instrument of torture."

Educating Ada and leading her gifted and rebellious daughter toward a happy marriage gradually became the central focus of Lady Byron's life. Ada had inherited her mother's mathematical acumen as well as her absent father's imagination and instability. As Ada, Countess of Lovelace, she would write the first computer program in the 1840s, more than a century before the computer as we know it existed. It is only now, in the twenty-first century, that Ada is receiving wide recognition for her accomplishments. Her mathematical genius has recently spread a wide net, and Ada Lovelace Day has become a day of recognition for all women of science and intellectual accomplishment. It is a joyful day, though hers was a short and complex life.

So many myths, so much "steam punk" literature, has risen around Ada. No longer is she defined by one line of her absent father's poetry: "ADA! Sole daughter of my house and heart." Still, no recognition is given to the fact that she was raised by a complex and brilliant single mother whose mathematical prowess was similar to her own. It was as if Ada had sprung full blown from the brow of Zeus—something Ada, being Ada, might not have minded. However, she needed her mother in so many ways, and the relationship between mother and daughter twists and turns through the years, ending in bittersweet recognition and moving reconciliation, as we shall see.

However, common misconceptions remain. One of them is that Lady Byron kept her child from knowledge of her father and his poetry, and another is that Ada led an exemplary, if tragically short life, devoted to scientific and mathematical study. In truth, Ada, encouraged by con men, would turn her prodigious talents toward gambling and programming the outcomes of horse races—to predictable results.

A daughter who most certainly did not lead an exemplary life was Medora Leigh, the child of Lord Byron and his half sister Augusta Leigh. Medora was less than a year old when Lady Byron married Lord Byron, and at first Lady Byron believed her husband was attempting to upset her as usual when he said Medora was his child by his sister. This did not stop Lady Byron from loving the beautiful, intelligent infant, and years later it would be Lady Byron, not mother Augusta Leigh, who saved Medora from certain death and then lived with her for a season in Paris before returning to England with her. The love Lady Byron felt for her husband's child brought back emotions long suppressed, and she was the first to admit Medora's resemblance to Lord Byron was part of the reason she considered Medora her adopted child. At the same time, the dramatic love-hate relationship between Lady Byron and sister-in-law Augusta flared yet again. It runs like a live wire through these pages.

Ada had always regretted not having a sibling, and when Lady Byron informed her adult daughter that she had a half sister, Ada was delighted. She met Medora in Paris the Easter of 1841 and was close to her for most of the time that Medora spent under Lady Byron's protection in England.

Lady Byron's relationship with her two daughters plays a large role in her life and in this biography, as does her relationship with her grandchildren. Ada had little time or patience for her three children in the years in which she studied mathematics. "I wished for heirs, never wanted a child," she complained memorably to her mother. It was Lady Byron who suggested her first grandson should be named Byron. She raised her second grandson, Ralph, and all but raised her granddaughter, the later explorer of the Middle East and saver of the Arabian steed, Lady Anne Blunt. Ada's growing recognition of her motherhood will correspond with Lady Byron's during the wrenching months of Ada's tragic illness.

Others played central—and dramatic—parts in Lady Byron's life: her once-adored son-in-law the Earl of Lovelace; the first art historian and esteemed travel writer, Anna Jameson; playwright Joanna Baillie; Sir Walter Scott; the eccentric and creative thinker Charles Babbage, whose ideas for an Analytical Engine predated the computer; Lady Byron's first cousin Lord Melbourne, whose wife Caroline Lamb once had a mad affair with bad Byron; the young Queen Victoria who relied on Lord Melbourne as her Prime Minister; the charismatic young minister and champion of the working man, Robertson of Brighton, who became Annabella's second Byron; the freed slaves Ellen and William Craft; and Harriet Beecher Stowe—to skim some of the cream from the cream. Lady Byron's intelligence, her calm articulation, her liberal views, encompassing knowledge of her times and her incredible psychological understanding of others—not of herself—were evident to all who came to know her.

I have attempted a biography of a misunderstood yet difficult woman of genius whose main failing was her inability to delve into the darkness in her own nature, though she could understand and condone the darkness in others. She wasn't the angel her large circle of devoted friends considered her. Nor was she the demented and dull-witted demon that her twentieth-century critics and biographers painted. She was a flawed human being, albeit an exceptional one. The third act of my biography portrays her in her later years, when the grandchildren she loved surrounded her and Harriet Beecher Stowe entered her life—to explosive results.

In her last decade, Lady Byron brought together all her papers in order to attempt a memoir of her marriage. She hoped to offer a fair and balanced account that could be read by her adult grandchildren after she was gone. Robertson of Brighton, her dearest friend in those years, urged her not to "repress" her emotions. He helped her to order her papers and he recorded their "Conversations." It was he who would witness her dramatic and final meeting with sister-in-law Augusta Leigh when both of them were old and Augusta next to death. Robertson, more than a score of years Lady Byron's junior, would have been her perfect collaborator, but once more fate intervened—and all her papers were returned to her.

After her death, grandson Ralph, whom she raised, would spend decades attempting to redeem Lady Byron's archives from the resisting hands of ancient executors. Ralph's friend, author Henry James, witnessed Ralph's struggles and reshaped them into his masterpiece of a novella, *The Aspen Papers* (1888). When Ralph gained control of all Lady Byron's papers in the 1890s, he grappled with whether or not to suppress the evidence that his grandfather Lord Byron had an incestuous relationship with his sister. It took him until 1905 to decide not to censure, but to print truthfully what he hoped would be a privately circulated biography of his grandparents' ill-fated marriage, *Astarte*.

Among the papers Ralph preserved were the many "Statements" Lady Byron wrote but never succeeded in turning into a memoir. In the one Ralph found most poignant, Lady Byron wrote that she had long realized that at least some of the animus directed toward her came from the fact she never defended herself in public against Lord Byron's brilliant and bitter accounts of her in his later poetry, nor from the critics who continued to degrade her in print. Still: "I have no cause to complain of the world's unkindness; on the contrary, I am grateful to it.

In personal intercourse I have *only* to acknowledge the kindest and most generous treatment, and if I have sometimes been condemned by strangers without evidence, I have certainly been acquitted equally without proof by those on whom I had no claim, of the charges of listening to informers against Lord Byron, sanctioning treacherous practices, etc. There can be no *media via* to such accusations. The woman who could be guilty of any one of them could not be trust-worthy witness in matters relating to the husband she had injured and betrayed. Read then no further, you who hold this sheet in your hands, unless you can relinquish all prepossessions of that kind. Think of me, as Memory, not as a Person, for I desired not sympathy but an impartial hearing.

When I look at the accumulation of difficulties in my way, I feel that the truths I may bring forward will but partially dispel illusions, so long accepted as realities, and that even if not as fruitless, it is yet an ungrateful task to translate fascinating verse into bare fact. Apart, however, from any view to benefit the unknown Reader, who may have little disposition to attend to me, I naturally desire to leave a few counter statements for the information of my grandchildren, for I own that on that point the opinion formed of me does touch me.

Think of me as a memory not a person . . . it is an ungrateful task to translate fascinating verse into bare fact. . . . Usually it is in her poetry—and she wrote poetry all her life—that she touches on her emotions, at times brings personal darkness to light. In this "Statement," she came close to the heart of the matter.

Of the loves Lady Byron found and lost in her later life, all had some relationship to Lord Byron, as we shall see. She was, as the song says, a one-man woman whose man got away. A brilliant woman who did much for those she loved and for England itself, she had happiness as well as tragedy in her later life, though not unlike that other genius, her husband, she often got in her own way.

After the death of her own mother and the early death of Lord Byron, Lady Byron had something that very few women, if any, had in her day: Enormous wealth under her own control. It gave her, in her own words, more ways of doing good for others. That's what she did through her liberality and her liberal views all her life—she helped others. She remained conscious of the fact that she received more than she gave, and that, as she wrote, the poor saved her from herself. I have tried not to save Lady Byron from herself. I think of this biography published two hundred years after that fateful marriage and two hundred years after the birth of Ada, Countess of Lovelace, as the celebration of a worthy but complex woman who led a big life that is still unsung. My hope is that her story will resonate today.

November 19, 2014
New York City

O World I have known Thee! And ere my farewell
Of thy scorn and thy kindness I frankly would tell.
Thou cans't not forget me: embalmed by *a Name*
I must live in the record of honour or blame.

Lady Byron, *On My Sixtieth Year*

Part One

ON HER OWN

*I*t was quite a row she had with her mother and, like many a dutiful daughter, she regretted it the next day. Still, she did not want to stay at the family home at Seaham in County Durham for the social season. She was nineteen, months short of twenty, and loved her London, no matter that two years before, she made disparaging remarks about her own "coming out" there.

Anne Isabella Milbanke, always called Annabella, was born on May 17, 1792, to middle-aged parents who had long since given up hopes of having a child. Judith thought she was going through menopause at first, but she was still months shy of forty and in good health. As her old aunt Mary Noel told her, the common notion about change of life was that it began thirty years after the first period "and I think you were sixteen at least when it began." Old Aunt Mary had been a mother to Judith and knew she was pregnant before Judith did. Judith's brother, Lord Wentworth, was pleased as well when pregnancy was confirmed, for now he would have a *legitimate* heir and couldn't help wishing, truth be told, for a boy. Still, when Annabella was born, he celebrated with Annabella's good-looking and good-natured father, Sir Ralph, and his favorite and oldest sister, Judith. Lord Wentworth was going to have women, first Judith, then his niece Annabella, as heirs. Women could inherit in his line. Better than nothing—much.

Annabella's parents were unusual for the times. They were fashionable people, belonged to the ruling class, yet theirs was a love match and neither took lovers—hardly the rule in the eighteenth century or during the Regency that followed. They hobnobbed with royalty. Annabella's first name, Anne, was that of her royal godmother, the Duchess of Cumberland. They went to balls, gave dinners, and spent every season in London at their home at Portland Place, as Sir Ralph became a Member of Parliament two years before Annabella's birth and remained such for twenty-two years, right up to 1812, the winter of the row.

Annabella's parents were unusual as well for raising their own daughter. Not that there wasn't help, and from an early age Mrs. Clermont was always there, even sleeping in Annabella's room on the scant occasions when Judith had to be away from home. Judith appreciated the fashionable life she had led, the grand tours, the spas, the balls, the London seasons, the *ton*. But once she had a child, she no longer traveled to London with Ralph when Parliament was in session. In her forties she simply preferred being with her child. Annabella, she wrote, grew more precious, precocious, and amusing every day. And their comfortable home in Seaham was by the sea, which both mother and daughter loved—and who could doubt the benefits of sea air? Annabella grew healthy, balanced, strong. Her first ballet master couldn't get over her immediate grace, drive, ability to learn. Such a report pleased the mother. There was truth to it as well.

When Ralph and Judith traveled together, they also brought the child and, in those early years, only accepted invitations to homes at which young children were welcome. This was so unusual that it must have sent some tongues wagging. There was probably no such phrase in the late eighteenth century, but the Milbankes were a tight-knit family.

By the time Annabella was six, she was old enough to be brought to London for the Parliamentary season. London was love at first sight for Annabella, just as the sea had been when she was an infant. A few years later her father set up an allowance for her of 20 pounds a year, to be delivered quarterly by a Mr. Taylor, and for which the child would fill in a receipt. She would save almost all to spend when she was in London. Though Seaham would always be the home of her heart, it wasn't London. And particularly in 1812, when she was a young woman close to twenty, with friends galore in town, she didn't want to spend the season in the north country with the old folk.

The circumstances were these. Her father Sir Ralph, whom she adored, was not well and was about to give up his parliamentary seat. A Whig, and of the most progressive part of that party, he had backbenched it through his whole career. As much as his daughter loved him, she knew he was not meant for the world. In his sixties, he was ruddy-faced and good-natured, given to tell (repeat) a story, help a neighbor, drink and eat too much. He had a poetic streak, and he and Annabella teased each other, told jokes, especially when they both were a bit tipsy. There was something grandfatherly in his love.

He was all for his neighbors in Durham, the region he represented. Soon, in retirement, he would work on improving sanitary conditions there. They loved him in Durham. But in the wider world of affairs, he was considered genial and ineffectual. Annabella herself described him as an Uncle Toby, but with many more qualities and depth. In 1812 he wasn't well at all, most probably an acting-up of his gout. This ill health might have been exacerbated by financial worries. It was rumored he had ruined himself with these many expensive runs for Parliament. There had also been bank failures, problems on his estates, Napoleon. Earlier, he even had to sell some land at the bottom of the market. February of 1812 was not Sir Ralph Milbanke's finest hour.

Wife Judith was made more for the world. She was quick, sharp, understood politics and science and the dark side of human nature. She could keep accounts, run an estate. She was up to date, believed in inoculating infants—Annabella had been inoculated. Judith offered to pay for anyone on her estates or in the region who would have their child inoculated as well. No one took her up on it. She was extremely progressive, against war with France, adamantly antislavery. She made speeches on the hustings for her husband. Annabella attended as a child and wrote that her mother was more effectual than her father, adding that of course a woman making public speeches was an event in itself.

*Sir Ralph and Lady Milbanke and their precocious
daughter Annabella.*

The sharpness of Annabella's mind, her brilliance in mathematics and science, her ability to speak plainly and well, owe something to her mother. Perhaps the streak of poetry in her, the love of classic learning and languages, come from her father. From both she received what she would practice all her life: "zealous" attention "to the comfort of the labouring poor." The best doctors attended their tenants, the "finest Claret" selected for them when sick. "I did not think that property could be possessed by any other tenure than that of being at the service of those in need." This would turn into a philanthropy notable throughout her life.

Still, Judith was always hovering, wanting the best for her daughter, concerned she was too idealist. She wished for a good marriage. In that quarter Judith might have had less concern than she evidenced. For Annabella at nineteen had close to a battalion of suitors. She had grown up to be as graceful as she had been as a child. She had long, rich brown hair and blue eyes. She was small and well formed and had a remarkable texture and glow to the very fair skin of her rounded face. Added to this, she was a prodigy in mathematics and languages, and rather than speaking in lisping fashionable slang, she spoke her mind straight out with no airs at all. Her lineage stretched back to Henry VII and one day she would be a baroness. During the previous season in London she had refused the hand of many of the most eligible men in England—some of whom never married afterward. She wasn't beautiful, but she was very pretty, and with her strong mind, moral views, and intelligence added to her prospects, she was enthusiastically sought after. She was kind, she appeared calm, and perhaps more than one man—and his mother— understood that in an age when fine superficialities abounded, she was quite uniquely herself.

She was also used to getting her own way. Going to London, an unmarried girl, alone? Judith objected. Leaving when her father was ill? Adding concern to her mother?

Of course she wouldn't be alone. A dear family friend, the older Lady Gosford, was most desirous of Annabella staying at her home.

And another, Mary Montgomery, Annabella's closest friend, was in London. MM, as she was always referred to in Annabella's letters, was an invalid with all sorts of health problems, including a very bad back. Annabella didn't know how long she would survive, and she wished to be a comfort to her during these sad days. (Ironically, MM would be the only one of Annabella's early circle who would outlive her.)

Annabella regretted her row with her mother and confided in a family friend, Dr. Fenwick, who had been with her when she had scarlet fever as a child. He wrote that if she felt she had any fault in her conduct toward her mother she should repent it: "I know you have a warm temper to struggle with; I have seen you subdue it & have been sensible of the effort it cost you." Annabella took his advice and had a calmer talk with her mother. After it, she wrote a letter to Judith, on February 9, admitting she was well aware her mother's concerns were not self-involved, but stemmed from fears for Annabella's safety. She knew she shouldn't leave Seaham until her father's health was improving, or else she would be flying from "one anxiety to suffer from another." She would wait a fortnight to make sure her father was making progress: "I cannot express how calm & contented my mind has become since your kindness last night," she ended her letter, allowing one to assume her mother had already more or less given way to her headstrong daughter.

So on February 21, Annabella left Seaham to go to London, for the first time without her parents in tow. She wrote to her mother not to worry. "If I should die," she had already equipped her maid with "fifteen pens" with which to let Judith know instantly. Meanwhile, she ate heartily on the road, and when she got to London she was in fine health and thought she never looked better. MM perked up when she saw Annabella, but who knew how long improvement would last. And Annabella let her parents read over her shoulder, as she had in 1812 a brilliant social season.

"I am *quite the fashion* this year," she wrote home, sharing her experiences in letters audacious, energetic, joyful. Not only was she coming into her own, but she had an audience of two to whom she had to prove her maturity, at the same time knowing her every encounter and thought would be of interest to them. Ah, to be young, invulnerable, and the apple of one's parents' eye. It lasts only for a moment, but given the censure she received from some later scholars for her youthful exuberance and self involvement, one wonders—had they never been nineteen? Or popular?

The suitors—and their hopeful parents—seemed to meet Annabella the minute she stepped off her coach. There was a General Pakenham, who was in his thirties and amused her with stories of his brother-in-law Lord Wellington—she refused him, hoping they could still be friends. There was Augustus Foster, the son of the present Duchess of Devonshire's first marriage. "An icicle," the Duchess, who had earlier been the Duke's mistress, would come to call Annabella for refusing her son. Annabella had no intention of marrying beneath her station, or adding to the financial woes of her father. Lord Jocelyn was as warm as he was funny-looking. He was an heir and she liked him. His previous engagement was broken off when his fiancée realized "insanity is very strong in the family." Enough said. There was William Bankes, also an heir and a Cambridge friend of that young poet Byron: "Mrs Bankes visited me the day before yesterday, in order to make an oration on the merits of William my suitor." Another source leaked that "the youth had £8,000 per an, independent of his father whose heir he must be." She obviously thought that would amuse "Sir Ralph," as she sometimes called her father.

Womenkind considered her "somebody," she confided. She thought about it and came to the conclusion, "without jest," that she was liked more in company than on an individual basis as "I am stronger and more able to exert myself in the scenes of dissipation." One doubts she meant that she could drink anybody under the table, more that she spoke her mind, was herself and, as the mountain was constantly coming to Mohammed, she certainly didn't flirt—or need to.

Things were going so well that she decided, early on, to open her parents' house on Portland Place for an evening in order to give a dinner party for fourteen. Her uncle Wentworth and his wife would be in town, and she jested that "the admirable manner in which I shall do the honors of the House may procure me a *wing of the estate*." Though she joked about the future inheritance, she certainly knew how to get her mother "to approve this *extravagance*."

She hadn't called on her father's only sister when she arrived, but almost immediately bumped into her at a ball. So on March 2 she felt it her duty to call at Melbourne House, though her aunt, Lady Melbourne, had ignored her brother's illness. Hadn't sent Sir Ralph a word.

ELIZABETH MILBANKE, unlike brother Ralph to an extraordinary degree, had left the north country as soon as she could, married the very wealthy, extremely undistinguished Lord Melbourne when she was sixteen, and headed to London. Tall for her times, strikingly attractive and sensual, brilliantly malicious, Lady Melbourne became a political force through the powerful men she drew to her, becoming the most influential Whig hostess of the day. (No back-bencher she.) She resembles, in her friend Richard Brinsley Sheridan's play *School for Scandal*, Lady Teazle, who came from the country and learned how to get the upper hand of her husband, informing him that ladies of fashion in London were accountable to no one after they married. The current saw was that a woman of fashion owed her husband an heir of his own blood, and after that first son she was free to suit herself. Lady Melbourne complied.

Annabella and her parents knew the rumors about Ralph's sister were true, that after first son, Peniston, each of her successive five children were by a different man, from intellectual aristocratic to the Prince Regent. "Prinny," as the future George IV was called, had an affair with Lady Melbourne that resulted in many perks for her husband as well as in a fourth son (George). During the Regency, it was Judith's and Ralph's fidelity that was "odd." There were so many children carrying the noble names of men who were not their biological fathers that they were called "children of the mist."

Lovers to one side, Judith simply didn't trust her fashionable sister-in-law, though she could never convince her husband that his sister disrespected him and that she begrudged Annabella's birth. Annabella's sudden and late arrival robbed Lady Melbourne of a paternal inheritance she thought would come down to her. The families were not close. In hindsight, one might wish "If only." If only it had stayed that way. But it didn't. Annabella's subtle aunt came to play loose and free with her niece's fate.

Lady Melbourne's intelligence, sensuality, and intense ambition for her children, her very worldliness and ability to please the men who were important to her, were one side of her character. She was also a practical woman much like sister-in-law Judith, who knew about farming and improving estates. It was joked that she was the only woman in London able to make a profit from her garden. She was given a less kindly botanical nickname "the Thorn" for the prick of her tongue, and there were those who said there wasn't a happy marriage she could abide. She and her friends, such as the earlier Duchess of Devonshire, Georgiana, were often grist to the newspapers of the day. She knew the world, was charming, dangerous, manipulative, glamorous, bigger than life. She and her brother's family did have one trait in common: an unusually hearty appetite. There was not a Milbanke or Melbourne who picked at food. They gobbled chops. Annabella never referred to fashionable clothes but to many a meal in her letters. Lady Melbourne was sixty-two years old and still attractive. That morning in March, however, when she greeted Annabella, her head was shaking as if she had some sort of paralytic episode. Her niece, who understood anatomy and medical symptoms, reported this home—to a mother who also understood anatomy and medical symptoms. Her aunt's health might offer some excuse for her having failed to inquire after her brother, Annabella opined. A few weeks later we find a reluctant Annabella dining at Melbourne House *en famille*. At that dining table were two more who would become enmeshed in her drama. One was Lady Melbourne's particular favorite, her second son, and Annabella's first cousin: William Lamb, living on the first floor of his parents' mansion with his wife Caroline (number two).

William, who was attracted to young girls, knew his wife Caroline in the days when she was a child and he seemed to form an attraction to her early on. They married when she was twenty. Thin, boyish, with a freckled nose and reddish blond hair, Caroline was some six years older than cousin Annabella. Raised in the lap of luxury, "Caro," as she was called, was bright, talented, and hugely unstable. We'd call her "bipolar" today. When she was a child, her aristocratic and adored grandmama, Lady Spencer, diluted opium into lavender to calm her down.

Annabella reported home: "Caroline seems clever in every thing that is not within the province of common sense." There was a golden cord of propriety that ran through these freewheeling Regency lives. One did what one wanted—discreetly. Discretion Caroline lacked. In the past, Annabella considered Caroline "silly." What she realized at that dinner was that the silliness wasn't a byproduct of Regency artificiality, but instead part of Caroline's hyperactive personality. She was no fool, though she certainly could be foolish. What was to stop her from indulging her whims? Her life was buttressed by footmen and servants. Caroline would later blame the wealth and privilege into which she was born for her recklessness.

William was tall like his mother, a dark, handsome man in his early thirties. His mother was ambitious for him. He had the finely tuned intelligence her husband lacked. His biological father, Lord Egremont, "was the pattern grand seigneur of his time," according to biographer David Cecil. "Egremont spent most of his time at his palace of Petworth in a life of magnificent hedonism, breeding horses, collecting works of art, and keeping open house for a crowd of friends and dependents." He didn't marry until late in life because of Lady Melbourne's influence. He was restless, genial, and almost surprisingly erudite, characteristics shared by his biological son William, who often dropped by the palace for a visit.

William loved the child in his wife and probably would have married her earlier if he had had anything to offer her, but he was a second son. Here, fate took an ironic turn. Peniston Lamb, Lord Melbourne's firstborn, died of tuberculosis. Suddenly, William became heir. Lord

Melbourne took out his profound grief in rage and by the means he had at his disposal. Whereas Peniston had received a yearly allowance of 5,000 pounds, Melbourne retaliated by allowing his son-in-name-only, 2000. Didn't give a damn that such a slight could not go unnoticed. Glad of it. Usually, Lady Melbourne could have her way with him—his attentions were habitually elsewhere. But his anger and grief were so overwhelming that she dared not try. William's prospects, though, had suddenly shifted. Now first son and heir, he married the girl he was attracted to when she was fourteen and he twenty-one. Years later, when William became Lord Melbourne, the teenaged Queen Victoria's first Prime Minister, and adored mentor, he and Annabella would be friends who shared, as others couldn't, the pain and knowledge of the past.

At this intimate family dinner, however, Annabella was not at all impressed by lanky, handsome, loud-laughing William, thought him self-involved in his informality. Caroline, on the other hand, showed surprising consideration, Annabella wrote to her mother.

Caro, or Caro William, as she was called, was giving a small party that week and invited Annabella, with the caveat that Lady Holland would be there. Perhaps her mother would not want her to attend? Lady Holland was a divorcee, and though all of male Whig London dined at Holland House, known for its brilliant conversation and political influence, the Lady was not widely accepted socially. Wasn't that considerate of cousin Caro, Annabella wrote to Judith. She had responded—and here breeding shows—that she would not object to being in the company of anyone Caroline saw fit to receive as a guest, though, of course, if she was asked to be introduced to Lady Holland, she'd refuse. She was sure her mother would agree "no one will regard me as corrupted by being *in the room* with her." With that, Annabella answered *for* her mother and, discreetly, went her own way.

After the party, Caroline invited her cousin to a bigger one she was giving at Melbourne House on 25 March 1812. Annabella accepted. An exciting occasion indeed; the man of the hour would be there. At cousin Caroline Lamb's fashionable, slightly risqué morning waltz (for waltzing had just arrived from Vienna and was considered improper by some in the *ton*), Annabella Milbanke first laid eyes on Lord Byron. It was also the first season women danced in men's arms.

THREE WEEKS PREVIOUSLY, twenty-four-year-old Lord Byron awoke to find himself famous. His book-length poem *Childe Harold's Pilgrimage* had just come off the press, yet already two editions had sold out. Editions were small in those days. Still, the first copies were eaten up, leaving an appetite for more. His fame spread like wildfire—a literary contagion unlike any that had come before. Caroline had read the poem in proofs and raved. It was all people spoke of; Annabella caught up, reading *Childe Harold* a few nights before the morning waltz.

John Murray, his publisher, had urged Byron to cut some of his most savage satire, particularly concerning religion and politics. The sex, perhaps Murray knew, would sell. But Byron refused, just as, though he was in terrible financial straights as usual, he passed his royalties on to another. A poet should not accept money for his poetry, something he accused Walter Scott of in an angry satire, "English Bards and Scotch Reviewers," written three years previously when his early work was badly reviewed. Important as well, he considered himself, first and foremost, an aristocrat. His dysfunctional family traced back to Norman times—and he had inherited an abbey at Newstead to prove it. A Lord Byron didn't *work* for a living—neither did his untitled father Mad Jack, who fleeced two wives amid other scandals before he died.

In truth, *Childe Harold's Pilgrimage* was a thinly disguised self-portrait of a brooding young aristocrat-in-training (for that's what "Childe" meant in medieval days), and its unflinching realism, delicious wit, and carnal exploits caused a sensation. The blatantly autobiographical elements heightened the fervor. That it was Byron's story was undeniable—at first he thought to title the poem "Childe Burun," using the medieval form of his own family name. His revealing depiction of a young man "sore given to revel and ungodly glee" fleeing in exotic, picturesque travel from the sexual adventures of his misspent youth turned him into something new. He was now not only a poet and a lord, he was a "celebrity," the very first of the ilk. That Byron was exceptionally handsome with his dark hair, grey eyes, dark moods, and unpredictable nature added to his glamour. So did his strong plea for the national independence of enslaved nations in *Childe Harold* and his scathing rant against Lord Elgin for stripping the Parthenon of its sculptures and sending the plunder home as *his* marbles. Byron's fame brought him swift entrance into the highest level of Regency society. Aristocrats who hadn't paid attention to him previously, now lisped their fashionable baby talk his way.

Byron didn't waltz. At Caroline's fete at Melbourne House, one can picture him leaning against a fine drawing room mantle, most likely designed by Chippendale—once Lady Melbourne's favorite. Byron often leaned against mantels and let the world whirl while he observed. He was very sensitive about his lameness. His right foot was deformed, the calf of that leg withered, the leg itself shorter than the other. The handsome, brooding poet loped along, adding even more dark romance to his persona, but adding nothing to his sense of self. He never forgave or forgot his cursed deformity. When he was a child, his mother put him through all sorts of excruciating fittings and crampings and cures that didn't work. He was an agile swimmer, and raised hell at school, but of course, his lameness made him red meat—even for boys who liked him. Imagine the transformation at the age of ten, when lame, plump George Gordon suddenly came into his title. One day boys teased, headmasters threatened, the next day they bowed, they flattered. Lord Byron's fate, as his nature, lay in extremes.

Annabella watched the women at Caroline's morning waltz throwing themselves at Byron. She had written home of having read his poem, finding in it deep feeling and some mannered expression. In London that season, she had already met the movers and shakers of the day, so many that she was rather bored by them and didn't spend much time discussing them in her letters. But Byron! Everyone was abuzz. In her youth she had created her own magazine for her family at Seaham; now she had the human interest story of the season to report to her adoring parents: "All the women were absurdly courting the author of *Childe Harold*, and trying to *deserve* the lash of his Satire." She, on the other hand, had no desire to be portrayed in one of his poems and refused the chance to be introduced to the man who had all London at his feet. He was cynical, she wrote, she saw it in the twist of his mouth, and she perceived an anger burning within him, what she called "the violence of his scorn." He attempted to control it—often by bringing hand to his curling lips as he spoke. For herself, she couldn't "worship talents" that were unconnected with respect for one's fellow man.

Cousin Caroline's impressions were more pithy. In her diary Caroline Lamb wrote that the moody poet was "mad, bad and dangerous to know," encapsulating the young Byron for posterity. Then she quickly jumped into an outrageous affair with Byron, outrageous not that she had an affair, but that she knew no boundaries in her sexual pursuit of him. If there hadn't been a Byron, Caroline might have invented one. She had found the objective correlative for her hyperactivity and constant need of attention.

Annabella had previously spent a weekend with cousin Caroline at the Melbourne country retreat at Brocket Hall and wrote home that Caroline didn't do justice to the strength of her intellect, hiding it behind a childish manner that "she either indulges or affects." That "childish" facade that Annabella perceived was Caro's luck, in a way. For it was the child in her that found its way into her husband's heart, the child he could indulge and, later, could not totally abandon.

Caroline cut her short hair even shorter, donned her Page attire— she enjoyed cross dressing—and slipped past servants into Byron's bedroom. She also mailed Byron curls of her pubic hair and asked for "blood" in return: "I cut the hair too close & bled much more than you need." For at least four months Byron fell madly in love himself, and the two exchanged over three hundred, mainly lost, letters. He found her bohemian, quixotic nature unique among womankind, and

The talented, erratic, erotic, and married Caroline Lamb
would enter Lord Byron's bedroom disguised as a page.

most probably, in her ambiguous sexuality and outrageous disregard for the mores of her class, he saw himself

As early as the morning waltz, Annabella witnessed Caroline flirting with Byron, trying to imitate his gestures, and was inspired to write a short poem of her own, naming "Caro" outright as she portrayed her cousin's "silliness," as well as that of the many other women who crowded and crowed about Byron. They all smiled and sighed over Byron, hoping to imitate each of his strange grimaces and to replace them with "a wilder Passion." Was human nature to be cast anew because of this man, she wondered, in *Byronmania*:

> Then grant me, Jove, to wear some other shape,
> And be an anything—except an Ape!!

Annabella in London.

Annabella would make "no offering at the shrine of Childe Harold," she had assured her parents, adding, however, that she would not refuse his acquaintance should it come her way on a less hectic day. Lord Byron came Annabella's way the next month, but not before another party at which she astutely observed that Lord Byron was actually very shy. Annabella would have all through her life a most uncanny instinct for the psychology of others, particularly when she kept the other at arm's length. When she came too close, it became her conviction as she grew older and wiser, it was she who got burned.

Byron's shyness, coupled with the annoying presence of William Bankes, that suitor she could not shake off, kept her from intruding on his privacy. However, the very next night, the two met at a supper party and spoke to each other for the first time. Interesting conversation. How handsome he was. How noble his manners. Still, he didn't have that "calm benevolence" she was looking for in a husband. Even without it, his conversation became the best she ever knew as the season progressed. It took her a while to arrive at a less articulate version of cousin Caroline's "mad, bad, and dangerous to know."

"I think of him that he is a very bad, very good man," Annabella informed her parents, artlessly, accurately. Her empathy for him had swelled. She overheard him at a party abruptly asking those about him, with his usual abandon, "Do you think there is one person here who dares look into himself?" Though those words echoed her feelings about fashionable London, they didn't "bind" her to him. It was what followed: "I have not a friend in the world," he proclaimed. He knew all London sought him out for his fame, that these people were moths to his talent, and that the women of the *bon ton* were curious to bed him. The rumor that he was extraordinarily well endowed did not detract from his charms.

Annabella was different. (Or thought she was. Cousin Caroline had been attracted by the poet's claim of friendlessness, as well as by his other attributes.) There and then, in a sudden rush, Annabella made a secret vow to herself: She would silently, in her heart of hearts, be Lord Byron's devoted friend: "He has no comfort but in *confidence*, to soothe his deeply wounded mind." If her disinterested friendship could offer him "any temporary satisfaction" from his obviously troubled state, wasn't it almost a Christian duty to comply? Not that she'd seek to be more than a friend: "He is not a dangerous person to me," she wrote to her alarmed parents.

From their first meeting there seemed to be a spontaneous understanding between Annabella and Byron—often they seemed not to need words. "It is said," she would write, "that there is an instinct in the human heart which attaches us to the friendless." Jove had indeed granted her another shape. For Annabella, friendship was not fawning acceptance, but honest exchange. She would hold to this through her life—that she had been and always would be Byron's true friend. Of course, in the fullness of time, she'd recall that when she made her girlish vow: "I did not pause—there was my error—to enquire why he was friendless."

That season, she spoke with Byron one human being to another. If she didn't agree with him, she told him what she thought. She was the antithesis to Caroline, who was causing scenes, threatening destruction, burning facsimiles of his letters around a fire at Brocket, servants in tow. The next season, when Caro cut her hand at a ball while wielding jagged glass at him, running out in hysterics, blood splattering her fine dress, her antics hit the papers. Caroline couldn't or wouldn't control herself. As intrigued as Byron had been by her rashness, unconventionality, and sexual ambiguities, Byron couldn't control her either.

It might have been quite refreshing for him to be with Annabella, this accomplished young woman, who swatted off suitors like flies (some of whom, like Bankes, were his friends), could speak intelligently on everything from the Greek historians to the parallelogram, who took an honest interest in him as a human being, and didn't seem inclined to jump into bed. There were times when Caroline's unbridled sexuality went beyond him. Frightened him? In *Childe Harold's Pilgrimage* he bemoaned the death of his one true love—actually John Edelston, a choirboy at Cambridge.

Byron's homosexuality did not end with his years at Harrow. John was also the model for Byron's love poems to Thyrza, three of which were appended to the first edition of *Childe Harold*, though he changed John's sex for public consumption. Leaning against one mantel or another, watching graceful Annabella, surrounded by her own entourage of admirers, abounding in moral ideals, talking sense on many a subject without any airs at all in a society that doted on affectation, he might have felt quite safe—sexually that is. Byron didn't pursue women; they pursued him: mainly older, married, experienced women.

Annabella might have felt safe as well, clad in the armor of friendship and knowing Byron was bedding her cousin. Caroline warned her, rather shrewdly, to "shun friendships with those whose practice ill accords with your Principles." Warned her that if she succumbed to Byron she was tossing herself into stormy seas. She had intuited that her mad, bad lover seemed to fancy her country cousin—especially when he was positive about poems Annabella sent him for criticism. Byron might have meant his praise—or at least have been surprised by the subject matter. Annabella's early poems could be moody and dark and deal with the early death of poets. Byron had satirized the melancholy, roaming, lower-class poet Joseph Blacket, the "cobbler poet" who was sponsored by the Milbankes and lived and died in a cottage Annabella's parents lent him free of charge at Seaham. It was rumored he was in love with Annabella. After his early death in 1810, Annabella wrote:

> I left thee Seaham, when the winter's blast
> Had o'er thy summits bare in fury past!

When "Nature's troubled spirit call'd aloud," and "admidst the torrents' rush," Blacket's voice was still heard. The dead poet's nature was "congenial with so rude a scene." He was "a bard of genius speaking mien," but "keen suffering quelled" his "native fire."

The year before, in 1809 in one of her earliest poems, she wrote about the Irish poet Thomas Dermody, who drank "himself to madness and death in 1802," when Annabella was ten years old:

> Degraded genius! O'er the untimely grave
> In which the tumults of thy breast were still'd
> The rank weeds wave, and every flower that springs
> Withers. . . .

So serious a young woman. Caro had nothing to fear from her.

There is no doubt that Byron confided in Annabella, spoke openly of his errant ways with other women. For in her diary she wrote she would continue her acquaintance with the poet "additionally convinced he is sincerely repentant for all the evil he has done, though he has not resolution (without aid) to adopt a new course of conduct and feeling." In aiding Byron to reach toward his better self—and encouraged by Byron to do so; he probably couldn't resist leading her along this path—she had become the very good girl determined to save the very bad man. It's an oath not taken without a burst of virginal eroticism and youthful narcissism. Annabella had no idea she was falling in love.

Her mother did, and didn't like it one bit. Judith, sharp and protective, had a more sophisticated understanding of the world. Annabella, in the year of the waltz, could write poems about silly women fawning over a poet, but she hadn't a real idea of the games these people played, even though by then she was with Aunt Melbourne almost every day. Intellectually she might have realized that the most exciting, most titillating game for the *ton*—outside of reckless gaming—was Love. But she was almost "addicted" to the good in human nature, to the good in herself. Judith was right to fear her daughter was swimming with the sharks.

Because of this concern, and despite her distrust, Judith wrote to her sister-in-law. She told Lady Melbourne in the *strictest confidence* that she was not at all pleased by this supposedly Platonic relationship between her daughter and the poet. Lady Melbourne responded that she could not disagree with Judith and would keep an eye on the situation and on her niece. Then she turned right around and let Byron read the letter. It was dangerous to show someone as unstable and proud as Byron that he was mistrusted and disliked. It upped the ante in the game of Love.

By the autumn of 1812, the Milbankes had taken up residence in Richmond, a suburb south of London perhaps more economical than Portland Place. Annabella joined them, MM in tow. There, Annabella received a letter from Dr. Fenwick warning that Aunt Melbourne was in many ways "unworthy" of her: "She may in some instances exhibit the Appearance of Sincerity, You Must Not forget that she Can deceive, & has been in the habit of deceiving." In the next breath he mentioned Byron's latest poem as if unconsciously linking the Lady's deviousness to the poet.

Lady Melbourne and Byron had forged a relationship so strong

*Lady Melbourne, the middle witch, flanked by two other
fashionable ladies around the cauldron.*

that season of his success that many wondered at the extent of it,
though Byron was forty years her junior. The Prince Regent thought
it quite peculiar that Lady Melbourne was the confidant of the man
who was cuckolding her son, and that she was the confidant of her
daughter-in-law as well. William was often away from Melbourne
House and had as well a characteristic that his biographer David
Cecil would trace from his earliest days up through the time he was
Prime Minister of his country. Intellectual, genial William avoided
controversy whenever he could. If Caro had adhered to the rules of
the game, had kept the golden cord of propriety intact as she saw to
her pleasure, things would not have come to a head. But Caro was
besotted; some thought her out of her mind when it came to pursuing Byron.

It was not as if she were some teenager without a care in the world.

Lord Byron, the young Romantic poet.

She and William had one surviving child, a boy, Augustus. At the infant's christening dinner, the erratic playwright Richard Brinsley Sheridan made a loud guest appearance, literally crashing the event. He had been the longtime lover of Caro's mother, and he had an erratic temperament at times veering toward madness—not unlike Caro. Did he think he was the infant's biological grandfather and had a right to be there? Whoever his grandfather, Augustus was mentally deficient. Caroline and William loved him dearly. He grew big, was destructive, but they refused to send him away.

For Caro, even beyond this sobering responsibility, it was Byron, Byron, sexual surrender, erotic slavery, love, love. In less than half a year it was all spilling over. Lady Melbourne realized that it might wash away with it her son William's political prospects. A stop had to be put to the affair. Byron himself didn't know how to get it to end. Caroline stalked him, forged letters. Finally, toward the end of the year, Lady Melbourne, who often quoted "Life is a tragedy to those who feel and a comedy to those who think," convinced Caroline to leave England and go to Ireland with William, her child, and her mother, hoping distance would lessen obsession.

All through the year, the correspondence between Lady Melbourne and Byron was full of lighthearted banter. Byron, for all his pride, played the role of the charmed supplicant. But suddenly Lady Melbourne was incensed. Why had Byron promised to write to Caroline now that she had finally been convinced to go to Ireland! Letters would only encourage her! Byron responded, assuring Lady Melbourne his affections lay elsewhere: "I was, am, & shall be I fear attached to another, one to whom I have never said much, but have never lost sight of." He had wished to marry this other woman, but he heard she was already engaged. "As I have said so much I may as well say all." Then the Byronic twist: "The woman I mean is Miss Milbanke."

Her niece?

He knew "little of her, & have not the most distant reason to suppose that I am at all a favorite in that quarter, but I never saw a woman whom I *esteemed* so much."

Was he joking? He who fell in and out of love every three months?

"Miss M. I admire because she is a clever woman, an amiable woman & of high blood, for I have still a few Norman & Scotch inherited prejudices on the last score, were I to marry. As to *Love*, that is done in a week (provided the Lady has a reasonable share) and besides marriage goes on better with esteem & confidence than romance, and she is quite pretty enough to be loved by her husband, without being so glaringly beautiful as to attract too many rivals."

He had no high opinion of her sex, he informed Lady Melbourne, "but when I do see a woman superior not only to all her own but to most of ours I worship her in proportion as I despise the rest."

How much of this was written for shock value, how much had the kernel of truth? In her *roman à clef*, which became a bestseller four years later, Caroline Lamb wrote of Byron in her eponymous novel,

Glenarvon: "That in which Glenarvon most prided himself—that in which he most excelled, was the art of dissembling." He could "turn and twine so near the truth," with such supreme subtlety, that none could readily detect that he *was* dissembling. In Byron's letters to Lady Melbourne he was turning and twining quite near the truth, whatever one intuits of his motives or his sense of play.

"I see nothing but marriage and a *speedy one* can save me," he wrote to Lady Melbourne, as Caro was still pursuing him. If her niece was attainable, he'd prefer it; if not, the first woman who looks as if she wouldn't spit in his face! He had no idea if Annabella would have him: "I wish somebody would say at once that I wish to propose to her."

That Byron respected Annabella is true. He admired her intellect, her lack of affectation, he enjoyed talking with her and, being extremely competitive, he would have liked to succeed where many of his friends had failed when it came to winning Miss Milbanke's hand. He saw her as a superior woman. Through her life many an intellectual and artist and grateful supplicant idealized her as such. Caroline herself admired her cousin. And for the moment Byron hoped to run past himself while he still had the chance. Albeit a genius, he wouldn't be the first man to attempt marriage as a cure. Wealth and position enter into it of course, but that would be true of any women he'd consider marrying—and he insisted he did not care that Sir Ralph was in a bad way financially at the time. Basically, beyond the fun of calling Lady Melbourne aunt, Caro cousin, and being able to spite Annabella's mother, Byron liked Annabella, was rather taken by her—and her lineage—and, most important, thought she would be safe.

Lady Melbourne actually did intercede, showing her niece selected letters from Byron—possibly reading sections to her as she would have to cull carefully from his other love interests and bawdier remarks. Then, she went further and literally proposed *for* Byron. He had expected Lady Melbourne to see the lay of the land, not offer Annabella his hand. Looking at it from Lady Melbourne's point of view, it must have been irresistible to propose for him. It would solve the Caroline problem, annoy her sister-in-law, and keep herself in control.

What apparently surprised Annabella most was not the proposal (she had so many) but finding out that Byron until recently thought she was already engaged. Lady Melbourne knew she wasn't engaged to George Eden, her childhood friend, as much as he and his family wished it otherwise. (Eden, later Lord Auckland, never did marry.) Why hadn't her aunt told Byron the truth? Lady Melbourne, as usual, quickly used her head: She "was very sorry for all this," Annabella wrote, "but not being in my confidence she could not decidedly declare the contrary." Annabella rejected Byron. To Lady Gosford she shrewdly observed, even without other objections, "his *theoretical* idea of my perfection" would end in his disappointment.

To her aunt she wrote she'd be unworthy of her dear friend Byron if she didn't tell the truth without any feminine coyness. She was "predisposed" to believe her aunt's testimony in favor of Byron's character. It was "more to the defects of my feelings than of his character that I am not inclined to return his attachment." She wished Lady Melbourne to forward her letter to Byron, and let him know that she would like to remain his friend if possible. Because of Byron's pride, Lady Melbourne assumed Byron would cut Annabella out of his life.

Cut her, my dear Lady Melbourne? "Mahomet forbid!" Byron responded, sounding quite relieved. "I am sure we shall be better friends than before & if I am not embarrassed by all this I cannot see for the soul of me why *she* should." He called Annabella the "fair Philosopher," and in another letter to Lady Melbourne called her "my Princess of Parallelograms," referring to her mathematical talents and to the fact that "we are two parallel lines prolonged to infinity side by side but never to meet." Tell Annabella that "I am more proud of her *rejection* than I can ever be of *another's acceptance.*"

Refuse Byron? It made what Lady Melbourne considered her niece's "odd" nature more intriguing and she could not resist asking her to write her, in strict confidence naturally, what exactly *were* her qualifications for a husband. Serious Annabella sat down in Richmond and composed a list of admirable qualities—duty, respect, good

Annabella's shrewd and complicated aunt,
Lady Melbourne, Lord Byron's confidante.

humor, etc. The usual suspects. Lady Melbourne responded by telling her niece she would never marry if she didn't get off her stilts—or as we'd say, her high horse. And later, of course, when the timing was right, she shared Annabella's private letter with Byron.

Annabella took her aunt's rebuke as justified and answered with humor, attempting to show that she wasn't on stilts. Couldn't she just be viewed as being on tiptoes (a pleasantly unselfconscious reference not only to her ideals but to her height—just under five feet.) Still, Annabella had refused so many suitors. Had it become a reflex action?

There was one point in Lady Melbourne's response to her niece's list of sterling qualities that gives a sharp insight into her own success in the world of men and to her own strength as a mother. It was a rebuke Annabella took to heart, as we shall see. Annabella had confided that her nature was actually a warm one, and her moods often depended on the moods of others. A certain empathy moved her to be sad when others were sad, happy when they were happy, etc. And she had a temper when provoked.

Lady Melbourne admonished her niece. Allowing herself to be irritated when others were out of sorts required "correction in the highest degree." With common acquaintances it might be of no consequence, "but if your Husband, should be in ever so absurd a passion, you should not notice it at the time, no Man will bear it with patience." If she maintains her good humor, when he regains his, he will calm down, listen to her with patience and realize the obligations he has toward his wife. In fact, until Annabella can attain this power over herself she had no right to require it in others. "I have stated this rather strongly, from my persuasion of its importance, & I am sure it is not difficult to acquire, I speak from experience."

This was Lady Melbourne at her best. It reminds one of the time when the Prince Regent was dining with her and news was brought that his father, mad King George, was failing. Prinny, who had no interest in his insane father's mortality, wished to continue his meal. It was Lady Melbourne who forcibly persuaded him that he must return to the palace and let the populace see his humanity, his concern for the father he loathed. Though he demurred, she'd have none of it, and called for his carriage. Later that night he came back to thank her for her advice.

On this note let us allow 1812, the year of the waltz, to end and for Annabella and Byron to go their separate ways. Is each age more influenced by its entertainments—or imitative of them—than the other way around? Annabella would accept her aunt's invitation to the Melbournes' box at the opera, where as Annabella put it her aunt flirted and singers screeched. Onstage the actors wore their elaborate wigs and swished in their fashionable costumes and cross-dressed, girls turning into pages, pages into girls. The passions were overriding or ironically muted, death and love and marriage and betrayal all took their turn against an artifice of elegance and jewels. Fate hung on a lie, or a misplaced letter, or a false friend. In moments of passion

The young Princess Charlotte and husband Prince
Leopold among the fashionable set seen at the opera.

or jealous deception the music swelled. First acts often ended incon-
clusively, as this one did when the curtain came down on Annabella
Milbanke's first London season on her own. But the tragedy—or the
comedy for those who think rather than feel—had hardly begun. For
Byron and Annabella, *non è finita*. No, not finished at all.

❧ 2 ❧

LETTERS IN LOVE

*R*eader, prepare for a train wreck.

It wasn't until the following spring in London that Annabella came face-to-face with Byron once more. She became extremely agitated and without thinking held out her hand. She saw him turn pale as he pressed it—the first time they touched. The more they met at one social function after another, the more pain she felt. She was listless, often unwell, confiding in her diary that she felt *dead*. She would not consciously admit it, but she was in love.

She retreated to Seaham, preferring solitude, read a lot: Cicero and the still-anonymous Jane Austen. Refused another suitor or two. Couldn't get Byron off her mind. When she heard he would soon be sailing to Italy, she wrote to her aunt, asking Lady Melbourne to tell the poet that she would always take pleasure in hearing he was happy. Lady Melbourne delivered the message to a distracted Byron, who answered in a postscript: Send his regards to Miss Milbanke and "say what is proper." Aunt Melbourne couldn't resist turning Byron's curt disinterest courtly.

Not that Annabella needed much encouragement to do something quite unusual for any young woman of her generation. She initiated a correspondence with a suitor she had rejected, writing to Byron that her aunt had assured her he felt satisfaction at being remembered by her. Lady Melbourne had previously relayed that Byron wanted to render his conduct in conformance to Annabella's wishes, just as if his marriage proposal had been accepted. Now, as a friend, she claimed that right. She acknowledged the strength and generosity of Byron's feelings, knew his instincts were toward the good, but that he could not reach that goal on his own. She assured and reassured Byron with example after example that it wasn't love, but sincere friendship that drove her to write to him, a friendship beyond that of the admirers who were in love with his celebrity. It was an "unreserved friendship" based on encouraging him to accept and reach toward his better self. There was more, she wrote with an air of mystery. She could suffer as he could suffer. Had society allowed it, when they had met in London, she could have freely told him that the strongest affections of her heart had been rejected. The only thing she had left to offer any man was friendship. Her parents understood this and approved her writing to him on that basis. Others might not be as liberal. She asked Byron to keep her correspondence a secret from all, especially from her aunt Lady Melbourne who would not understand the simplicity of her motives.

Byron received the naïve, awkward, rambling letter at a time when his own affairs were a shambles. Annabella might have invented a phantom lover, but Byron's love life was as real as it was convoluted. Idealistic country virgins weren't his meat, though he had consciously played on Annabella's wishes to "save" him, letting her believe her goodness held power over him, and perhaps in his heart of heart's wishing it did. Still, in his life, he gravitated to older, married women. Out of England and in the East there were the young boys who stirred his soul. What he did for homosexual companionship in his homeland remains blurred. One imagines with older, married women the sexual practices he might have preferred were more acceptable. In his mid-twenties, he tended to hide not only *in* the skirts but *behind* the skirts of these women. Lady Oxford, in her forties, is a good example. One wonders if Annabella knew that in 1813, as she offered her bon voyage wishes, Byron was planning to follow his mistress, who had just left for the Mediterranean with her unsympathetic husband and family.

It had been with this mistress, Lady Oxford, twenty years his senior, that he conspired to get out of his endless mess with Caroline, who would not stop stalking him, causing havoc when she could. He and Lady Oxford composed a letter in which they told Caroline his love lay elsewhere and that *her* love had been a "truly unfeminine persecution." He hoped to remain her friend and as first proof offered her scathing advice: "Correct your vanity, which is ridiculous; exert your absurd caprices on others; and leave me in peace." The phrasing of the letter certainly showed a woman's hand, especially to someone as literary as Caro. Added to this, she saw Lady Oxford's seal on the stationery. To allow Lady Oxford to partner in rejecting her? She was devastated, and even given her penchant for melodrama, broke down at this rejection. Was she aware that Byron had previously played another trick on her? She had asked for a curl of his hair—from his head this time—but he sent her a lock of Lady Oxford's hair instead. It was childish, of course, but that was Byron at twenty-four. At odds. Planning to go abroad, but for one reason after another, not making a decided move on his own.

Lady Oxford, for her part, had boarded ship worn out by Byron's change of moods and by Caroline, who now knew her as an enemy and would be capable of scenes in London. Added to that, Lady Oxford had found Byron attempting to seduce her eleven-year-old daughter and she was far from amused.

It was in this unsettled state in the summer of 1813 that Byron received that first overlong letter from Annabella offering to be his disinterested friend and moral guide. He wrote back irascibly that in Lady Melbourne's "zeal" in his behalf, as friendly and pardonable as it was, she had to some degree gone beyond his intentions when she made a "direct proposal" of marriage to Annabella. He had to be candid: He didn't think he could be Annabella's friend as she had asked. Then he softened his harsh rejection of friendship with "I doubt if I could help loving you."

Annabella got the rebuke and it must have stung. In one simple and direct paragraph, she responded that she couldn't forgive herself for intruding on him. "I will not regret the friendship which you deem impossible, for the loss is *mine*, as the comfort would have been *mine*. God bless you."

That humble reply was moving in its simplicity, and soon Byron wrote again. She had misunderstood him. He would never deny that he had aspired to her hand or that he had failed. In fact, he and his friend Bankes found out they had been refused within weeks of one another. He wasn't rejecting her friendship, not at all. He was willing to obey her. If she marked out the limits of their future correspondence, he wouldn't step beyond them.

Byron seemed genuinely to enjoy their ensuing correspondence, in great part a dialogue about himself. She was right about his restlessness, but he did hate stagnation. She was right that he never tried to justify himself. Yes, his laughter could be false-hearted as she claimed. And he had to plead guilt to the charge of pride. For him "the great object of life is Sensation—to feel that we exist, even though in pain." (Annabella had plenty to say about that.) In November he wrote in his journal that he received such a "pretty letter from Annabella." Theirs was such an odd situation and friendship! There wasn't even a spark of love on either side. She had rejected him, yet he felt no coldness to her, just as she seemed to have no aversion to him. What a superior woman! She was very kind and generous and gentle and seemed almost without the pretensions of the women of her class.

However, as the correspondence continued, Annabella became increasingly aware that her phantom lover, created to assure Byron of her solely Platonic feelings, now kept him from proposing again. For Byron's habit of falling in love with the moment and writing what he imagined others wanted to hear had impressed her as the God's honest truth. She counted that on *three* occasions in his letters to her, Byron declared that he would now never marry, since "the only woman to whom he could trust the happiness of his life *has disposed of her heart to another.*" Three times! And now, because of her lie, he was convinced he could never resume his courtship. (Which of course, Byronically, allowed him to lay it on thick.) Whatever should she do? she asked her confidant, Mary Gosford. She had lied to a man "who has undoubtedly practised no deception with me."

Annabella wrote various versions of a confession for her duplicity, inventing one obscurity after another, until she wrote such a convoluted paragraph to Byron that he quoted it back to her verbatim and asked her whatever did she mean. However, through the miasma of words, he discerned a glimmer of interest at a time when his life was taking a disastrous turn. It was 1814, and he told Annabella he was once more preparing to sail toward his "magnet"—Italy.

What he didn't tell Annabella was that he planned to go abroad with his half sister Augusta Leigh, a married woman six years his senior, mother of three children—and pregnant now with his child. Byron was madly in love. Augusta stayed with the poet in London. The two went out into society together; his poetry developed incestuous metaphors. Even his best friend, John Cam Hobhouse, was beginning to suspect the unthinkable. Just as Caroline Lamb had broken past the lax morality of the time by forsaking the silken cord of propriety, Byron was close to flaunting the one sin his times found a crime against nature. When Medora was born, Byron wrote to Lady Melbourne the child "wasn't an ape." His society assumed the child of incest would be a freak. For those who use their heads, this scenario wears the mask of Comedy: the young woman in Seaham tortured by one girlish lie to the man who is secretly sleeping with his sister. Aunt Melbourne, though "the Thorn," was appalled. She warned Lord Byron that if his affair with his sister came to light it would ruin him—and Augusta too. The only solution was Comedy's last act: He *must* marry.

Sister Augusta agreed with Lady Melbourne. She had a young friend whom she'd like Byron to wed. Lady Melbourne had other brides to suggest. Byron assured Lady Melbourne he wouldn't even consider marrying her niece if Lady Melbourne objected. He joked about the situation of the year of the waltz being in reverse. Perhaps the niece was ready to say yes and the aunt, no! Lady Melbourne didn't believe Annabella would be a wise choice, but she didn't say no.

The possibility of such a marriage might have amused her. It was too delicious! She sent Byron Annabella's confidential list of the sterling moral attributes she expected in a husband.

While not confessing her feelings to Byron in a clear way, Annabella had her father invite him to visit them at Seaham. As this visit would bring their friendship into the light of day, she discussed with Byron different ways of informing her aunt of their correspondence. She had no idea her aunt was privy to every one of her letters. Perhaps all comedy revolves around self-interest: Byron with his tangled love interests, Annabella with her one girlish lie on her girlish conscience. On both sides artifice ruled—and a sort of mental coitus interruptus, setting off a weird aura of sexual frustration. These two people, as far as we know, were never alone in a room together, never had a conversation without the swirl of the fashionable waltz about them. Had once touched hands. The entire relationship was built on words, and the hollowness at the core of them and the expectation at the heart of them becomes more tragic than comic as one reads on.

Byron accepted Sir Ralph's invitation to visit. Annabella and her parents waited. One thing after another delayed him, until the family had to leave for Halnaby where Aunt Wentworth was quite ill and Byron found he wouldn't be coming north that year after all.

All this expectation and subtle duplicity was too much and Annabella broke through it finally. She hinted that she was no longer eternally committed to her phantom lover. By then, the young woman Augusta had chosen for her brother to marry had bowed out of the picture. Others as well. As a result, Byron wrote Annabella a cautious letter. Was he to believe that the "objections" to which she had alluded were no longer unsurmountable? He didn't want her to promise or pledge herself to anything, but only wanted to know if there was a possibility of such a situation. He found himself addressing her for a second time on what he called "this subject."

Receiving the stiff missile, Annabella rejoiced. "I *dared* not believe it possible." Immediately she discarded pretense like an old dress flung off, looked in the mirror, and became herself: "It would be absurd to suppress anything—I am and have long been pledged to myself to make your happiness my first object in life *If I can* make you happy, I have no other consideration. I will *trust* to you for all I should look up to—all I can love. The fear of not realizing your expectations is the only one I now feel. Convince me—it is all I wish—that my affection may supply what is wanting in my character to form your happiness."

She had already made him happy, he replied: "Your letter has given me a new existence—it was unexpected." He counted the reasons for loving her—always a bad sign: Superior human being, not only from what he observed, but from the observations of others. Worthy. Virtuous. Difficult not to love. He hoped to adopt whatever conduct he needed to to make her think well of him. Actually he had received Annabella's joyous letter at his estate at Newstead, where he was having halcyon days, secluded by the snow with his pregnant sister. He handed Augusta Leigh Annabella's letter, saying, "It never rains but it pours."

Annabella continued to pour: How foolish her phantom lover seemed now that she was engaged. Had she known of Byron's true feelings, she would have dropped her pretense earlier. Yet, on second thought, had she not "conjured" this lover into being, her impulse to write to him would probably not have prevailed. Still the folly was all hers. How that letter reassured him, Byron responded. He had been convinced her heart was taken and lived under the delusion that he had reclaimed his. Her explanation lifted a weight from his heart, a restlessness in his brain that would have made him "I know not what. Now I am yours." She would be his "first friend," his adviser, she would reprove him when necessary. She would improve his conduct, erase his errors. However, Annabella was becoming less the pillar of virtue Byron imagined, more the twenty-two-year-old virgin in love. He would eventually tell Lady Melbourne, with obvious annoyance, that the flesh-and-blood Annabella he finally visited at Seaham was, of all things, a "Romantic."

That visit to his fiancée was constantly delayed. His letters became progressively more businesslike. He had to stay in London to take care of a suitable settlement on her, to sell part of Newstead (an ongoing drama of real estate near-misses), to speak with his lawyer. . . .

Meanwhile back at Seaham, Uncle Wentworth, now Byron's future benefactor, had arrived to meet the poet, and he and her parents waited as one thing after another kept Byron in London through all of October. Imagine the scene, Annabella wrote to Byron. She, the bride-to-be, was in the position of calming the old folks, the twenty-two-year-old advising patience to those in their sixties. In fact, Uncle Wentworth told her, Byron could do all his business as well from Seaham as from London. She attempted another lure. His sister had written her such a warm letter: Perhaps he could bring Augusta with him?

His sister couldn't come, he replied; she was nursing infant Medora.

On and on it went, until Uncle Wentworth could wait no longer and went home. How Byron regretted this! Whether or not the lawyer arrived, he would set out later in the week. However, with business unsettled he couldn't stay at Seaham "above a few days." He was planning his escape even before he arrived.

The lawyer came. Byron left. However, sister Augusta so wished him to stop by on the way to Seaham that "I shall make 'mine inn' at her abode for a short time—and thence to our Papa's." The attempt at intimacy is cloyingly synthetic; even a great poet could not bring these words to life: "mine inn"—"our Papa"? On the other hand, there's a more nuanced reaction to Byron's constant referral to Lady Melbourne as "our Aunt."

Byron deserves sympathy as he drags himself toward Seaham. It is just as psychologically damaging to be committed to someone you cannot love as it is to be romantically in love with someone who doesn't love you. Pushed forward by his sister, Aunt Melbourne, and circumstances, Lord Byron reached Seaham in the evening of November 2, 1814. Annabella was reading in her room that night when she heard his carriage. The servants led Byron to the drawing room, and he was standing, as at that morning waltz where she first saw him, by the side of the chimney piece. He didn't move forward as she approached him, but took the hand she extended and kissed it. They were both silent, until he said in a low voice, "It is a long time since we met."

She could hardly speak and left the room, using the excuse of calling her parents. After that, she remembered the night as full of general conversation. They all knew the theater. The actor Sarah Siddons was a great friend of hers and her parents. Byron was a fan of Edmund Kean and was soon to be made a manager of London's Drury Lane. As they said their goodnights later on, he whispered, "What time do you get up in the morning?"

"About ten," she replied, and went off dreaming of the embraces the next morning would bring.

She woke up and dressed well before ten and waited. He didn't stir from his room. It was close to noon when, disappointed, chilled by premonition, she went out to walk by the sea. Her engagement had been greeted with people "hoping" for her happiness rather than assuming she would be happy. Ugly stories circulated. The bookies took odds on whether the marriage would take place. She warded it all off but, walking on the beach, much of this came back to her. She even wondered at the absorbed way in which Byron played with his watch chain last evening. Was he in fact self-centered, vain? He certainly was in no rush to hold her in his arms.

By the time she returned, Byron was up and the family about him. In company he was charming. Even her mother seemed to lose some of her nervousness about the match. That nervousness hit Annabella instead.

His visit was full of disappointment. He was strange, moody, unpredictable. He did his best with her parents, and of course, everyone loved him, even Judith, though he secretly hated her for her earlier slur—and got enormous pleasure later on when he would accidently knock off her wig. Often, he took his rifles and went out shooting—sometimes shots were heard in the house. At times Annabella and Byron walked by the sea together or read together in the library—that was good. But he was so often out of sorts, so often wished to be by himself. She spoke to her mother and to Dr. Fenwick about her doubts. Though fine in public, Byron was very dark and moody and unpredictable when the two of them were alone. They attributed his behavior to his poetic nature, wedding jitters, business problems. . . .

Byron wrote to Aunt Melbourne after a few days that things were going well with Annabella, but by the next week he was full of complaints. His fiancée's moods changed from sun to cloud according to his. Was she doing something wrong? She would ask him. He complained that during the first days of the visit she was very silent. It unnerved him. Then after a while she talked too much. She came down with vague sicknesses every three days. There was one hysterical scene, he said, reminiscent of Caroline Lamb's behavior—it was too petty to record. Lady Melbourne knew how he hated scenes!

Byron was the cause of that scene. Annabella was no fool, and Byron's behavior was getting to her. Something was not right. One evening when they were alone she asked him to trust her, that she was, as she said in her letters, first and foremost his true friend. She wanted him to tell her openly whether after so much time had elapsed his feelings about their marriage had changed. He needn't say more. She would not delve into whatever he did not want to tell her, and she was willing to take it upon herself to break the engagement if that was what he wished. A well-bred woman breaking her engagement was unheard of in those days. It was a solemn commitment, particularly in Scotland where Byron was raised.

Byron's reaction? He fainted.

Had Aunt Melbourne warned her niece? Or had it been Caroline? Caroline knew that he was in love with his sister and that they had an infant daughter, Medora. As he told incredulous Lady Melbourne, these confessions had been his method of warding off Caro.

"You don't know what you've done!" Byron cried out after Annabella revived him. He was in "a frenzy of despair." She begged him to forgive her, but he remained "inflexible, petrified." He kept referring to the past and to fearful mysteries. Whatever his words, he had fainted at the very thought of losing her, hadn't he? She could have broken with him before this scene, but after it she believed it would be abandoning him to suffer his imagined demons alone. She would marry him and attempt to ease his despair: "Little did I dream that I was to aggravate those sufferings, & form the bitterest drop in his cup."

Though Byron stayed at Seaham much longer than the two days he envisioned, he left earlier than he planned. He had been quite surprised by Annabella's sexuality. Disillusioned too. He had expected the voice of disinterested reason. He found instead someone who had her own moods up and down, according to what she perceived he was feeling. The only thing that steadied her, he wrote to her aunt, was what he and Lady Melbourne had always called their own "calming process." It worked so well on Annabella that it amused him, Annabella turned into a contented child when they made love. Not that they had intercourse, but came close—it was Byron who resisted. Their inability to control themselves while together became part of Byron's reason for leaving Seaham early and staying away almost up to the moment of the January wedding. In actuality, it was Annabella, jarred by his moods, who needed what we call "space," and asked Byron to leave.

She was warmer than we imagined, he wrote to Lady Melbourne. Surprise showed in letters to others as well. She was not the cold princess of parallelograms, the intellectual bitch of his later poetry. She was an inexperienced young woman passionately in love. Hardly what Byron was looking for in a wife. She wasn't really safe at all.

Marriage contracts were drawn up. Byron had arranged it so that they could be married at her home at short notice. He wanted as little fuss as possible. He and his best man, John Cam Hobhouse, set out toward Seaham from London on Christmas Eve, 1814, but they parted for the night, Hobhouse to visit Cambridge, their alma mater, and Byron to stay with his sister nearby at Six Mile Bottom. Unfortunately, Augusta's husband, Colonel Leigh, was home for the holidays, so Byron hadn't the freedom he would have wished for. Being with Augusta and Medora, however, gave him further doubts about the ensuing marriage. If it hadn't been for Augusta's insistence, he would have sent a letter to Seaham backing out. Before Augusta saw him off the next day, they carved their initials on the old oak tree.

Hobhouse remarked, "Never was lover in less haste." Meanwhile, Annabella and her family had been waiting for Byron's arrival day by day over the Christmas holidays. Never were nerves more frayed, particularly those of Lady Judith, who realized Byron hadn't presented her daughter with a token of affection. Of course there was the marriage settlement. But a gift, a sentimental token? A ring? Nothing at all. Byron did give Annabella his seal before the marriage. It read: "Malgré tout" and Byron told her it referred to a secret. "'No one knows all that those words mean.'" The seal portrayed two clasped hands encircled by a serpent. Above the image, the inscription "Despite everything."

The reluctant bridegroom and his best man didn't arrive at Seaham until December 30. Judith was so agitated she went to her room. Hobhouse felt foolish trying to explain to affable Sir Ralph why the simple trip from London had taken so long. Annabella had not yet appeared. Byron went to his own quarters, and when she heard him come from his room, she ran out of hers to greet him, threw her arms around his neck, and burst into tears. She was much more sensible by the time they walked downstairs. She greeted Hobhouse, frankly, openly, with no airs, and her delight in Byron was noticeable. And Byron? Well, as Hobhouse put it, "Byron loves her when present, and *personally*, as it is easy for those used to such indications to observe."

It became jolly enough. On New Year's Eve they did a mock wedding with Hobhouse as the bride. On New Year's Day Byron said, "Well, Hobhouse, this is our last night. Tomorrow I shall be Annabella's." And tomorrow, January 2, 1815, arrived, with bride and bridegroom kneeling on cushions in the Seaham drawing room, only the family and those closest to them in attendance. They were married by the Reverend Thomas Noel, who was Uncle Wentworth's illegitimate son. Annabella, in a simple white dress, was firm as a rock as she recited her responses steadily, looking all the while unflinchingly at

Byron. That was how Hobhouse saw it. Before the ceremony, however, Annabella, who had her doubts, had an indelible premonition of
disaster, but she went ahead.

When they got into their wedding carriage, Annabella might have
noticed that, even as they started off, Byron had difficulty letting go
of Hobhouse's outstretched hand. As they drove along, bells of the
neighboring church chimed and a six-gun salute followed them. It
may have been those ringing bells that agitated Byron. His first words
to her in their wedding carriage conveyed the message that if she had
married him the first time he asked, two years before, she could have
saved him. She might have made him anything she pleased. Those two
years had ruined him. It was all her fault! He sang, he made strange
noises, went from high humor to despair. He told her straight out she
would find she had married a devil.

Arriving at her family estate in Yorkshire for their honeymoon,
Byron jumped out of the coach ahead of her, leaving Annabella to
descend and to greet, by herself, the servants and tenants of Halnaby
who lined the way. She had known these people since childhood. Many
remembered that strained scene and passed it from one generation
to the next. One old man recounted the bride had tears in her eyes,
another that she smiled. Annabella remembered that for the first time
in her life she experienced what it meant to be alone with her God.

However, once doors closed, and Lord and Lady Byron were by
themselves, the calming process appeared to have been put to good
use. Byron, with his usual, uncanny lack of discretion, wrote that on
their wedding day he had Lady Byron on the couch before lunch.

∞ 3 ∞

THE UNDERSIDE OF THE MOON

She left on her wedding trip looking like a flower, Mrs. Clermont, Annabella's childhood governess, reported. She returned to Seaham after a three-week honeymoon looking as if she cared for nothing in this world. She had lost weight—untypically had had no appetite on what Byron called their *"Moon."* On the way to her parents that late January—they were to celebrate Byron's twenty-seventh birthday together—Lord Byron told her he presumed she now knew what not to talk about. She certainly did. "He made a point that I should write to every one of my happiness . . . I did to some." First and foremost to her parents—she wanted to shield the "old folk" from the truth. When they had been alone at Halnaby, Byron acted as if he hated her.

The newlyweds had slept together that first wintery night of their *Moon*, even after Byron told her he hated sleeping with any woman, but that she could do as she chose. One animal, he said, was as good as another, as long as she was young. That, Annabella was—twenty two. They would sleep together often through their marriage, though it was usual for those of their class to return to separate rooms. Late that first night, Byron startled her out of sleep. The fire from the fireplace was flickering, and, half awake, Byron had mistaken the red glare from the crimson curtains surrounding their marital bed as flames. "Good God, I am surely in hell!!" he cried out. He was not there alone.

It was an icy cold hell. Snow covered the grounds of the Yorkshire estate, the blanket of white isolating Annabella even more from the warmth she once knew. She was determined to marry a man with no insanity in his family? Byron chided. Well, his own maternal grandfather had committed suicide and a cousin had gone mad and set fire to his house!

Lady Melbourne had told Annabella that she would hold that list of qualities Annabella looked for in a husband in close confidence. Annabella's list had ended with one resolute determination: No history of madness in the family. Oh, you have done very well indeed! Byron mocked. The result of this taunt was that on the first full day of her marriage, Annabella realized her aunt betrayed her.

That same day a letter came from Byron's sister. "It affected him strangely, and excited a kind of fierce and exulting transport. He read to me the expression, 'Dearest, first and best of human beings,' and then said with suspicious inquisitiveness, 'There, what do you think of that?'"

"My answers on all such occasions appeared to convince him of my unsuspecting good will."

A few days later, another letter from Augusta. "He admired it as poetical." He missed "Gussy," or "Guss." That was what he called his half sister. She was the only one who understood how to make him happy. Still, he called her "a fool," stupid, unprincipled. "Goose" was his other nickname for his sister. Bell or Bella was what he called his wife—or Pip, referring to her smooth-complected face, as round and glowing as an apple. To both women he was often "Duck."

Bella, Bell, Pip, Gussy, Guss, Goose, Duck. All was peachy keen on the surface of the *Moon*. Yet when Bella innocently spoke of the unknowing incest between siblings in Dryden's *Don Sebastian*, Byron's "terror and rage were excessive." Frantically he asked, "Where did you ever hear of that?" She "quietly explained." With that: "He took up his dagger, which with his pistols, lay on the table," and slammed out.

Each day he attempted to tear Bella down. The leitmotif was that he had committed an unforgivable crime. How had she been fool enough to marry a man of whom she knew so little? he'd ask as his guilt ran over. At night he would "walk up and down the long Gallery in a state of horror and agitation," and threaten suicide. When he saw her depressed "by his unhappy state of mind, he would say 'Don't be sentimental,' and treat my affection for him sarcastically, as very troublesome." At the same time, everything was her fault, her responsibility. The mysterious evil would have never happened if she had accepted him two years earlier. If one didn't know better, one would have assumed that in the year of the waltz he ran to her with roses and went down on bended knees, not that Aunt Melbourne had gone further than he had expected and proposed for him by proxy.

One night Byron took out some of Annabella's letters to him—those before the engagement, when they were on "friendly terms." He pointed to one in rage. She wrote she wished she could be the means of "reconciling him with *his conscience*." What ever did she mean by that? He was in a frenzy, threatening revenge. Why hadn't she married him when he asked? He was becoming so violent that to stem the tide, she used her head—"first impulse" she called it. She threw herself on her knees, put her arms around his neck and said, "'You forget we *are* married, I believe.' This calmed him."

In the same red portfolio he took out a letter from Lady Melbourne to prove to her what "a good woman" *their* aunt was, "for there were things she will stop at!" He was "on the brink of a precipice," Lady Melbourne warned, "and if you do not retreat, you are lost for ever." He took part of Aunt Melbourne's advice, hadn't gone off to Sicily with his sister. Would that he had taken all of it, he continued with a look of "anguish and horror."

What was she to think? That something terrible had gone on between him and his sister? Something well known to her aunt! She blurted this out to her only companion at Halnaby, her maid Jane Minns, a farm girl, recently married, whom she had known since childhood. Jane advised her to write to her father, tell Sir Ralph how she was being treated and what she suspected. Ask Sir Ralph for advice. Instead, Annabella spent her time regretting that she had spoken out of turn to Jane. The duty of a wife was never to talk of her marriage, and she swore Jane to secrecy, which Jane kept through Lady Byron's entire life.

Her mother had been right about her aunt, Annabella realized, from many things Byron said and read to her. Lady Melbourne had felt malevolence toward her niece. Perhaps her financially savvy mother wasn't being vindictive when she said her sister-in-law was jealous of Annabella's being born, as it deprived her of an inheritance. Actually, Annabella found some solace in Lady Melbourne's bad opinion of her. Her aunt wrote to Byron that her niece was "a Spoilt child" that needed taming. Perhaps Byron was only pretending to be angry in order to correct her. In bed, almost as a joke on "our Aunt," they turned this into a fantasy in which Byron played Petruchio to her Katherine, a sexual *Taming of the Shrew*. The soft bondage in their lovemaking shadowed the sadomasochistic sexuality running through Byron's earlier sexual relationship with Caroline Lamb, which would soon be portrayed in her novel *Glenarvon*: "Calantha," said Lord Glenarvon, taking her hand firmly, and smiling half scornfully, "you shall be my slave. I will mould you as I like; teach you to think but with my thoughts, to act but with my feelings, you shall wait nor murmur—suffer, not dare to complain—ask, and be rejected, —and all this, I will do, and you know it, for your heart is already mine."

Out of bed, Annabella's sense of self was not that of a slave. She decided to speak truth to their situation. She told her husband she was sorry for him having married a woman he did not love. However, she loved him and would be what she always said she was: his true friend.

"Then if I were unfaithful you would not resent it?"

She had been taught a wife "better not notice deviation."

"Then you would *let* me be unfaithful?"

"Even as your friend I should love you too well to *let* you do what would injure yourself."

Then she didn't love him—a woman cannot love a man unless she loves his crimes as well. "No other love is worthy of the name."

Unlike Caro Lamb, Annabella refused to agree to that.

"I thought you had been more *malleable*," he responded in a tone she said she would never forget.

She quickly learned to steer as far from discussing religious faith as possible. "Come on—Convert me," he'd taunt. Hobhouse sent her a gift, but Byron would not allow her to send even a short thank-you note in return. He wanted no communication between them—nor did he want her to write to her own friends. She had to be careful of what she said when she did write. With Guss, however, who knew her brother so well, Bella could be herself, could write about what was going on, could communicate freely. And since Byron, with a look of shame, refused to write to his sister, it was Bella who became the conduit of news between Goose and Duck.

It was a relief to talk over Byron's superstitions and terribly black moods. Guss was accustomed to them all and gave the best advice. Keep things light. Jolly him out of darkness. Guss made fun of her brother's antics, imagining the look on his face in the wedding coach when the Durham bells peeled for them. She perfectly understood all that and downplayed it as "B's *fits of vexation*." And those superstitions of his—about traveling on Fridays, about Annabella having placed a black ribbon in her wedding ring to make it fit . . . well, it could all be very amusing. Keep it light. Bella did: For example, Byron told her he had two natural children and another wife. Where was that wife, she inquired. "*Somewhere*." Somewhere? She laughed in response.

"He desired me to write to Mr. Hoar to make his Will, for the purpose of leaving every thing he could devise to his sister, and as I was not mortified, but said I thought he was very right, he seemed disappointed." She knew that Augusta Leigh and the family needed financial help. Colonel Leigh, a turf man to the Prince Regent, was more a gambler than a provider. Mr. Hoar responded, by the way, that Lord Byron would have to make the will out himself.

But was it all an attempt to tame her? Was he proving to her that she was a Spoilt Child, as her aunt told him, spoiled by all the affection she had been shown through that unquestioning love of her parents, through the constant attention and admiration of friends, through the many suitors? Had she been spoiled into an unjaundiced view of humanity, and her husband's rough treatment meant to disabuse her? "I *would* not believe him worse than the actor of a most unkind part." Though Aunt Melbourne had "stimulated" Byron "to correct me as a spoiled child," perhaps all Annabella needed was patience. Certainly, Byron would see how mistaken he was about her character as he became better acquainted with her.

"If your Husband, should be in ever so absurd a passion, you should not notice it at the time, no Man will bear it with patience," Aunt Melbourne advised her niece. Actually, Annabella's calm under duress drove Byron to distraction and led him to further provocation about the mysterious crime that was her fault.

Annabella observed that Byron's blasphemy against God, his belief that he was cursed and predestined to hell, his rages and talk of hereditary madness, were somehow connected to his lameness. Slowly she broke through his defenses and got him to speak to her of what he called "his little foot." He was able to relate that deformity to his "superstitious terror"—or his Calvinistic assumption—that God wished him to suffer. His rages, she came to believe, were a result of his terror. It's to her credit that as a young woman, treated as badly as she was, she went beyond the personal assault and looked for the earlier, psychological roots for the fury he exposed her to. She called it being his friend. Also, as noted before, she was uncommonly psychologically astute—except when it came to herself.

How much did he confide in her? We know he did tell her of his bitter feelings against his mother, who once reproached him for his limp. Byron's upbringing had been the reverse of her loving one, and in her opinion, a terrible influence on his development. He was raised fatherless by a mother whom he considered erratic, stupid, temperamental, sensuous, and fat. Mrs. Byron was prone to hysterical outbursts and violent accusations—though one imagines it was not easy to be Byron's mother. He was headstrong, unruly, ungovernable from his earliest years—and lame. Mrs. Byron certainly couldn't outsmart him. It was only when she died, shortly after he returned to England in 1811 and after he delayed a visit, that his grief and sorrow overwhelmed him, and he rushed to his mother and mourned hour after hour over her dead body.

Were there things Byron told his wife that she would not put down in words? Did he go back to the time when he was nine and John Hanson became his mother's adviser? If there was any man at all in Byron's boyhood days, some trusted male presence, who took a fatherly interest in him, it was Hanson. Often the young Lord Byron stayed with the Hanson family in London. It was Hanson who chose a first school for the child and escorted him there. On the way, the eleven-year-old confided in the man, telling him of the mistreatment he received when he stayed with his mother. For the past two years, the young Scottish girl who acted as his nanny at Newstead, May Gray, had read him Bible stories, then come into the boy's bed and played what Hobhouse would later call "tricks with his person." The boy spoke of his terror to Hanson, asking him to talk to his mother. He did not want to go home till May Gray was sent "a packing."

Hanson did write to Mrs. Byron and followed it with a visit. Her son told him May Gray was perpetually beating him, stayed out late at nights, drank, fornicated, "But, Madam, this is not all; she has even—traduced yourself." Hanson couldn't tell Mrs. Byron the underlying reason for the child's terror. Byron swore him to secrecy; Hanson kept the secret until after the poet's death. Without knowing of the sexual abuse, and perhaps thinking her son exaggerated, Mrs. Byron took her time in firing the girl. Finally, May Gray was sent a-packing and Byron went home.

As a child, Byron feared his abuser; as an adult, he boasted in his journal: "My passions were developed very early—so early, that few would believe me, if I were to state the period, and the facts which accompanied it." Hobhouse reading his dead friend's words, spoke of the sexual awakening as something "less romantic." Today one gleans in those words that sense of isolation and singularity common to sexually abused children. The effect of Byron's early molestation on a

Lord Byron's mother.

particularly sensitive and extremely impressionable child—further complicated later on by the fagging system of Harrow—is rarely referred to, as his biographer Leslie Marchand noted years ago—and part of which, at least, his wife understood two hundred years ago.

"One night at Halnaby, I tried to make him consider the past as reparable, and solicited him to make me the sharer of his griefs, assuring him that I had been too conversant with the strong passions of human nature not to pardon the excesses to which they might have led him. He said I could know nothing of the things to which he alluded—good women could know nothing." He spoke of a seduction "far worse than what he had confessed to me." When Annabella asked him if Augusta knew of it, he became quite alarmed: "'Oh, for God's sake don't ask her!'" He said he was going to sleep, but if "I would ask him after breakfast in the morning he would disclose to me what he meant."

The next morning, however, he attempted to avoid the issue. "I pressed him to trust me unreservedly. He seemed torn by conflicting passions, and as my tenderness increased his eyes filled with tears, but none overflowed. He resisted my affection, and rising from the sofa where he had been stretched in agony, he stood before the fire with that terrible blackness of countenance" that she always "associated with remorseful recollections." He'd tell her the secret if she insisted, "But he bade me remember Caleb Williams and threatened me I should be miserable for life and the victim of another Falkland."

Caleb Williams (1794) was a suspense novel, still in print today, written by the radical political thinker William Godwin. The Falkland Byron alluded to was an antihero, a country squire of "considerable opulence." His early love of life and brilliant promise darkened after his return to England from a trip abroad. Byron, who said he could only write of characters whom he resembled, read of a tormented man of sensibility quite like himself, though without Byron's physical beauty. Caleb Williams, Falkland's private secretary, was a young man of humble birth who had risen through his industry. Curiosity ran deep in Caleb and he attempted to discover the secret that had so effected his beloved master's periods of gloom and isolation. After finding out the extent of Caleb's curiosity, Falkland cursed him by confessing that he had committed murder. Once Caleb knew the truth, Falkland pursued him in a relentless and ruthless drive to destroy him. Falkland's high place in society gave him enormous power and credibility among the admiring populace as he stripped this young man of an inferior class of every right and advantage a fair social contract would have offered.

Lady Byron knew Byron's own great-uncle, "The Wicked Lord," had killed a man but used his rank to escape being tried for manslaughter. After Byron warned his wife that she'd become the victim of another Falkland if he told her the secret that haunted him, Annabella pressed no further. "*Murder* was the idea suggested to my mind." What a "*Moon*," as Byron called his honeymoon, when he wasn't referring to those three weeks at Halnaby as his treacle moon.

THINGS WERE BETTER at Seaham, though at first Byron attempted to send Annabella there alone and spend his birthday in London looking for their new home. Here she put her foot down. No argument worked until she asked him: How would it look to others? Once at Seaham he told her he loved her better in company, because with people around he wasn't expected to love her too much. She took that as a hopeful sign. "He felt I was a comfort to him in some respects, if merely from habit of which he is so much the creature. He was not content if I was away from him."

They were sexually active, if we can judge by Annabella writing to Augusta that Byron's ardor hadn't decreased since the *Moon*. Guss replied, quoting Annabella, that she suspects Byron rejoices at discovering his wife's " 'ruling passion for mischief in private.'" Sleeping together in fact saved Byron's life two weeks later. He had stayed up writing and had thrown water on the coal fire in the next room—coal from his father-in-law's collieries—not realizing he was breathing in fumes from the embers. When he got to bed, he was incoherent, spoke wildly, then he fainted. Annabella somehow sat him up, revived him. She "sluiced me with Eau de Cologne and all sorts of waters besides," he wrote to Aunt Melbourne. If she hadn't, their aunt would be wearing black "for your loving nephew." How Bella herself was not overcome by the fumes that seeped into the bedroom, he did not know. "She is alive, and thanks to her so am I." Her lungs may have been affected in the long run, for she developed chronic bronchitis.

One of Annabella's fondest memories of her marriage would be what Augusta labeled the couple's "conjugal race." Byron could become a boy when far from scenes with "painful associations," as Annabella put it. Often they'd take a run in the sands. His pronounced limp didn't seem to bother him as he picked up speed. Annabella, who had lived an active outdoor life, bounded after him. He loved to climb, "a wild mirthful boy," scampering up rugged rocks. There was a crag called Featherbed jutting out from the sea and isolated at high tide.

Byron challenged her to a "scramble," and she climbed, following him up the steep incline. They stood on the summit together, breathing hard, at peace, far from the swirling waters below. Years later she'd have a close companion, the art historian Anna Jameson, do a drawing of Featherbed for her. As she put it, the shadows of her youth flitted around in the sea spray.

Memories of his youth seemed to come over Byron at the time. One night he said to Annabella, "I think I love you—better even than Thyrza," referring to his love for John Edleston. Yet it was at Seaham that he wrote the plaintive, "There's not a joy the world can give like that it takes away. . . ." It's not that Byron's homosexuality ended with his youth, but the freedom and wildness of it, the ideal of it, seemed like the golden past to him. His youth could never be reclaimed. No beautiful young boy would ever again—in the old way—bare his breast to him. The married man certainly felt old before his time.

Still, at Seaham, there was a shaft of light.

How delightful "your 'ramble-scramble tumble-sum-jumble,'" Augusta responded to Annabella's description of an evening party, calling her "Sis." "Only think! of B. Playing at Drafts!" Byron was roundly spoiled at Seaham, Bell reported, and Guss responded she was glad to hear it "because he would have it nobody could spoil him but me." They were sisters to one another though they were yet to meet. Sisters compete—Annabella wrote of her sex life, Guss boasted of her singular power to please her brother.

"The *Moon* is over," Byron wrote to Aunt Melbourne from Seaham, "but Bell & I are as lunatic as heretofore. She does as she likes and don't bore me." Lady Melbourne was sensitive to a seeming coldness and tartness in Annabella when she did answer her letters, and one wonders at the significance of Byron responding to their aunt, "I won't betray you if you will only write me something worth betraying." But of course he had already betrayed Lady Melbourne to Annabella, showing her letters that were supposedly private, revealing that Lady Melbourne considered her niece a spoiled child.

The couple stayed at Seaham for close to six weeks, and when it was time to go, the same scenario was reenacted in reverse. Byron would send Annabella to London on her own to find a house, while he stopped by his sister's at Six Mile Bottom along the way. Once more Annabella insisted she would accompany him. Guss seemed reluctant about their visit. The house was "small," and of course there were the children—four of them at the time, ranging from eight to under a year. Because of the lack of space Guss suggested the couple rent nearby.

Speaking of space, Aunt Melbourne had been busy. She wrote that she had rented the Duchess of Devonshire's house for the couple in London   the Duchess, now a widow, being in France. At first their aunt would not take such an expensive place. She went instead to the "great House brokers" and found that many of the places they had to show were "indifferent" and few of those came furnished. So like many a house hunter in a big, important city, she soon saw you could get very little for a very high price. "I am rather in a fright at what I have done." She leased them the Duchess's mansion on Piccadilly Terrace—700 pounds for the year. A huge price, a huge place. Not that the rent was ever paid. With Byron's Newstead estate still unsold and creditors mounting, the couple were to live way beyond their means. It was far from the small establishment Annabella had imagined in earlier letters, looking forward to their shared frugality; her only fear, she told Byron, would be living beyond their means. "Could not B.—content himself with a *small* house in Town," Guss wrote, "*till* he *could* have a *great* one!" Still, her husband had left, another guest hadn't shown, there was room for them in her "widowed state."

Again Byron tried to convince Bella to go on to London while he visited Augusta. She wouldn't have it, and, after three days, they were still on the road. "You lazy Travellers!" Her mother wrote. Judith would have "*dined* at Six Mile Bottom that night." Whatever reprieve was offered at Seaham was spent. Byron was agitated and often called his wife a fool for going to his sister's with him. He exhibited "the same ferocity of manner" that he had while traveling to Halnaby on their wedding day. By now Annabella was skilled in making him what Guss labeled "less disagreeable." She feigned lightheartedness, acted as if she were cheerful and gay, and within hours he became less violent. Still, she was a fool and Guss more than a fool, he said.

They arrived at Wandsford on the last leg of their overlong journey, and late that night, in bed together, his mood changed. "You married me to make me happy, didn't you?" he asked. They were the kindest words she could hope to hear and she answered him warmly. "Well, then," he said with passionate affection, "you *do* make me happy." She stayed silent in the dark, but she believed he could feel her joy as she wept. Then he seemed to pity her for some impending inevitable misery. That unrelenting pity, she would one day say, was worse than his insults, as it made her feel the "*hopelessness*" of her situation more profoundly. During the *Moon*, after pacing up and down the drafty halls in extreme agitation one night, Byron had come back to bed, and Annabella put her head on his chest.

"You should have a softer pillow than my heart," he said.

"I wonder which will break first—yours or mine," she responded.

THE NEXT day they arrived at Newmarket, and just before their carriage reached Guss's home at Six Mile Bottom: "I feel as if I was just going to be married," Byron said. The words slipped out and embarrassed him. He hadn't meant married to Annabella. Waiting in the drawing room for Augusta Leigh to make an appearance—she hadn't come outside, and was not even downstairs to greet them— Byron blamed his increasing agitation on finding a letter awaiting his arrival. In it, another complication in trying to sell Newstead and raise money. Finally, Augusta appeared on the landing and walked down the stairs. The timidity, the family shyness was there. That day in mid-March slim, graceful Bella was twenty-two, in the flush of youth. Hope existed. The night before, her husband making love to her, said she made him happy. Augusta Leigh was thirty-one, mother of four, with an eleven-month-old she still nursed. Older. Matronly. Concerned. No matter that some of Byron's friends called her "Dowdy Goody"—in life a Camilla often aces a Diane. When she finally reached the two, Augusta kissed Byron with affection and then shook Annabella's hand.

Byron went his own way in the house he knew so well, while Guss took Annabella upstairs to their rooms. There was already a place in Bella's heart for her sister-in-law. Judith had raised her dead sister's child Sophy Curzon, who had been like an older sister to young Annabella—until Annabella was eight. Then at eighteen Sophy married and left Seaham. Suddenly, Annabella was alone. Her sense of abandonment overpowered her. She was bereft, inconsolable, and being reprimanded for being selfish, she learned to hide her feelings, her anger, her despair at the loss of love.

> Unhappy age! when secrets all unguest
> Dwell, and accumulate within the breast
> And the poor child is deemed as freed from care
> As birds new fledged that blithely mount the air!
> For seldom even a parent's eye discerns
> For what the young heart sickens, throbs and yearns.

Now there was a new sister and for once Annabella took the initiative. She told Guss how happy she was finally to be with her and she made the first move: She kissed Guss. Later, without much thought, which was her way, Guss told Byron of Bella's affectionate gesture.

Why hadn't Guss kissed his wife in greeting? Byron railed. There was a maliciousness and a sense of mystery in the way he kept up this taunt. It was up to *her*, not to Annabella, to give that first kiss. Why had she shook her hand as if she were a stranger. It went on and on. Guss stayed composed under the assault, "timid and guarded." Eventually things calmed down and Annabella, with her usual discretion, left the two, as she imagined they'd have much to talk over. When she returned, Byron's mood had once more shifted. "We can amuse ourselves without you, my charmer," he said, and sent Annabella up to bed after dinner, while Guss, guarded and reluctant, did nothing to further acerbate the situation. When Byron finally did come to bed, he was in a frenzy: "Now I have *her*, you will find I can do without you." He had told Annabella not to come along with him, hadn't he? He had passion for his sister and he planned to indulge it, he ranted.

Yet the next morning, Guss appeared so calm and unconcerned in the way she greeted the two of them, unselfconsciously kissing each, that Annabella's suspicions of her sister dwindled. That same day, in the presence of both: "Well, Guss, I'm a reformed man, a'nt I?" he said as a way to express exactly the opposite. Here, Guss looked disconcerted, but said, "I *have* observed some improvements already." Annabella could only hope that his knowing way of talking of his love for his sister was "but another cruel experiment on my feelings."

Guss was always kind. Whenever she could, without inflaming Byron, she stood up for Annabella. But for the two-week stay it was more or less the same. Annabella was dismissed curtly, sent off, except sometimes Byron said "We can amuse ourselves without you, my dear," rather than "my charmer." She was humiliated. But really, what was either woman to do? They had continually written of Byron's shifts and how to jolly him, how to hold steady under his taunts. He told Guss that his wife had had no idea how brandy effected him, and when he first wished for some on the *Moon*, she went to her own supply and brought it to him. See? He was still drinking brandy, though even the smallest amounts could turn him brutal. He taunted Bella with what she didn't know, Guss with what she knew. He was erratic in his behavior, pointed to his knife and his guns, insisted to both that he might kill himself.

Byron had a captive audience, two women who loved him, and in front of both he spoke of the intrigues he carried on during his engagement. He could always confide in Guss—she was the opposite of a demanding lover, and her careless ease, cheerfulness, her ability to live and let live, was solace to him. He made his sister bring out the letters he'd written to her over the years. Even before he knew Annabella, he wrote to his sister of never marrying except for money. After the engagement he wrote to ever-agreeable Goose of his sexual adventures and of his aversion to actually marrying Annabella. He even sent his sister one of Annabella's letters to show how deluded Bella was. He made Guss hold it up to his wife: "All the time you thought I was dying for you," he taunted.

Earlier letters from his youth were not spiteful, but an occasion to remember, and together the three looked them over as one might a family album. As a schoolboy, his letters to his older sister "were romantic and open-hearted." Something changed between the age of sixteen and seventeen, they all could see as they rummaged. He acknowledged it with a sense of "mysterious horror." In one of the letters Annabella read, he told his sister that the change was not own- ing to love, but during his first year at Cambridge he acknowledged that he no longer had the carefree heart he once had and from then on, Guss told Annabella, he was a cause of misery to her. The sisters discussed much of this in Byron's presence.

In a light moment, Guss took out some youthful drawings of Byron at Harrow to show his wife. From there the women discussed portraits of him and what the best view of his face would be, as Byron looked and listened. Annabella said she would like a portrait of him painted that captured the lovely tenderness of expression on his face when he looked down at Medora Leigh—a world-class conversation stopper that.

On their walks together, the sisters confided in each other. Guss never gave Annabella reason to think Byron married her for love. But when Annabella said that immediately after the marriage she realized Byron did not care for her, Guss replied that she hoped Annabella was now of a contrary opinion. Annabella confided that at Seaham Byron had gotten terribly angry with her if she showed the slightest cour- tesy to any man. Guss replied that once at Newstead, Byron got very upset when she shook hands with their own cousin, George Byron! Ignore Byron's protestations, Guss advised. Besides, she told his wife, Byron's dark moods were often a result of indigestion. Weight gain had always been a problem and he attempted to solve it by starving himself, living on soda water and biscuits. Then he'd gorge himself and purge with overdoses of magnesia. This eating disorder and his tendency to grow quite fat plagued him through his life. Ironically, Annabella herself gorged and purged at highly emotional moments, though she remained slim. On another walk Annabella enquired about some specific details of Byron's amours before marriage, telling Guss Byron had desired that she ask. Without blinking an eye, Guss said she had no idea what her brother meant.

"Aunt Melbourne does not like my being here," Byron would say in front of both of them. Annabella realized her aunt had not written a word while they stayed with Augusta. It was obvious that at Six Mile Bottom Byron delighted in what he called "working them both well," and Annabella could see that Guss was in his power as well as she and that he was making cruel use of it. "Ask Augusta if I've been a virtuous man," he taunted.

"I'm afraid there's no such thing as a virtuous man in these days," Guss answered. She wasn't such a goose after all.

"Augusta, you're my only friend," he'd say. In a tone of suppressed wretchedness, she'd answer, "I fear I've been your *worst*."

Both women might writhe, but they competed: "He would lie down on the sofa and oblige her and me to kiss him by turns," Annabella wrote, "but I was sensible that he was more warm towards her than me." One day while kissing his sister on the sofa, he asked her, in front of his wife, if she remembered the signs they used when alone at Newstead to warn of another approaching.

The sexual tensions of that household! The kissing games. The innuendoes. The watchful eyes. The competition. Annabella spoke to Guss as if "there were a tacit understanding" between them. Without words, the two women communicated sexual knowledge—and it drew them to each other in a deep, visceral way, as they watched each other bend to Byron's will. Kiss me, Bella. Kiss me, Gussy. Kiss me, Kate.

On most nights when he left his sister, he came to Annabella in a rage. One night, however, he told Annabella he liked night more than day as he could spend more time being with his wife. "Spare your profession!" she snapped. He seemed alarmed by that.

"Where are you going?

"To my own room."

Perhaps she should have done that more often. Gone to her room. Challenged his words. Ripped off the disguise of calm and spoke her mind.

Her critics still quote Byron's manservant Fletcher: "It is very odd, but I never yet knew a lady that could not manage my Lord, except my Lady." Repetition doesn't make it true, judging by Byron's treatment of Caro, Lady Oxford (remember her adolescent daughter?), and his sister too. Two guns, one dagger, and a volatile nature were always within reach.

Alone that night in her own room, Bella wept herself into what she called "that peace which even my friendless and fearful prospects could never entirely banish."

Still, "She shall do for me," he said to Guss at Six Mile Bottom. Annabella was more malleable now than on the *Moon*. His wife went to her room on command. She took her turn on the kissing couch. Annabella repeated Byron's "She shall do for me" to Guss once they were alone. He's mistaken if he thought her character unformed, she told his sister.

Only late in the visit did Byron have sex with his wife. In that bitter heat, their daughter, Augusta Ada, may have been conceived. Nine months later, superstitious Byron would wonder if that were so, looking into "Augusta Junior's" face for some resemblance to his sister. At the possible time of conception, Augusta Senior had her period, and evidently had enough. For she sent the couple a-packing and they had to travel on Byron's forbidden day, a Friday. It doesn't rain but it pours. At their leased mansion on Piccadilly, facing Green Park—they found it to be No. 13. The house might be leased, might be absurdly grand given Byron's financial situation, but there they were, just about three months into their marriage, for the first time in their own home— and they had a very good week. Annabella couldn't remember when Byron was so kind to her. She wrote to Guss of the comforts of their new home, of the view, of being presented as a couple at Court. In fine spirits, marred only by her worry concerning Uncle Wentworth's health, she extended an invitation to Guss to visit. "Byron had proposed to her in my presence that she should visit us—and I renewed that offer of accommodation."

"Dearest Sis," Guss replied the next day: "I do not require your account of the view from your windows as an inducement to pay you a visit. You will perhaps be a better judge by and by whether I shall not be a plague—and you must tell me *truly* if I am likely to prove so— you know I should not be 'affronted.'"

"The more one sees of this world," Annabella wrote to her father, "the more difficult it must appear to judge what is really best, when there are in everything such *pros* and *cons* as Reason can hardly balance."

It did make some sort of sense that if your only sister-in-law and your niece, eight-year-old Georgey (Georgiana), were coming to London, and you were living in a mansion, you'd invite them to stay for a while. The Honorable Augusta Leigh had just been made Lady-in-Waiting to the bedchamber of Queen Caroline and had to come to London to finalize arrangements. Eventually this would give her and her brood rooms at St. James's Palace and 300 pounds per annum.

There was some logic in the laundry list of reasons Annabella would one day write out for her lawyers: How would it have looked to others if her sister-in-law didn't stay? How would she escape Byron's tormenting her by questioning *why* Augusta wasn't welcome? False excuses wouldn't appease him. Was she to tell him the true reason? She suspected that at some time before the marriage "some fatal and unrepeated *hour*" of "criminality" had occurred. Why, that would have "fixed his malignant temper" into what she called "a rooted hatred of me." She then would have no influence over him at all, for she would have made herself "too much the object of suspicious dread to be regarded as a friend." The variations of insinuation would be endless. He'd hound her.

The fact that Guss accepted her invitation pointed to innocence, Annabella opined. She wouldn't have if there had been something shameful going on. Wouldn't she have? Annabella didn't reverse the proposition: How would it have looked if Augusta refused? Whatever sense one attempts to make of Annabella's invitation to Guss, short days after leaving such a humiliating situation as Six Mile Bottom, kissing games and all, one fails. Lady Byron might later count her reasons when she spoke with her lawyers, when she spoke with friends, but Bella, Bell, Pip, young, pregnant, and passionately in love with a man who did not love her, was not using her head. Augusta and Georgiana arrived less than two weeks after the couple left Six Mile Bottom under duress. Byron was agitated, greeted his sister darkly, but after a bit of time passed grew quite affectionate. "You were a fool to let her come," he said to his wife in front of his sister. "You will find it will make a good deal of difference to you *in all ways!*"

Now *that* made sense.

13 Piccadilly Terrace

There is a sameness in most abusive relationships that is both distressing and predictable. There are threats and violence, there are tender regrets leading to sexual reconciliation. The pendulum—and pendulums are mechanical—swings back and forth. There is hope. At least when Annabella returned to London at the end of March 1815, there was hope, with Byron being as kind to his wife as he had ever been. If she hadn't gotten pregnant that last stormy week at Augusta's, she might have had that first happy week in London.

From the outside the marriage looked good, surprising the skeptics and the bookies. In public Byron was company-kind and hardly left his young wife out of his sight. They made a handsome couple, he darkly charismatic, with that curled lip and romantic limp, she pretty and graceful and, as everyone remarked, so knowledgeable, yet without pretension. Both aristocratic, in love. When the young American historian George Ticknor met Lady Byron, he thought her nineteen, the age she'd been when she first saw Byron at Caro Lamb's morning waltz. In all London, Annabella was spoken of "goldenly," Ticknor reported.

Byron introduced his wife to his publisher, John Murray, no innocent abroad. Murray was as enthusiastic as Ticknor. "She is a most delightful creature, and possesses excellent temper and a most inordinate share of good sense." The married woman no longer had to tiptoe for permission to be in a room with Lady Holland, the previously divorced wife of the Lord at the center of Whig politics during the Regency. Instead, Annabella wrote to her father in amusement that at a banquet she was told Lady Holland's constant amiability when in Annabella's presence was not her true nature. "She evidently does not know what to make of me, and handles me as fearfully as if I were a Hedgehog."

The writer Leigh Hunt remembered Byron after marriage as looking the "finest" he had ever seen him. Not only was he in trim physical shape, but in high spirits and quite whimsical. Byron couldn't resist jumping on Hunt's son's rocking horse to play. During one visit in the spring the two men were having so much fun that Lady Byron had to call up twice that she was waiting. She was taking her usual ride to Henderson's Nursery to choose flowers.

The surface view has value, for like all of us, Annabella, off to pick out flowers, had a day-to-day life. Though Hunt had not met Annabella formerly (he'd just gotten out of jail), he glimpsed her once and mentioned her earnest look and her "pippin face." That he used a variation of her pet name indicates that Byron, when speaking of his wife to others, appeared devoted. He had the best wife in the world, he told his friends—but don't get married.

Every night sister and brother stayed together a good hour after Annabella retired, and she would hear them laughing together downstairs. Byron and his sister spoke their own language. Duck would become playful, acting like the delightful, mischievous child he could be, Goose joining in the fun. When Byron was in one of his bad moods, Guss most often could jolly him out of it with their special brand of baby talk. From the way they acted, one would think they had bonded early in life. This was far from the truth.

They shared a father, "Mad Jack" Byron. From all accounts Mad Jack was a charming, degenerate gambler and womanizer, usually broke, living off women, and one of a long line of Byrons known for mad and bad behavior. As Peter Gunn wrote, "The profligacy and the utter contempt for the world's opinion" were the mark of "three generations of the family," and might "suggest the presence of some common element in their heredity." Augusta's mother, the beautiful Amelia, Baroness Conyers in her own right, was married to the future Duke of Leeds. He sued for dissolution of the marriage after Mad Jack became his wife's lover, and she supposedly said it was "perhaps the most lucky incident of her life." She took her clothes and jewels and moved in with dashing Jack Byron. They got married a month before Augusta Byron's birth. Amelia died before the infant was one, and Augusta's father was soon off to Scotland to marry Byron's mother, and squander as much as he could of her money before he died four years after his son's birth.

Before that birth, motherless Augusta lived with Mrs. Byron, though her father was rarely at home. When Mrs. Byron was pregnant, the four-year-old was sent to live with her grandmother, Lady Holdernesse, and spent much of her childhood at the palatial home of her mother's titled siblings, at their pleasure of course. If Augusta's morality became one of everything being permitted as long as everyone was kept happy, she came by it honestly, as she herself must have spent a lot of her orphaned childhood keeping her mother's first husband, her half siblings, and her strict grandmother pleased to have her around.

Augusta's life hadn't changed much. She was "The Honorable," but because of her beautiful mother's actions, she did not have the advantages of her titled half siblings. With her own multiplying brood of children and her gambler of a husband, she was making the best of her aristocratic connections as she attempted to make ends meet. Becoming Lady-in-Waiting to Queen Caroline was such a perk. When she and her half brother had come together again as adults, it must have been a thrill for each to find a part of selfhood in the other. One wonders if after Byron's marriage the half siblings shared some secret or unconscious envy of that other only child, born to every advantage and the apple of her adoring parents' eyes. Was it *so* unfair that Bella was alone and obviously upset in her bedroom while they were in the drawing room finally having fun? Byron often admonished Annabella for the ease of her charmed life, leading her to think that his constant derision might be his way of opening her eyes to realities from which he thought her sheltered.

Annabella would lie awake waiting for Byron's footsteps on the stairs. Either she'd hear him finally stride up to her in passion, his "terrific energy" evident as he bounded, or she'd hear Augusta and him leisurely climbing the stairs together and would catch the "flashes of merriment" between them. There was plenty of time to listen because it was a very steep staircase.

Lady Melbourne had warned them of it when she leased the stately town house. She sent them a rudimentary floor plan and advised the couple to sleep on the ground floor, which had four large rooms, two of which could be their bedchambers. After all, the Duchess of Devonshire had slept downstairs. But they chose the four large rooms above, despite the need for finer furnishing, and the steep climb.

"One night when Byron and Augusta were later than usual and my Imagination was on the rack, I could not lay still any longer, but got up and walked about. They heard me below, and he sent her upstairs to see what was the matter. I was in an agony of tears and tried to conceal them as I heard her approach—but the thought of his dagger lying in the next room crossed my mind—I wished it in her heart. It was an instant of revenge, and her voice of kindness extinguished it— yet if I should ever go mad perhaps these remembrances would be prevailing ideas." What saved Annabella from madness she believed to be what she called "a principle of Forgivenesss . . . under circumstance that made my brain burn." It was not altruism. She called it "Romantic forgiveness," conscious "of it being *necessary*—in its utmost extent *to myself*." She "was almost mad," but Augusta "never saw it."

When Annabella had to leave 13 Piccadilly to sit vigil at her dying uncle's bedside, she admitted even this came as a relief. "Dearest," Byron wrote, "Now your mother is come I won't have you worried any longer—more particularly in your present situation which is rendered very precarious by what you have already gone through. Pray come home." Back she went. Uncle Wentworth died soon after without legitimate issue. Annabella's mother inherited half of his

Augusta Leigh, Byron's half sister and lover.

considerable estate and with it the stipulation to take his name—her maiden name. Judith and Ralph became Lord and Lady Noel. Ticknor believed Annabella a baroness of great wealth, which would some day be true. In 1815, however, the Noels were, as others in that day, land rich and cash poor. Bank failures, declining property values. No one in the country had money, Judith said. Whatever was sent to market came back unsold.

Byron was deeply disappointed. He blamed his mother-in-law for the continuing necessity of having to sell both Newstead Abbey and Rochdale. By then he had been made a manager of the Drury Lane Theatre, so in public he would on occasion share his box with his in-laws, but he would no longer see them in private. He even refused to attend the family dinner they had for Annabella's twenty-third birthday in April 1815. He took out his rancor against Judith by keeping Annabella as much as he could from her parents. He continued in

Annabella around the time she married Lord Byron.

not wanting her to be in correspondence with her own set of friends, and they were not welcome at 13 Piccadilly.

Before Augusta arrived, Guss had written to Bella that if she turned out to be a "plague" as a house guest, Bella must tell her truthfully. Two months and counting, Annabella told Guss it was time for her to leave. Annabella stood firm, would not hear of any other solution. On June 25, Augusta Leigh and Georgey returned to Six Mile Bottom. As soon as his sister and niece were gone, Byron again showed affection for his wife, and they took up what Annabella called "a sort of conventional language of nonsense." It was the type of playful childishness and baby talk that Byron and Augusta constantly shared. Now Byron and Annabella became children together, as they had on certain carefree days at Seaham, bounding along the beach. In the midst of this, Annabella remembered him suddenly interspersing the frolic and levity of his banter with the deepest reflections. "The transitions had all the grace of Genius." These times of happiness stayed with her through her life.

From Six Mile Bottom, Augusta wrote to Hobhouse that her pregnant sister-in-law was not looking or feeling well when she left her. The couple "go out little, I think (and Lady B. thinks) almost *too* little." Too little, because of Byron's attempt to cut his wife off from her own circle. To Lady Melbourne, he went alone. Bella had little desire to see her aunt—or for him to see her—but when his moods blackened, she was content if those visits offered him some relief. When the Byrons did go out socially, it was to his friends, where his company-kindness was evident and he showed her off. Annabella didn't lack compassion for Byron. She saw the struggle in him and believed he would have loved her had he been able. Her passion for Byron ran deep, but she was not only *in* love—she loved.

Judith certainly wasn't blind to Byron's attitude. When the new Lord and Lady Noel took up residence at the Wentworth estate at Kirkby Mallory in mid-August, she wrote to her son-in-law that she was so sorry not to have seen him their last night in town to say goodbye, particularly since she wished to prevail on him to visit them at Kirkby. Seaham would be free as well and there had been talk of the couple escaping the dunning of creditors and the expenses of London by staying there for the birth of the child. Though Byron had already refused to go, Judith still held out hopes. She emphasized that Annabella required "Country Air, her looks shew it." It would do them both good. Annabella, however, "manifestly requires it—and *that* is the first thing to be considered at present." No one who knew her well at that period thought Annabella was looking good.

Judith was pleased that her daughter had chosen Mr. Le Mann for her London doctor, as giving birth "is not a business of *fashion* but of *Nature*, and I believe Le Mann very clever." How did those who served the *bon ton* obtain their reputations and lucrative medical careers in the first place? "By going abroad and attending fashionable ladies giving birth and *keeping their secrets*." She didn't think Annabella would suffer more than necessary in labor. Not only was her youth in her favor, but she was in shape, having exercised since childhood and having never led a sedentary life. Whatever the pangs, "I believe that the first cry of a fine Child will cause you to forget them, as the Sweet Sound of yours did me, tho' from my Age (40) I suffered long and much."

In other circumstances Judith's upstaging her daughter as to the severity of labor pains might have irked Annabella. Instead, as Annabella attempted to shield her aging parents from the woe that was in her marriage, she felt a sense of responsibility for her mother's joy and also a sense of displacement for keeping her in the dark. As for "little *Pip*," Judith continued, have *him* dressed handsomely and send her the bill: "As I shall have pleasure in decorating the little Byron."

Cheerfully, Annabella wrote that Byron was "vastly entertained with the thought of making you a Grandmamma." Byron was actually vastly entertained by the thought of Grandmamma dropping dead. His venom had increased since before the marriage when he wrote to Hobhouse wittily that not only wouldn't Annabella's parents and uncle die, they all seemed on the verge of sprouting new baby teeth!

Annabella kept up a front in her letters to her parents. She joked about how big she had become, of how she'd write more if she could find a desk shaped like a shaving bowl, of how at Hyde Park she got stuck between two poles! To her father she wrote that she was sure her mother would insist on coming for the birth and would fidget while she squalled.

The real estate market remained stagnant and Byron was greatly in arrears. A would-be buyer for Newstead Abbey didn't have the cash to cement the deal. Annabella, after having remained steady and having downplayed financial concerns, made enquiries of everyone she knew, both for her father and her husband, to see if mortgages could be had for any of their properties. No luck. She went to Hanson personally to see if any mortgage at all could be provided for Newstead. Again, no luck. This was at the end of August. "Do you know I'm a Widow for a day or two? Byron is just gone to Augusta, which I am glad of," she informed her parents.

Guss tried to prevent her brother's visit on the basis that if by any chance he did sell Newstead, her husband might work on Byron for immediate money. It would then be lost for her and her children in the future. Byron had done what he threatened during the *Moon*. He made a new will after Uncle Wentworth's death, and officially signed it in July. His personal worth would go to his sister and her children— not to his wife and their children. As it turned out, he would have a daughter, but it was particularly odd that he was willing, before- hand, to leave his own son and heir nothing but a title. Judith was appalled, not Annabella. She knew Augusta's needs were greater than hers would be, and approved of the will on that basis. It was Augusta herself who had reservations, sensitive that her attachment to Byron might be looked on as mercenary.

In the days before he left to visit his sister, Byron's mistreatment of his wife escalated. "Perfectly ferocious," Bella recorded. She was seven months pregnant and emotional. When they slept together, he'd keep her awake all night with cruel remarks, till she lost her self- command and, sobbing convulsively, left him. He told her he was leaving for the Continent as soon as the child was born because every- one knew once she gave birth she'd love it more than him, mothers always do. You'll make me hate my child, she replied.

Right before he went to Six Mile Bottom, he asked Bella to forgive him his ferocity, his apology "half in earnest & half in jest—but a kind word from him was then too precious to me to be rigorously examined." She wrote to him as soon as he left. His kind words made her feel that Byron had turned from self-loathing and again "loved *himself*, which does me more good than any thing else." She hoped while he was away he'd call out "'Pip, pip, pip'"— now & then." She was sure she'd hear him and she promised not to "grow lemoncholy."

Before he received Bella's letter, he wrote that his man Fletcher had forgotten to pack "certain phials" labeled "drops." Would she send them on? "Ever most lovingly thine B," he signed himself, add- ing "(not *Frac*)," meaning not in a fractious mood. The "drops," by the way, were laudanum. Five days and some affectionate letters later, Byron returned and was as affectionate to Bella as he was angry at

Guss, who wrote to Annabella that her brother's rage was the result of her defending Annabella's parents against his abuse of them. During one of those harmonious days of homecoming, on a carriage ride together, Byron interrupted the couple's intimate babble and pronounced as if it were a fate he was doomed to fulfill: "I shall break your heart and Augusta's after all."

There was a noticeable decline in Byron's stability as the theater season progressed. He was drinking brandy, which he could not tolerate. By November he was sleeping most regularly with a minor actress at Drury Lane, Susan Boyce, whom he threatened to bring home to copulate while Bella gave birth. Later he would say of his affairs at Drury Lane that at the time sex was a mechanical act for him—a performance, not a passion. His laudanum would have helped that along. Drinking, drugging, whoring, on occasion taking a swing at a buddy, Byron was spiraling out of control. Certainly he had pressing financial difficulties, human dilemmas, but for Byron all of his problems had external, cosmic causes—they existed in the stars, not in himself. He was cursed, doomed. He was, as so many of his protagonists—and so many a charming addict—a tortured soul.

Annabella tried to make some sense out of his inner chaos and knew that the Calvinism of his Scottish upbringing encouraged his fatalism. She also saw his "habitual *passion for Excitement*" as part of his ardent temperament. Boredom of any kind was exactly what drove the "best-hearted people" to the "most dangerous paths," she wrote to Guss. Her husband might seem to be acting out of bad motives, but he was actually trying to escape from mental suffering by any external stimulus at his disposal: "Drinking, Gaming etc." Also, "The love of tormenting arises chiefly from this Source," the love of tormenting *her*:

> She listens yet to hear his voice—
>   Is that his coming tread
> What used to make her heart rejoice?
>   Such power, alas! Is fled.

But still her cheek will flush and fade,
    For still those sounds are dear;
And all she feels is still betrayed
    When bursts the silent tear.

Too soon that withered heart of Love
    Must wear one lifeless hue—
The winter of Despair above
    Shall weep no drop of dew!

During her winter of despair, Annabella copied out Byron's new poem *Parisina* in her clear handwriting, a fair copy to send to publisher Murray. Byron handed her the poem saying she could think of it what she wished. It portrayed the incestuous love affair in Ferrara between Parisina the wife of the Marquis of Este and his bastard son Hugo. The lovers met recklessly at night:

Who that have felt that passion's power,
Or paused, or fear'd in such an hour?
Or thought how brief such moments last?
But yet—they are already past!
Alas! we must awake before
We know such vision comes no more.

Murray admitted to being alarmed when Byron hinted the theme of his poem was incest. Seeing Lady Byron's handwriting, however, he tore open the packet in relief "and have found in it a Pearl."

"I am very glad that the handwriting was a favourable omen of the *morale* of the piece, but you must not trust to that," Byron responded. "For my copyist would write out any thing I desired in all the ignorance of innocence." He was blind to the fact Bella was consciously protecting herself through feigned ignorance.

Byron's debts were such that a bailiff was assigned to live in the house. Incredibly, Byron thought he was *hiding* the fact from

Annabella, as she wrote to Augusta in amazement. The live-in bailiff left a day before Annabella gave birth in December, though Byron made the strange threat that a bailiff was coming to her bedroom to claim her bed. Then I'll have my confinement on the floor, she said.

The month before that confinement was one of unspeakable rage. The dysfunction that had been in the marriage from the beginning now played itself out. She was in physical danger by November. Her confidence that she could always "stare him down" had lessened. Once, he took the dagger he always carried and held it over her head. All she did was stare up at him. He said, "If anything could make me believe in heaven it is the expression of your countenance at this moment." He probably thought she was ready to die for love. He misjudged her, she told Guss. She was *not* a timid woman, she was not afraid. Such lack of fear, however, can become foolhardy. Byron was not in control in November and he was threatening to take his own life, while others in the household feared for his wife's. Would a day come when she could not stare him down?

God knows what I suffered yesterday, she wrote to Guss. Byron left the house telling her he was going to abandon himself to every sort of desperation, he upbraided her for having married him when he didn't want to marry her, and that as a result she was answerable for any drinking or whoring he did. He hoped their child would be born dead: "O Augusta, will it ever change for me?"

The next day? He returned from the Drury Lane Theatre and was kind to her again, but rather odd. She wished some man with common sense, perhaps cousin Captain George Byron could come and laugh Byron out of his excessive horror of the live-in bailiff, "which he seems to regard as if no mortal has ever experienced anything so shocking; and *we* can do less because he thinks that women don't enter into those sublime grievances." These days he "loves or hates us together," she told Augusta. At the height of anger, he called his sister *Mrs. Leigh*: "I expected you would soon be 'The Honorable.' I ought to have laughed at this; but I took it as another misery, fancying that *I* was in some way responsible."

The household staff had eyes to see. Fletcher guarded Byron's door at night in the weeks before the baby came. Mrs. Clermont, that family friend and Annabella's old governess, arrived and took the room next to hers. The baby nurse hired was now living in and, without being told, was taking precautions for her mistress. The person Annabella needed in order to control Byron was *Guss*. She was certain Byron would not bring his actress into the house to bed if his sister were present. Five months after asking Guss to leave, she asked her sister-in-law—who had often offered—to return. One caution: Whatever Guss experienced of Byron's violent abuse, do not risk his displeasure by defending Annabella. It would not be the act of friendship, because it wouldn't do Annabella any good, and it would tear away at Guss's influence over her brother. Do not appear afraid "for my carcase," she wrote in the down-home language of her letters to her father. "Let me see you the middle of next week—at latest. . . . My dearest A.—I feel all your kindness." On November 15, Augusta and Georgey moved back to 13 Piccadilly. Byron was insulting on his sister's return, insisting he meant to vex her as well as his wife. "Ah, you don't know the fool I have been about him," Guss told Annabella.

Everyone in the house practiced caution, but Byron, who was acting deranged, was not inferred with or confined in any obvious way. Annabella continued to see her husband alone. "Life had then lost some of its value to me, not that I wished to die." Annabella's mother had arrived in London for the birth, but became critically ill with erysipelas and was confined to her hotel room. It spared her the knowledge of a household living in fear: Augusta, Mrs. Clermont, Fletcher, and a baby nurse, all focused on protecting her daughter.

A few hours before going into labor, Annabella went to tell Byron she'd soon be confined. By the way, he asked, how long after the birth did she plan to remain at 13 Piccadilly? Later he'd say he was prone to pose questions at the wrong moment. During her confinement Byron acted out. From the room below hers he flung soda bottles against the ceiling and threw furniture against the walls. Her "squalls" during labor were answered by his racket. Their child entered this world amid chaos. The day after his daughter was born, Byron came to Annabella's room.

"The child was born dead, wasn't it?" he asked. When the nurse brought the bundled babe into the room, proving otherwise, he looked at her and said, "Oh! What an implement of torture have I acquired in you!"

Augusta Ada Byron was Sunday's child, born on December 10, 1815. For the first months of her life she was called Augusta Junior. "Oh dear! She pinches me," Annabella wrote to her mother while nursing, saying she shared these details for her mother's pleasure, not her own. Lady Noel had survived illness and was recuperating at Kirkby. Annabella hinted that she and Byron and the baby might suddenly descend on them.

However, on the night of January 3, 1816, a year and a day after they married, Byron came to Annabella's room and talked of his sexual relationship with actor Susan Boyce, told his wife of his intention of continuing with her despite being tired of her personally, and went on, as he had done often in the past, to reiterate his determination to do everything "wicked," repeating varied possibilities and using violent language. In the midst of this he told her that a woman had no right to complain if she hadn't been beaten or confined by her husband, and she must *remember*: "I have never done an act that would bring me under the Law—at least on this side of the Water." For someone who would kill the lawyers first, he was well versed on current marital law. Annabella broke into tears. It was the last time Byron came to see his daughter. Three days later he sent his wife a note. She should choose a convenient day for leaving 13 Piccadilly. The sooner she could do this the better, as he was breaking the household up. "The child will of course accompany you." Byron's letter still in her hands, she told Mrs. Clermont. "Although I expected it I cannot help feeling this—to *think* that I have lived to be hated by my husband."

She consulted with Matthew Baillie, her friend, the playwright Joanne Baillie's brother, a doctor of high standing in Regency society. His book on morbid anatomy was the first systematic study of pathology. Perhaps her husband wasn't responsible for his actions and if so she would not leave him. Byron believed himself to be guilty of a dreadful crime—and if he hears or reads of any allusion to it, he identifies with it, be it a person or a character in a book. He goes through a violent struggle, and his remorse remains constant as he tries to find out if his wife suspects this real or imaginary crime. "I am certain my life depends on my seeming unconscious," she told Baillie. "When he uses me the worst he seems most sensible that I do not deserve it—and speaks of me as the most perfect of human beings, with passionate affection—at times—at others he expresses loathing and hatred—. . . . I am convinced that my removal will compose him for a time." She wished "to defer any attempt at restraint." But even after she left, if he were still intent on fulfilling "his intention of going abroad to the spot with which I know his most maddening feelings to be connected," should he be restrained "if I can impose it?" That "spot" was Turkey and the "maddening feelings" were homosexual and she knew it.

Baillie advised that no "young woman" ought to be left alone with him. He also suggested that she consult her doctor, Le Mann, as well. There were possible maladies of stomach, of liver, that might have effected Byron's brain. She did consult Le Mann and they examined physical causes in medical books together. She then went to see John Hanson, who had known Byron since boyhood, and presented her concerns. This was an age that believed insanity was inherited. Byron boasted of his and Augusta's crazed ancestors. If it were a mental disease, should it be caught now, before it progressed further?

If she were suggesting that Byron be restrained, Hanson advised against it adamantly, saying it could lead to catastrophe. The fact that Byron always kept two pistols and a dagger by him, the fact that he had fears of persecution in the night, well, he had been that way since a child. Wouldn't go to sleep till someone looked under his bed. His bottle of laudanum? He always carried one with him. Hanson did ask her if she had any personal fear for her own life, to which she answered, "Oh no, not in the least; my eye can always put down his," and hinted it was Byron's threats of suicide that she feared. She begged Hanson to use his influence to have Byron follow her to Kirkby as soon as possible.

Annabella, in fact, for all her earlier intentions, was conflicted about whether to stay or go. By then George Byron had come to stay at 13 Piccadilly at Augusta's request. He saw Byron's accelerating violence and insisted Annabella leave at once for her own safety and that of her child. If she refused, he would take it on himself to inform her parents of the situation.

So it was that on the night of January 14 Annabella came to Byron's quarters to say goodbye. Augusta was in the room with him. In a mocking tone Byron asked his wife, "When shall *we* three meet again?" They had journeyed past the underlying eroticism of *The Taming of the Shrew* to the opening lines of *Macbeth*. The curtain rises on a miserable night. The first witch asks the others round the cauldron:

> "When shall we three meet again
> In thunder, lighting, or in rain?"

"In heaven, I hope," Annabella answered without missing a beat. She turned and left.

"I fell into a sound sleep on the last night, as I believe is often surprisingly the case in such cases of deep sorrow. Next morning I woke exhausted. I went downstairs—the carriage was at the door. I passed his room. There was a large mat on which his Newfoundland dog used to lie. For a moment I was tempted to throw myself on it, and wait at all hazards, but it was only a moment—and I passed on. That was our parting."

DEAREST DUCK

*L*oyal Mrs. Clermont had seen mother and child off that morning. In the afternoon, stopping at Woburn, Annabella wrote to assure her former governess that she was now more in her senses and she was not to oversympathize with her. Byron had told her to communicate with him only through his sister, but she disobeyed and had already let Byron know their child was well and the best of travelers. "Ada's love to you with mine—Pip." Dr. Baillie had warned her to be soothing in tone and not jolt him. However, he wasn't a lawyer—or a woman in love. She had made her first mistake.

Then she wrote to friend Selina Doyle, who knew of the woes in her marriage. Selena was from Yorkshire, and she and her family were lifelong friends of Annabella and her parents. Although Byron would not let Selina visit his wife at 13 Piccadilly, they communicated. He had no idea she had asked for the advice of Selina's brother, Colonel Francis Doyle, a well-known mediator in marital affairs. Frank had already advised that Annabella should take Byron's letter dismissing her and her child, and leave for good. She should not write a word to him directly.

After posting her letters, Annabella changed horses and went on, exhibiting that restlessness which would pursue her for the rest of her life. She arrived, not at her familiar Seaham, but at the extensive Noel estates at Kirkby Mallory, and her parents' new residence. Perhaps because it was very late, and she was fatigued from the long trip, the Noel staff escorted her to the kitchen rather than the drawing room. When the mistake of position was rectified, her woken parents were shocked by their daughter's gaunt appearance. The very next day, however, Annabella's milk was flowing more freely and she saw Ada respond to that nourishment and to the loving adoration of doting grandparents. Country air was having an immediate effect. Annabella had a surge of hope; these palatial new surroundings were sure to suit Byron.

She wrote a second letter to Byron, believing it to be in the same cheerful vein recommended by Dr. Baillie. She joked about her being mistaken on arrival for a servant, she extolled the mansion's cutting-edge water closet—no mean attraction in 1816. She pointed out the large and gracious private space Byron would have to use as a sitting room or *sulking* room if he joined the family. Byron was delighted with this jolly letter, Guss informed her. "Dearest Duck," it began. Just after she sent it, a letter from Selina Doyle arrived. Brother Frank again urged that Annabella confer with legal advisers immediately. But Frank didn't know Annabella as well she, Selina wrote, quoting Annabella, who told her that if Byron should prove insane, she would not forsake him.

It was definitely time for the male point of view Frank Doyle offered: He told Annabella in plain language that her husband committed outrages on her in order to test that she loved him for himself. He was a jealous man, as Annabella well knew. He was experimenting with her feelings, presenting himself as the most guilty of human beings, wanting Annabella to prove her love by becoming complicit in his sexual exploits. She was perhaps not the first woman he had attempted to corrupt, but would he love her any more or would he instead despise her if he succeeded in conquering her "strong sense of virtue"?

Byron was not simply expecting his wife to take a lover while he took a mistress in proper Regency fashion. He was much too jealous for that. One has to trace what was left unspoken in the marriage by referring to Caro Lamb's novel, *Glenvaron*. The sexual slavery that

Glenvaron expected of the woman who loved him was portrayed in detail. His conscious aim was to corrupt her moral sensibilities, so that she would succumb completely to his sexual imaginings. In a similar way Byron attempted to strip Annabella of her sense of self and her self-respect. Frank Doyle knew Annabella had been tempted.

Her mother asked to read the letter from this close family friend. It was only then, after months of subterfuge, that Annabella found a way of letting her parents know what was going on. She handed the letter over.

"Outrages?" Judith demanded. "Ill treatment?" Annabella broke down. Her father was more angry than she had ever seen him, more angry than her volatile mother, who might have had her suspicions. While Sir Ralph fumed, Lady Noel prepared to take Frank Doyle's advice. She would go to London immediately to speak with him and to seek out legal counsel. In the meantime, she cautioned her daughter not to write another word to Byron. What Annabella needed to write was a statement about the marriage for Judith to bring with her to London. In her "Statement to my Mother," she admitted in general terms that there was no vice Byron hadn't attempted to familiarize her with, often saying he planned to "teach her a few things." When she wouldn't succumb to his scenarios, he was contemptuous and blasphemous. She didn't include that she was no longer fearless, believing she could control her husband with her steady look if she returned to him: "He knows he has injured me too deeply ever to forgive me," she told Mrs. Clermont.

Having her mother leave for London was a relief. Without Judith's constant stream of advice and anger, Annabella had but one "wild fit" in the succeeding days. Her mother, unlike herself or her father, acted out emotionally, expressing outrage in bursts of passion, and she was given to drink. As Judith consulted with lawyers and spoke with her friends, Annabella asked Mrs. Clermont to keep her sober: "She will break my heart if she take up the thing in *bitterness* against him."

Annabella wanted to take time before deciding whether or not she'd ask for a legal separation. She had all the doubts any woman might have having left someone she loved and with whom she had a child. Perhaps Byron would mend his ways, perhaps Byron could not help himself, perhaps he was mentally ill. She couldn't just abandon him in the latter case, could she? How would *he* feel? All of this she agonized over in the journals and letters of a highly intelligent and idealistic twenty-three-year-old. Why shouldn't the world see she still loved her husband? she wrote to her mother. The more they saw this, the more they'd realize she had reasons stronger even than her love for leaving him. None of the gossiping Regency elite would have to know what those reasons were. "The temperate are always believed."

Judith rolled her eyes at her daughter's naivety: "I have some-times thought (and that not only lately), that your mind is too *high-wrought*—too much so for this world; only the grander objects engage your thoughts. Your character is like *Proof-Spirits*—not fit for com-mon use. I could almost wish the tone of it lowered nearer the level of us every day people."

Her mother had no idea there had been an incestuous attachment between Byron and his sister, and Annabella wanted it to stay that way. For Judith, money was Augusta's motivation for staying at 13 Piccadilly after Annabella left. In those days, a father had exclu-sive legal rights to his offspring's "body." If Byron gave his child to Augusta to raise, as he threatened, the guardianship of "Augusta Junior" would give the pregnant Augusta Senior a new and constant income stream—the 20,000 pounds in the marriage settlement vested in the child.

At Kirkby, Annabella received daily reports from both Guss and Mrs. Clermont about Byron's state of mind. He had gone to the the-ater the night of his wife's departure, where he talked nonsense about the Cooke sisters and said he wanted to marry the heiress Mercer Elphinstone if he could get out of his present situation. His "flirting" at Drury Lane became so flamboyant and odd in the next weeks that people wondered about his sanity. Some days he didn't drink brandy. Some days he stayed up late with his friends and drank himself stupid. His memory often failed. If George Byron were to call, he told the servants to announce him, forgetting his cousin was living with him. George was soon to marry, so Lord Byron offered his cousin free use of Seaham as if the estate were his to give. One drunken night, after insulting his sister, he ran after her to make amends and fell face-first, sprawled up those steep stairs. It was Guss who emphasized her brother's erratic behavior as signs of madness in her letters to her Sis. The doctors were more concerned with his liver and his brandy.

Annabella's own state of mind grew worrisome; she wrote she was not fit to manage herself or to be left alone. She had suicidal thoughts, which she laced with Milbanke humor. Galloping wildly over the countryside one day, she felt a surge of good spirits when she realized "I was in danger of fracturing my sconce." To Augusta she wrote, "I am very low tonight." While nursing "my Augusta," she "happened to sigh," whereupon her infant "looked up in my face and sighed too." It was very odd. "I hope the Blue Devils cannot be sucked!"

In London, her daughter's plight energized Judith. At sixty-five years of age—an old woman in her time—Lady Noel scoffed that Byron might think her done in. If there were mother-and-daughter friction at home, there was no greater champion of her daughter's interests abroad. Fierce love of her daughter focused her considerable talents. The lawyers she consulted both admired and praised her on the advice she had already given Annabella. Why did her husband and daughter always underplay her formidable abilities? "I assure You *I am very Sane*, my Brains are particularly clear—like Byron I can collect myself on *great occasions*."

In less than a week in London in late January, Lady Noel spent hours in conference with mediator Frank Doyle, with Serjeant-at-Law Samuel Heywood, and later with old friend Sir Samuel Romilly, the eminent chancery barrister. The "trio," as Judith called her legal advisers, were of one mind and all repeated what Frank Doyle had said in the first place.

In 1816 and for most of the century, "married women's rights" was an oxymoron. It explains why Annabella, who left 13 Piccadilly with many doubts about separating, was forced to act so quickly. Her twentieth-century critics hold this against her and blame her parents' influence, as did Byron. If Annabella were living today, she could take her time. She might have seen Byron in a neutral setting to talk. She might have had him come to Kirkby Mallory, as she at first wished, to see if they could work things out. She might have had sex with him again. She might have given their life at 13 Piccadilly a second chance. Perhaps Byron would change. In short, Lady Byron would be free to make the mistakes women are free to make today. But she had no such freedom. Legally, she had to act immediately.

Divorce was out of the question; it didn't exist. A marriage could be "dissolved" by an Act of Parliament on the charge of adultery. This was a man's game. No woman could win such a claim, and through the centuries only two dared to try. Men sued for adultery. Powerful, titled men. Legal separation of bed and board was a possibility for a woman on only two grounds: adultery and/or physical cruelty. Byron had already informed Annabella she had no claim for cruelty "on this side of the water." A wife could charge adultery. However, any act or word that showed she had forgiven her husband after the adultery occurred was considered legal "condonation" and canceled the offense. Such acts included staying in the house after learning of it, writing to the husband in a loving way or admitting him to her presence after leaving his house. The ecclesiastical court could then force a woman back under his legal control. Annabella was already guilty of both staying and writing.

Hopefully, a private settlement could be arranged, the courts kept out of it all. Judith set up a meeting between herself and Byron's kin— sister Augusta and cousin George—at Mivart's Hotel, where Judith was residing. Selina Doyle and Mrs. Clermont were in attendance. Annabella worried that her mother would not stay calm and would insult dear Guss. But Mrs. Clermont reported that the only time she spoke harshly to Guss was when Guss talked of her brother. Feisty Selina Doyle, of an outspoken, direct nature, which behooves the daughter of a military family, knew more than Annabella's mother about Guss's relationship with Byron. She didn't think it necessary to spare Augusta's feelings. She told Augusta and George how Annabella willingly sacrificed the daily comforts of her own life to be of use to Byron, but instead of that insuring his happiness it engendered hatred until everyone in the house thought Annabella's life in danger.

Yes, that was true, Guss and George agreed. The accelerating violence of those last days was so fresh that Augusta went beyond—or hadn't time for—self-interest. She affirmed along with George that they feared for Annabella's life. Only Annabella's feelings were to be considered, they agreed. Then George was given the unenviable task of bringing up the subject of legal separation to Byron.

He went back home and found his cousin in the drawing room—waiting perhaps. George spoke of the meeting at Mivart's and the desirability of separation, reminding Byron that he himself wanted one, having forced his wife from his house. Byron was "astonished." He had *not* told Bell to leave. There was written proof he had, George answered.

"I asked her to stay *after*."

Did Lord Byron suppose Annabella could return to her parents looking as she did without informing them of his behavior? If she hadn't, didn't he think they'd hear of it from other quarters? Incensed, Byron threw his hands up and spit out: If she and *her friends* wanted a separation, let her have one! With this grudging consent, it seemed as if an agreement could be reached. Judith's mission in London appeared accomplished. However, her legal trio, covering all bases, advised her to see a lawyer who practiced civil law before she left. At the time only a small, tight-knit group of "civilians" handled marital disputes that went to court. These advocates were all doctors, holding degrees from Oxford or Cambridge and practiced in buildings close to St. Paul's Cathedral, nicknamed "Doctors' Commons." Lady Noel was referred to the young and rising star in his profession—Dr. Stephen Lushington.

The young Lushington, little more than half Judith's age, was reassuring during that first meeting. He agreed with Lady Noel's trio that a "quiet adjustment" would be best. He was happy that

Annabella was now in possession of her child, and if custody came to court, Byron's habits of life and "partial derangement" could be in his wife's favor. (Complete derangement would negate a legal separation.) Lushington was not unaware of Lady Melbourne's character either, he assured Judith. He also knew of actor Susan Boyce's exploits and feared if Lady Byron returned to her husband's bed, her *health* might be endangered—he was factoring in venereal disease. Byron's "extreme indecency of . . . language," might serve as well. He knew of reports that Byron's eight-year-old niece Georgey was often sent out of the room to protect her from her uncle's blasphemies.

Pregnant Augusta had Annabella promise that should she die in childbirth, Annabella would take care of this daughter. Byron had "intimated future designs in respect to Georgiana, and seemed anxious to corrupt the child's mind in a manner which made Augusta very uneasy." The sisters-in-law were aware of Byron's predatory nature. It was partly "this most wretched prospect," of future molestation that encouraged Annabella to promise Augusta she would offer Georgey "every protection in my power." Lady Oxford's pubescent daughter, Augusta's eight-year-old. . . . One wonders if the slightness of Annabella's frame, "almost infantile," Harriet Beecher Stowe would later describe it, contributed to the sexual pleasure Byron found in his wife.

At Judith's meeting with Lushington, Doyle's original advice was repeated. All contact between Annabella and Byron must be avoided. Annabella had written two letters to Byron right after leaving—could they be construed as "condonation" of Byron's behavior? Of course it would have been better if neither had been written, Lushington responded, but he seemed confident that each could be explained by the advice of the doctors to write kindly to a husband who might not be in his right mind. It would have been better if copies had been made of those letters, so that he could examine them himself. This brought Lushington to an important piece of legal advice. It was imperative that from then on Annabella make in her own handwriting and keep copies of every letter she wrote and every letter she received. Her parents were to do the same. What we call a "paper trail" had to be established, should the separation end up in court.

Later critics have often berated Lady Byron for making these copies and for what turned out to be a voluminous record of her life. Always a saver of her letters and journals, Annabella's habit was reinforced through these legal contingencies. Her twentieth-century biographer Malcolm Elwin would even fault Lady Byron for confiding the facts of her marriage to her lawyer. He called Lushington "a *stranger*." His opinion in 1962 was no different than that of the journalist James Perry, who wrote in 1816: "What! A Wife tears herself from the bosom of her Husband and acts by the cold caution of a Lawyer than by the dictates of her own heart!"

Lushington prepared a short legal letter that Sir Ralph should write out in his own hand to send to Byron. As her father prepared two copies of carefully convoluted legalese, twenty-three-year-old Annabella dreaded her husband's reaction to it, as well as the finality it represented—the "awful and afflicting change" that was about to come. Her marriage, she wrote in her journal, had been the least erring of her years. The images of tenderness Byron brought before her eyes were always "on the side of Vice." Had her trials been those of "Happiness," she may have indeed become complicit in what he put before her in order to corrupt her. Wryly she admitted her sorrow had enforced her chastity.

When Annabella's grandson, late in the nineteenth century, finally read these words, he came to believe that the grandmother who raised him left his grandfather because she was tempted, was afraid of what she'd become if she stayed. Lady Byron's belief in virtue and good works was the wellspring of her character. A year of moral corruption in partnership with a charismatic husband might turn into a phase in the development of some women in high society—especially in the freewheeling, albeit discreet, Regency. For Lady Byron it would have been the destruction of her character, in effect the ruin of her strong sense of self. Byron knew this. He hated himself as he attempted to destroy her, and when he failed to break her, he hated her as well.

Annabella wrote a long letter to her sister-in-law to prepare Byron for her father's separation letter. Let him know that she was separating for no other reason than the impossibility of making him happy, not from any resentment of his conduct toward her. On the other hand, be careful not to speak of her love: "Don't let him think I can be *worked upon* in any way." She ended "If I had lost the most perfect felicity of the world, I could not be more afflicted than by the duty of resigning those prospects of wretchedness. Strange!—but *you* will not wonder." In the clear light of day, and with her mother newly returned from London, Annabella realized that this letter could be construed as a declaration of love to Byron, an act of condonation. She didn't send it, but she did write a shorter note. Against Lushington's specific orders, she told her Sis that Sir Ralph's letter was on its way. She warned Guss that this must be kept secret, as it would legally "be prejudicial to me and mine" if anyone found out she had given notice to a third party before Byron was informed. Two weeks to the day after Annabella left London, Guss, forewarned, intercepted Sir Ralph's letter and returned it unopened to Bell, writing: "For once in my life I have ventured to act according to my own judgement—not without 10000 fears I assure you. But I do it *for the best*" only wishing "*a few days delay. . . .* I CANT write rationally." Nor did she.

Instead, Guss grasped hold of Lady Melbourne's skirts, telling Annabella that her aunt had given Byron a good dressing down for the way he had treated his wife. Just wait, she repeated in a second letter. If Annabella's father sent that separation letter again, what better "revenge" could Byron have than taking away her child. "And who could prevent him." Furthermore, Lady Melbourne could turn from champion of the marriage to dangerous foe.

Judith was furious! "Annabella is in a dreadful State and agitated in a degree that is become *terrifying*. Your *cruel wicked* Brother has broken her heart." Annabella was sinking under Byron's "*unmanly* and *despicable* treatment." Byron had plunged his dagger in *all* of their hearts, but for Annabella the wound might be fatal. As melodramatic as that might sound, Fletcher's wife, Anne, still in Annabella's service, wrote to Fletcher in London that her ladyship had rolled on the floor in agony. Annabella had steeled herself for Byron's receipt of the letter; now it was back in her hands because she had not listened to her lawyer. "Shall I still be your sister?" she had asked Augusta when she knew her father's letter would be sent. "You will ever be my own dearest Sis!" Guss answered. But Augusta wasn't her sister; she was Byron's sister—plus one.

Annabella did not let her mother send her two angry letters to Mrs. Leigh. However, because she had not followed legal advice, and instead trusted her sister-in-law, her distressed father would have to travel to London himself, consult with Lushington, and make sure his letter got into Byron's hands. The pain she was causing her aging parents through her own actions overwhelmed her. In her distraught state, after her father left, she confided in Judith, swearing her to secrecy.

Augusta thought Lady Melbourne could save her marriage? Byron had showed her letters from her aunt and taunted Annabella with the fact that he had had sexual relations with Lady Melbourne, more than forty years his senior, at the same time as he was bedding her daughter-in-law, Carol Lamb. It had been Lady Melbourne who "*proposed it to him*." How old was this Lady? "*So old* he hardly knew how to set about it."

Keep that a secret? Judith immediately wrote the above to Sir Ralph in London, warning him not to mention it in any letter Annabella might read. Despite Annabella's objections, Doyle and Lushington must be told as well. Augusta knew about this liaison and it was common knowledge in Lady Melbourne's circle, "but with *that Set* it is not *reprobated*." Byron had also showed their daughter a letter Lady Melbourne had written to him—and Judith quoted it accurately—stating that Annabella "has always been used to have her own way and has been flattered into a high opinion of herself—but *You* must break her of *this and subdue her*."

What a woman your sister is! Sir Ralph should go right out and buy the French epistolary novel *Les Liaisons dangéreuses*. His sister was just like la Marquise, who in an exchange of clever letters with the younger man once her lover, maliciously plotted and made grand sport of systematically ruining a virtuous young married woman who trusted them both. Judith ended her letter: "God bless You! My Dear. I shall only add—that from the time we married, the only unhappiness You have occasioned me, has been from seeing *the Sway* Lady Melbourne has at times had over You—and that before *I was able to oppose it*, or had courage to do so She has pillaged You of *tens of thousands*—recollect this—and *now despise her.*"

No wonder Judith had a new outbreak of erysipelas. Her head swelled and was so sore that she couldn't bear her wig on her head, and came to the dining table each evening in her nightcap.

On February 2— a Friday!—Byron received and read Sir Ralph's letter. He would not believe it. He told Sir Ralph his wife left London on "medical advice." He had begged her to remain until he could accompany her. "For the present at least, your daughter is my wife;—she is the mother of my child—and till I have her express sanction of your proceedings, I shall take leave to doubt the propriety of your interference."

That Annabella would demand a legal separation had never entered Byron's mind. As Mrs. Clermont put it: "That he wished for a separation I am convinced, but like every thing else would have it in his own way, namely that he should live as he liked and where he liked upon the money he has and is to receive upon your account and that you should live with your parents at their expense crying and sighing for his return."

Shocked by his father-in-law's letter, Byron wrote to Annabella directly for the first time. Byron's love letters commenced, and they were not like the strained ones of the courtship. Byron wrote beautiful, impassioned pleas to his Bell that would stir the hearts of future generations: "The whole of my errors—or what harsher name you choose to give them—you know—but I loved you—and will not part from you without your *own* most express and *expressed* refusal to return to or receive me."

"Kate!" he wrote, "'I will buckler thee against a million.'" The allusion of course was to *The Taming of the Shrew* and the sexual fantasy they shared of dominant husband humbling spoiled, headstrong wife. There were erotic undertones in his next letter as well, as Byron tempted his wife to see him: "Have no marks of affection—of the warmest and most reciprocal attachment passed between us." It was not a tame sexuality he referred to. It was "nau," as Bella hinted to Guss. Their marriage from beginning to end had an erotic edge to it that appears to have satisfied them both. "Were you then *never* happy with me?"

As she copied this for Lushington, she commented, "It is extraordinary what an effect those *words*, from former associations still convey, for one tender remembrance sweeps away accumulated injuries." However, Byron had opened his red portfolio to taunt her too often. He had demonstrated conclusively how cleverly he could manipulate meaning, twining so close to, yet turning so far from, the truth. "The absolute monarch of words," Annabella later wrote, saying Byron used them as his hero Bonaparte did lives, "for conquest." The mathematician in her likened his words to "ciphers." The more her husband expressed his love in these letters, the stronger Annabella grew in purpose, for his hypocrisy toughened her resolve.

She warned her advocate as she copied Byron's letters to send him, that her husband "particularly piques himself on a talent for equivocation which renders it impossible to disclose the real sense of his words." She would have preferred a continuation of his "tyrannical and cruel treatment" rather than this artful dissembling that he was ignorant of any ill treatment toward her, at the same time blaming his liver, his finances. The beauty of his words themselves convinced her that she'd rather go to court than "*remain in any degree in Lord B's power.*" She had a good memory, she wrote, "but it is sad to employ it in recollecting wrongs."

Since Byron would not accept his wife wishing a separation through an intermediary, on February 7 Bell was directed to write to him herself, using language Lushington advised. She did, but ended the letter in her own words: "It is unhappily your disposition to consider what you *have* as worthless—and what you have *lost* as invaluable. But remember that you declared yourself *most miserable* when I was yours."

That same day Byron wrote to her: "I will not compromise my rights as a husband—and a father." He cited the two letters Bell had written him after leaving 13 Piccadilly. Those letters had to be explained, she wrote to Lushington "as they *must* appear like duplicity—or extreme irresolution." Lushington, who had not read them, calmed her, advising her to maintain silence concerning them for the time being, as there would be another meeting at Mivart's Hotel in three days.

It began by Lord Byron's solicitor, John Hanson, lying to Lushington. He hadn't come at Byron's bidding, but on his own initiative, because of his sorrow and his hope that there would be some means for reconciliation. Byron knew his behavior had been blameable at times, but Hanson believed Byron shouldn't consider himself guilty by agreeing to a separation unless there were stronger reasons for it than Hanson knew. What were Lady Byron's reasons for leaving?

Ask Lord Byron directly, Lushington replied.

Byron's memory was "treacherous," Hanson countered and again he pressed for Annabella's specific complaint. What would Hanson think if threats had been used? Lushington asked. "Threats?" What specifically? Lushington would not be specific. Well, Hanson responded, if there were threats, if there *were* serious charges, how could Lady Byron have written her letter of January 16, 1816? With a flourish, Hanson handed Lushington the letter:

Dearest Duck

We got here quite well last night, and were ushered into the kitchen instead of drawing-room, by mistake that might have been agreeable enough to hungry people. Of this and other incidents Dad wants to write you a jocose account, & both he & Mam long to have the family party completed. Such a W. C. Such a *sitting-room* or *sulking-room* all to yourself. If I were not always looking about for B, I should be a great deal better already for country air. *Miss* finds her provisions

increased & fatten thereon. It is a good thing she can't understand all the flattery bestowed upon her, "Little Angel." Love
to the good goose & every body's love to you both from hence.

Ever thy most loving
Pippin . . . Pip——ip.

Lushington's heart must have sunk. This was outright condonation.
But he did not blink. The letter could be explained, he replied. The
meeting ended.

BY EARLY FEBRUARY, county air or no country air, Annabella's
milk had dried, and little Ada, still often called Augusta Ada, was
weaned—"easily," she wrote. Annabella had intuited that not only
had the proceedings stalled, but that Lushington himself was not
completely convinced a separation was inevitable, given the love
she expressed in "Dearest Duck." She would go to London to confer
with Lushington in person, while her mother stayed at Kirkby with
the infant. When Lushington advised against her trip to town, afraid
Byron would find a way to see her alone, which would void everything, she answered that there were things "I and only I" could tell
him, things she dared not confide to her parents nor commit to paper.
On February 22, 1816, Annabella joined her father at Mivart's Hotel,
and immediately set off to meet her lawyer.

"I wish you could know Lushington," Judith wrote to Annabella
before she left London. "He seems the most *gentlemanlike*, clear
headed and clever Man I ever met with."

Entering Lushington's office at Doctors' Commons, Annabella
found the advocate she had corresponded with was a handsome man
with an oval-shaped face, aquiline nose, and strong chin. The young
Lushington—he was thirty-four and would live to be ninety-two—
had short dark curly hair and side burns that rounded toward his
cheeks, emphasizing deep-set and penetrating dark eyes. He was a
Whig, a social reformer politically involved in abolishing slavery, in

*Stephen Lushington, Lady Byron's trusted lawyer
and friend throughout her life and beyond.*

animal rights, and in women's rights—or the lack thereof. A firebrand of a cultivated sort, highly regarded MP at times, Lushington brought to his extensive knowledge of the complexities of the law a quality the best lawyers share, a penetrating understanding of law's relationship to human nature.

On meeting his client in person, Lushington found Lady Byron's strong mind housed in a surprisingly small frame. The young woman was pallid and spoke slowly, her natural good looks and vitality weighed down by her plight.

It was a long meeting and at first they spoke generally of her situation. He was frank. Her case, legally speaking, was weak. It was a shame that so much had occurred while she and Byron were alone. *Two* accounts were needed for any claim of mistreatment. A new law, however, now said that the deviant behavior need not have been witnessed by two people at the same time. As subtly as he could, Lushington wondered, was there *no* possibility of reconciliation? He brought up the Dearest Duck letter, not as the legal hindrance it was, but as an example of tender feelings that might lead to marital resolve. That was why she had come to London, she responded. There were things kept from her parents, that "I and only I" could tell Lushington.

Some things she could not say out loud, some were coded and alluded to on paper, but by the end of the long interview Lushington was aware of the strange kissing games at Six Mile Bottom, Byron's referring to Medora as his child, the way Bell was sent to bed while Byron stayed with his sister. All this was referred to the "libel" drawn up should they be forced to go to court. The word "incest" itself need not have passed Annabella's lips, but it was communicated. By the end of that meeting, Lushington no longer considered reconciliation an option. In later years he wrote that he would have withdrawn from her council rather than be part of such an unholy reunion.

Byron was in such financial arrears that Annabella hoped he would find it difficult to refuse a more-than-generous financial offer, leaving her little as long as Ada stayed with her. She wrote to Lushington that she was willing to give anything, "and should feel so very happy to be secured from molestation with the child, that I scarcely think of any other advantage."

"Dearest," Byron responded on March 4. "Did I not love you—were I not sure that you still love me—I should not have endured what I have already." Byron mocked this "matter of pounds shillings and pence!—no allusion to my child—a hard, dry attorney's paper:—Oh Bell, to see you thus stifling and destroying all feeling all affection, all duties (for they are your first duties—those of a wife and mother) is far more bitter than any possible consequences to me."

Frank Doyle immediately deciphered Byron's words, writing to Judith that he feared an amicable separation would not occur and therefore it was of the upmost importance that the Noels at Kirkby never lose *possession* of their grandchild. He recommended that they guard the infant with every possible vigilance, as Byron might attempt to send agents to snatch her. Judith bought a pair of pistols, for defense, not offense, she informed her daughter, and workers on the estate were hired to guard the child, something long in the memory of those who lived at Kirkby Mallory.

Nothing but war remains, Annabella wrote to her mother. In Byron's camp John Hanson had begun to take depositions from the servants, as a preparation for going into battle. Fletcher's wife, Annabella's maid Anne, came to London. She deposed that Lady Byron had been detained at Kirkby against her will. Because Annabella realized the Byron camp actually believed it was not she but only her parents wishing for separation, she asked George Byron to come to Mivart's Hotel to tell him personally this was not true.

Byron's cousin was taller than Byron, good-looking, a decent sort about to marry, who certainly hadn't condoned Byron's treatment of his wife. Annabella felt comfortable around him, protected even. She told George that the decision to leave Byron was hers and hers alone. If her closest friends *knelt* and *begged* her to return, it would make no difference. She hinted that there were reasons she hoped would die with her, and that she had a duty to God not to return. Soon after, on March 5, Annabella did something Lushington strongly advised against, she answered one of Guss's many letters and agreed to a meeting, although by then the *bon ton* were whispering incest and it behooved her to stay away. In walked Guss, seven months pregnant, probably by the Frederick after whom this son would be named. She was full of sisterly concern—and shocked when she saw Bell. The only way to describe her appearance was to imagine Bell as having come back from the dead. "She is positively reduced to a Skeleton— pale as *ashes*—a deep hollow tone of voice and a *calm* in her manner quite supernatural. She received *me* kindly, but that really appeared the only **surviving** *feeling*—all else was *death like* calm. *I* never can forget it—never!"

In this trance-like state Bell made it clear to Guss that she had received all the letters from Guss and from Byron that she hadn't answered. Nothing was intercepted or kept from her. Her parents supported her decision, but she was acting on her own. Guss returned to 13 Piccadilly terrified. If her brother did not agree to a separation and Lady Byron went to court, would the undisclosed complaints include incest? Were they all to be ruined? Both banker Douglas Kinnaird, Byron's close friend, and John Hanson had convinced Byron he was being bullied into terms by agreeing that the Wentworth property would be divided between the couple after Lady Noel's death. They wanted Byron to change that clause so that the entire inheritance would devolve to him, and Byron would decide, through his well-known largesse, how much Lady Byron was to receive of her mother's estate when the time came. However, the clause about dividing the property that Byron had already agreed to was standard in the couple's situation, for it protected a separated wife from being forced back under her husband's roof should he alone hold the purse strings. Augusta was beside herself. She saw Byron's friends driving her brother to *destruction*. Lady Noel was an old woman. If the estates came down to Lord Byron in the following years they would be seized by the bailiffs and no one would get anything. "The two wise men," she labeled Hanson and Kinnaird.

Perhaps it was concern for his sister's reputation, added to Hobhouse's concerns, that persuaded Byron to bring the issue of the Wentworth property to the attention of a mediator. Hobhouse had heard another rumor the *bon ton* were chewing over. It was a crime so heinous that Hobhouse couldn't write it down. He called it "———" in his journal. He dared not speak its name. A mediator, Sir Samuel Shepherd, was agreed upon. A tentative separation agreement signed by Byron and Annabella was sent on to him to decide whether or not the original clause about waiting to divide property until the inheritance devolved to them should remain.

Public opinion was running decidedly in Lady Byron's favor. On March 17, Annabella wrote to her mother that her aunt Melbourne was "frightened out of her senses." Lady Melbourne had found out something through her daughter-in-law Mrs. George Lamb, who was and would remain Annabella's close friend. Caro George, as she was called, told Lady Melbourne that Annabella knew of her "misdeeds" toward her. Annabella informed her mother, "I have now the fairest reasons for cutting her altogether, and I don't know what good she can ever do me. What do you think of it? I have just read 'Les liaisons dangereux' which don't incline me more to cultivate her acquaintance." Break with her! Judith responded with gusto. Cut Lady Melbourne entirely.

Smelling blood in the water, Lady Melbourne wrote her niece a long letter three days later. Her heart ached for Annabella, although her dear niece was in London for ten whole days before she got wind of it! Lady Melbourne brimmed with kindness—and fright. She now knew that Byron had let Annabella read her letters to him, and she had tried unsuccessfully to have Hobhouse get them out of Byron's red portfolio and burned.

Perhaps in reaction to her mother's fury, Annabella's temperate nature reasserted itself. She would be wrong to cut her aunt after such a letter, she told Judith. More to the point: "I must beg that you hold your tongue. Lushington says the whole business might be undone, if Lord Byron could trace any report of an unfavorable nature to us—my honor being pledged for silence till this arbitration is settled." Rather than cutting Lady Melbourne's moorings, Annabella left her aunt bobbing about in half knowledge. At twenty-three, Lady Byron was similar to the young betrayed American heiress in Henry James's future novel *The Golden Bowl*, who after losing innocence wins the day through silent maneuvering.

Was it a coincidence that on the same day Lady Melbourne wrote her long letter stating her heart bled for her niece, Byron sent his wife the first poem he had ever written to her. She might think it an "affectation," he wrote to "Dear Bell," but he assured her it was not. Though his conduct toward her in the past had been that of lunatic and lover, let him now be her poet as well:

> Fare thee well! and if for ever,
>   Still for ever, fare *thee well*:

> Even though unforgiving, never
>   'Gainst thee shall my heart rebel.

On the poem went. If only she could see beyond his naked chest to his own "bleeding heart."

> All my faults perchance thou knowest—
>   All my madness—none can know;
> All my hopes—where'er thou goest—
>   Wither—yet with *thee* shall go. . . .

Annabella did not rise to the bait. Byron circulated the poem and somehow it was printed. "Very tender," Annabella reported to her mother.

Once Sir Samuel Shepherd judged Lady Byron in the right in regards to the Wentworth property being split after it devolved, Annabella received a bitter letter from Byron. He ranted on that Bell hadn't received "Fare Thee Well." Fletcher's wife told him her father had taken it—and Byron's latest letters to her as well. If this was so, he would be justified in stopping all legal proceedings. The next day he sent her letters from three friends attesting to how highly he esteemed her—and he found someone on whom to blame his entire marital situation: Mrs. Clermont. Annabella's former governess was Iago, a spy, a false witness!

> With eyes unmoved, and forehead unabashed,
> She dines from off the plate she lately washed.

Thus began "A Sketch from Private Life." This satire about Mrs. Clermont was circulated and printed as well. The poem certainly didn't aid his cause. That his Lordship would write so of a lower-class woman who had risen from service to a position of trust was considered despicable. Lushington was convinced these poems were Byron's attempt to get Lady Byron's attention and to lure her to respond to him before the separation agreement was final.

*This cartoon satirizes the Byrons' separation and
was part of the media frenzy accompanying it.*

Although she hadn't responded, Annabella doubted Byron would
sign the agreement. He was going abroad. What would compel him
to sign before he left? She had done all she could. Resolution was out
of her hands. Her "one or two days" in London had turned to two
months.

Then at the last minute, just before she planned to return to Kirkby
Mallory, she received a letter from Caroline Lamb, whose former
letters of support she had not answered. Caroline begged to see her
secretly before Annabella left London. Husband William would drop
her off and fetch her. That this was important enough for William
Lamb to bring his wife to her made all the difference, and Annabella
agreed to meet with Caroline at George Lamb's home, Caro George
in attendance.

Tremulous, redheaded, unstable Caroline Lamb entered dramatically, quite agitated and repentant. She would have confided
in Annabella before the marriage to save her from it, but Byron

had sworn her to secrecy, promising never to renew such "crimes" as he had confessed to her. From the time Augusta Leigh came to London in 1813, Byron hinted often that he was involved in a criminal intercourse: "Oh I never knew what it was to love before—there is a woman I love so passionately—she is with child by me, and if a daughter it shall be called *Medora*." Caroline responded that though she believed Byron capable of an enormity as great as incest, she could not believe it of his sister. This seemed to inflame his vanity, and in rage he assured her that the seduction had not been difficult, that his sister "was very willing." When Caroline still would not believe him, he opened his red portfolio: "Oh Byron, if we loved one another as we did in childhood—*then* it was innocent." In others there were cross marks in positions that could not be mistaken as other than avowals of sexual intimacy. Since then, Caroline had not been intimate with Byron, though she had been after he told her of "worse crimes."

Worse crimes? Annabella asked softly. Byron had previously confessed to Caroline that he had "perverted" three of his friends at Harrow and then had "corrupted" his young protégé Robert Rushton. She didn't think he had "committed this crime" since he returned to England, but he had plunged himself into sodomy in Turkey. Now that Caroline knew his secret, Byron had said, he would have to persecute her as Falkland persecuted Caleb Williams.

At these words Annabella became agitated. Falkland! Caleb Willliams! Caroline's report corresponded word for word with what Byron had told Annabella on the *Moon*, words she had repeated to Lushington and which were already in her libel. The secret hadn't been "murder" as had crossed her mind at the time. It had been sodomy.

Was it his homosexuality that Byron considered his mark of Cain, separating him from any chance of redemption? Was it shame of his sexual nature that he transmuted in his poetry to a battle between the doomed Byronic hero and an unforgiving (Calvinistic) God? In his own words Byron despised most women, though he needed them. His disgust and refusal to watch a woman eat and his remark that women should feed only on lobster and champagne has been taken as high wit. His lobster-champagne remark is often quoted as a brilliant bon mot. No consideration is given to the possibility that the poet might be repulsed by the bodily functions of womanhood, fearing her sexuality might devour him. Christopher Hitchens, a later wit, alone satirized Byron's words. The four most overrated things in life he wrote were "champagne, lobster, anal sex, and picnics." Lord Holland, an earlier wit, joked that Lady Byron might have left because Byron attempted to "————" her too. Later scholars have taken Holland's joke seriously, as if to discredit Lady Byron's sexuality and turn her into the prude Byron wished her to be.

Something else Annabella had told Lushington on their first meeting had been corroborated by Caroline. Byron had told Caroline that Medora was his daughter. It must have appeared odd, Annabella wrote to Lushington, that she reacted only to hearing Byron's allusion to Caleb Williams, not to what was said of Medora. However, hearing the exact words she herself had heard Byron utter repeated proved that erratic Caroline was telling the truth. "Before I went," Annabella reported to Lushington, "I repeated in the presence of Mrs. George Lamb—that I had declared *no* belief." Lushington responded he was speechless, except for congratulating her Ladyship most cordially on her "final escape" from such a "villain."

Annabella's declaring no belief, Dr. Lushington's "not knowing what to say," was coded Regency-speak. What occurred that afternoon would be passed on to Lady Melbourne and through her to Lord Byron with the speed of light. Caroline's accusations of sodomy and incest could be attributed to her insane temperament and thwarted love of Byron. But if Byron had spoken of or alluded to such "crimes" to his wife using similar language, something only Byron himself would know for sure, it was to everyone's interest that Lady Byron continue to declare she had no belief. Lushington was "speechless" because he knew the meeting with Caroline Lamb was indeed Lady

*Mrs. George Lamb, "Caro George," as a young
woman. She would become "a sister" to Lady Byron.*

Byron's "final escape." The lawyer had played the card dealt him well,
and now he was aided by last-minute luck. How much further could
Byron possibly afford to take the game? William Lamb, the future
Prime Minister of England, by bringing his wife to cousin Annabella,
had served Lord Byron up—cold.

Soon after, on April 9, Lord Byron appeared at friend Lady
Jersey's soiree, entering arm and arm with his sister. Gentlemen
turned their backs on the poet, and one after the other, like a flock
of penguins, trailed each other out of the room. Augusta herself was
shunned by Caro George. Though Lady Jersey was gracious to Lord
Byron that evening, she soon visited Lady Byron to explain that Lord
Byron's appearance was unexpected. Byron was no longer welcome at
the best houses.

Ten days later, on April 19, 1816, Lord Byron signed the separation

William Lamb, Lady Melbourne's brilliant
second son and Annabella's first cousin, later Lord
Melbourne, prime minister of England.

agreement. In returning it, he twittered a revenge tragedy: "I deliver this as Mrs Clermont's act and deed." Once again Lord Byron's fate was in his stars, light years away from himself.

He had an elaborate carriage built for his exit, based on Napoleon's, and costing 500 pounds. On April 24, 1816, he rode to his ship in style, with liveried footmen, his peacock, his Newfoundland dogs, his personal physician. That same day, bailiffs swarmed 13 Piccadilly and picked the grand place clean—including the squirrels, birds, and books fate and Mrs. Clermont forced him to leave behind.

"Fare thee well! and if for ever—/ Still for ever, fare *thee well*—" was turned to music. Harriet Beecher Stowe would remember that when she was a child it was "sung with tears by young schoolgirls, even in distant America." Madame de Staël said if she were Byron's wife, "*She* could have forgiven everything: and so said all the young ladies all over the world, not only in England, but in France and Germany,—where ever Byron's poetry appeared in translation."

> Would that breast were bared before Thee
> Where thy head so oft hath lain,
> While that placid sleep came o'er thee
> Which thou ne'er canst know again;

"Yes, that breast has been my pillow," Annabella wrote in her private "Answer to Lord Byron's 'Fare Thee Well'" :

> Yet a treacherous wound it gave,
> As the smooth deceitful billow
> Wrecks the bark that trusts its wave.

> Envy, dire foreboding slighting,
> Deaf alike to friendship's voice;
> Pride elating—hope delighting
> I alone was Harold's choice!

> Sad distinction, dear bought glory
> Was my heart's unstable prize;
> Now the theme of gossip's story
> Thus exposed to vulgar eyes.

> Yet 'twas not the sole illusion
> Fame's bright halo round thee spread
> Other dreams of dear delusion
> Faith and young affection fed.

> Not a suppliant world around me
> Could have lured me from thy side

No—the tender bonds that bound me
  Hands but thine could ne'er divide.

But 'tis done—that arm that held me,
  Late the cherished gift of Heaven,
Now unclasps, no more to shield me
  And—but no—thou art forgiven.

Never can the heart forget thee
  Which has felt a love like mine
Nor our smiling infant let me
  While she bears those eyes of thine.

O Farewell, fare well for ever
  Once in happiest hours we met
Now with blasted hopes we sever—
  Soon our sun of joy has set.

Who has felt the desolation
  Of the earthquake's dreadful reign
And would choose the same foundation
  For his peaceful bower again?

Her marriage over, Annabella returned to Kirkby Mallory and to her daughter. She had been away from Ada for half the infant's four months.

Part Two

6

DENIAL AND ISOLATION—ANGER?
BARGAINING—DEPRESSION—
ACCEPTANCE? GREAT SCOTT!

*L*ittle Augusta Ada didn't recognize her mother when she returned. Whenever Annabella entered the nursery at Kirkby, Ada cried. She had bonded with Grand Mama and Nurse Grimes. There was emotional reluctance on Annabella's part as well. The threat of Lord Byron claiming his daughter and having her raised by his sister haunted her.

> One bitter thought I cannot yet
>   Resign to Heaven's decree
> Nor in the dreams of Hope forget—
>   My child is not for me
>
> And heart-wrung I could almost hate
>   The thing I may not love
> And ask, while shuddering o'er its fate
>   If pity dwells above.

Mrs. Clermont, who had accompanied Annabella back to Kirkby Mallory, wrote: "The time is not yet come when it [the child] will love Mama." In the meantime, she should think of the pleasure the child's love was giving her grandmother. Devastated by her daughter's unfortunate marriage, Judith was proud of her place in her grand-daughter's affection and constantly gave Annabella advice on how to be a good mother, harder to take when one realized one was less loving. Annabella found it more difficult than ever to live at home and after two months at Kirkby she was on the road again. Ada at six months old was "stouter and stronger than any boy or girl" twice her age and "so good humoured" Annabella wrote that she had become "a very agreeable companion." Annabella felt weaker "now than during my greater exertions—Sleepless nights and headachy days." She left unspoken that she needed to break free of Judith and mother her child in her own way. She certainly didn't want to hurt her mother. Once on the road, her spirits picked up and she wrote playfully to Judith from Ada's point of view: "The people at Ely and Peterborough stared at us very much, and Mama said we were *Lionesses*."

Judith joked back telling her granddaughter how "delighted" the Dean's wife must have been, having given a personal tour of the Ely Cathedral to "so *notorious* a Person as Ldy B." Lady Byron and Ada were indeed notorieties, as they would remain for the rest of their lives. Whenever recognized, people gawked. Annabella's answer to Byron's "Fare Thee Well" read more and more true as years passed:

> Sad distinction, dear bought glory
>   Was that heart's unstable prize;
> Now the theme of gossip's story
>   Thus exposed to vulgar eyes.

By the middle of June, Annabella was settled comfortably with Ada "in full view of the sea and not many yards distant," at Lowestoffe in Suffolk "My health will improve in this quiet life and then I shall have more power to enjoy the blessings which remain, and of which I am most sensible." She wrote to her new friend, and Augusta's childhood friend, the Honorable Theresa Villiers, "You are right in thinking I am *not* unhappy."

One of the reasons that she was not unhappy was that the full weight of her separation from Lord Byron had not yet hit her. Another was the influence she was having—or holding—over his sister. Augusta had "thrown herself so completely into my hands that she cannot recede, and indeed she says I am the only human being in whom she has *wished* to confide." She had imposed no conditions on Guss, but let her know "any future intimacy" between her sister-in-law and Byron would "not be sanctioned" by a continued intimacy of "mine with her." The mere threat of Bella shunning Augusta in public, gave Annabella what she hadn't had while living with Byron—*power*. "I wish very much to see Augusta—and it has only been from consideration for her good, which may be best promoted by withholding *something*, that I have not yet promised to see her."

Annabella didn't withhold the gift of herself for long. "I shall put myself and bairn in a lodging somewhere between Knightsbridge and Green Street," she wrote, tearing herself from the sea to reunite with her sister-in-law. They met in London on September 13—a Friday. Augusta admitted verbally to Lady Byron that she had had sexual relations with Byron before, but never after the marriage. Annabella let Augusta know, as she had in previous letters, that her "ignorance" of the relationship was "feigned" in order to protect herself. With the truth established, Annabella was once more willing to be Augusta's friend—and moral guide. This did nothing to deflate Annabella's sense of righteousness, though Augusta held her own: Augusta showed her Byron's recent letters. She had previously "only suppressed them because of the bitterness towards me—they are *absolute love letters*, and she wants to know how she can stop them." After hearing this, Judith, who learned of the incest during the separation proceedings in March, warned her daughter: "*Once more* take care of Mrs Leigh; if I know anything of human nature she *does* and must *hate you*."

True as that might be, and as different as Lady Byron's life might have been had she cut Augusta out of it, this reconciliation allowed Annabella access to letters of Byron that revealed his true feeling. Publically, Lord Byron went around telling everyone that he wished to reconcile with his wife. By autumn, he was at Geneva, and enlisting Madame de Staël in his campaign to win Lady Byron back.

"I loved and love you most entirely," he wrote to Annabella. "Had I trusted you, as I had almost resolved soon after our marriage, all would have been better—perhaps well. However I am paying the penalty of my evils, and eating my heart." Four days previously he had written to his sister: "No human power, short of destruction, shall prevent me from seeing you." He called his wife "Miss Milbanke," and said she was "formed for my destruction," and was "the cause of all."

In other letters Augusta showed her, Byron spoke to his sister of the "tortures of the last two years and that virtuous monster Miss Milbanke, who had nearly driven me out of my senses, curse her." He called his wife "that infernal fiend, whose destruction I shall yet see." Augusta withheld that last reference for a time, not wanting to upset Annabella. She expected such, Annabella responded calmly. Had she? Even after reading Byron's letters to his sister, "I loved and love you most entirely" stayed with her; it was something she repeated to her daughter later in her life.

For all of Annabella's moral complexity and incipient narcissism, she was indeed "temperate" by nature. She never confronted Lady Melbourne, who was the chief instigator of her luckless marriage, who betrayed her niece's confidences to Byron, and who had made a "game" out her niece's "taming." When her aunt died in 1818, after an illness in which physical agony and mental deterioration combined, Annabella admitted to an unexpected sadness. Annabella had been passionately in love with Byron, and his rejection of her was crushing, yet as far as her letters admit—or she allowed herself to admit—she did not respond with hate, but with sadness and concern for his unhappiness. However, her reading of Byron's letters to his sister underscored the torture that awaited Annabella should she ever reconcile with him, as well as underscoring her failure as a wife.

The sisters-in-law became so close in London that late summer, that Shelley's letter to Byron could be taken as metaphor, though Shelley believed it true. He told Byron he heard his sister and wife were not only in harmony, but were living together. For a while they did meet everyday—until Annabella brought Ada to meet her aunt. Seeing her brother's child overwhelmed Augusta. She apologized afterward, telling Annabella she would control herself in front of the child, be calm thereafter, but Annabella was forewarned. What might Goosy Guss eventually tell the already precocious Ada about her "poor brother"? Caution reasserted itself. When Annabella returned to Kirkby in November for Ada's christening, she did not tell her sister-in-law of it or of the fact that Judith had replaced Augusta as the child's godmother.

Ada's first birthday came the next month, less than a year after Annabella left 13 Piccadilly:

> Thine is the smile and thine the bloom
> > Where hope might fancy ripened charms;
> But mine is dyed in Memory's gloom—
> > Thou are not in a Father's arms! . . .

"Thou Fatherless! who mayst not find a rest / Save in one frail and shattered bark. . . . Thou art not near a Father's heart."

The self-pity and ambiguity of her feeling toward her daughter was obvious. Judith remarked on it, and five days later Annabella wrote: "On a Mother Being Told She Was an Unnatural One":

> Forgive my Child, the seeming wrong—
> > The heart withheld from thee
> But owns it bondage doubly strong
> > Resolving to be free—

In this poem, her emotional conflict rang clear. Was she to give her heart away *again*, only to have it broken? "She pauses o'er those tender ties/And sees them formed to burst!" She confesses this to an infant who "Still may'st live to make me blest/And *dare* to cherish thee!" The complexity of Annabella's initial reaction to single motherhood, of Ada not being "in a father's arms," has a raw, albeit unpleasant, emotional honesty.

On the other hand, Lord Byron's love of Ada was unconditional. Within days of sailing from England, on shipboard he began the Third Canto of *Childe Harold's Pilgrimage*:

> Is thy face like thy mother's, my fair child!
> ADA! Sole daughter of my house and heart?
> When last I saw thy young blue eyes they smiled. . . .

He ended it more than a hundred stanzas later in an aesthetically stunning crescendo of stanzas to Ada:

> My daughter! With thy name this song begun—
> My daughter! with thy name thus much shall end—
> ·
> To hold thee lightly on a gentle knee,
> And print on thy soft cheek a parent's kiss,—
> This, it should seem, was not reserved for me;
> Yet this was in my nature: . . .
>
> · · · · · · · · · · · · · · · · · ·
> . . . though dull Hate as duty should be taught,
> I know that thou wilt love me; . . .

Poetry such as this soars beyond history. Within the year in which it was written, Byron had refused to see his newborn daughter, wished her dead, called her an instrument of torture, specifically sent her away with her mother, and had already impregnated Claire Clairmont, Shelley's stepsister-in-law with a daughter to whom he would be cruel. What matters fact in the face of inspired language? Through his words, the absent and seductive father she would never meet was reeling Ada in. He became the ghost of her father, even while he lived. His elements were hers. He claimed her as he sighed over what might have been. Reading his words, one would think the child was ripped from his fatherly arms.

Annabella's parents and her friends were infuriated by *Childe Harold*. It was on everyone's lips. Annabella was stung to the core by Byron's claim that she would raise their daughter in "dull Hate" of her father. How could Byron even think such a thing? What could she do to counter it, she asked Dr. Lushington. Nothing, he answered. Public silence had to be maintained. The formal separation was not even eight months old and Byron had been threatening he had power to annul it. Once more Lushington impressed upon Annabella that anything that could bring up the immorality that went on at 13 Piccadilly while she stayed on could go against her if Byron sued for the child.

"Let me know what you may hear" about *Childe Harold*, Annabella wrote to Theresa Villiers, who was in London, "and don't be afraid to send me any history of my hard-heartedness, for I am just now so soft-hearted that I think they may impart a little of their imagined qualities and be of service."

THE THUNDEROUS REACTION to *Childe Harold* did not diminish at Kirkby. Judith brimmed over with "Dull hate" of Byron all through the 1816 Christmas holidays. It was the last thing Annabella needed, and she realized once and for all something she had intuited since she went to London on her own at the age of nineteen: She and her mother could not live together. Their ideas were too different, she told her friends. She told her mother she needed a change of scene to improve her health. She no longer slept soundly, nor was her health robust as it had been before marriage. All this was true, but the main factor was that she had to leave her mother's influence, advice, and bitterness behind her. At the same time, she was acutely aware that once again her own actions, particularly separating Ada from Grand Mama, would cause her mother heartbreak. From the road she wrote to Judith:

I cannot send you Ada's smile
  Nor Ada's mother's fuller heart;
Yet would I each lone hour beguile
  And make you half forget we part. . . .

I seek for health, I follow gladness,—
  To bring any gather'd blessings home:
I would that every thought of sadness
  Away from you with me—could roam!
    Too oft indeed, I feel your feeling:
    When mine would turn to Heaven and rest,
So keenly, that no pow'r of healing
  Remains within my aching breast.

    To smile at grief—if such my lot,—
      When *yours* the grief, that smile must perish:
    I've deeply learn'd, yet measure—not—
      We weep the most with those we cherish!

While Annabella followed gladness to the house she had leased in
Hampstead near many friends, Judith, bereft of daughter and granddaughter, took out her anger and frustration in a peculiar act. It was
as if she appropriated the rage against Byron she believed her daughter should feel. During her daughter's engagement, Judith bought the
famous Thomas Phillips portrait of Lord Byron in Albanian dress at
auction, aware Byron wanted it but couldn't afford to bid. She couldn't
either, and sold her diamonds to purchase it for him. It was hanging
at Kirkby. She took it down and "deposited it in its case," she wrote
to Annabella. She hung instead smaller pictures of "Your Uncle, your
Mother and your Aunts, of whom in future days you may tell Ada
the stories." It wasn't a temporary venting of her anger either. In her
will, she stipulated that the encased portrait should not be seen by her
granddaughter until Ada was twenty-one. If Ada had been brought
up at Kirkby Mallory, this mysterious encasement might have added

*Lady Byron's mother bought this famous
picture of her son-in-law, Lord Byron, in
Albanian dress, but in anger "turned it
to the wall" after learning of Byron's
mistreatment of her daughter.*

another layer to the romance and mystery of her absent father. But though the fine mansion with its lovely grounds and adjacent estates would come down to Annabella, Kirkby would never be Lady Byron's prime residence.

Hampstead, outside of London, was then a rural neighborhood with plenty of country air and scenic walks on which Annabella could take her thriving daughter. "Ada is quite well," she wrote to her parents. To her "Dear Dad," because he was "fond of naughty jokes," she wrote "as elegantly as I can of some of Ada's mispronunciations." Ada "talks of *Puss* substituting an 'i' for a 'u'—and Horse is still worse for she omits the aspirate and turns 'o' into 'a.'"

To amuse herself, instead of composing poetry on the road, she had turned some religious phrases into the fashionable slang of the day: "To commune with one's own heart," would be taken by the *ton* to mean "To meditate upon a love letter"; "To be a doer of the word," would mean "To keep an assignation"; "Signs of *Grace*" would be taken as "The Devonshire drawl—and *Con amore* waltz."

Though by birth she could take her place high among these Regency aristocrats, her friends that season were intellectuals, artists, ministers, all disdained by her biographer Malcolm Elwin, who avoided mentioning the men, calling the accomplished women, including actor Siddons, her "usual gaggle of gossips." When Elwin wrote of Serena Doyle and other unmarried women friends he called them the "admiring virgins," just as he called close friend playwright Joanna Baillie and her sister the "older spinsters." It is a history lesson to see how easily unmarried women no matter their accomplishments were branded redundant by scholars in the 1960s. In 1817, after a certain age a woman was no longer a girl—she became a Mrs., a "Signora," out of respect; Annabella called the older Joanna Baillie "Mrs. Joanna," and her unmarried governess Mrs. Clermont. In earlier days, unmarried women were not turned silly—they were, after all, the only women who had control of their own money.

Annabella attended and hosted dinner parties, at the same time she was connected with the Reverend John William Cunningham, Vicar of Harrow, the author of the bestseller *The Velvet Cushion* and one of the leading evangelists of the Clapham Sect. She would attend his church often, as she had previously attended the church of his brother, the Reverend Francis Cunningham, Rector of Pakefield. Through her relationship with the Clapham Sect and with her interest in educational advances and social justice, she associated with laborers, Dissenters, and various middle-class advocates of reform. Because of these associations, the newspapers and journals, never tiring of using her name, wrote that Lady Byron had become a "Methodist." She joked about this to her mother, who was not amused. When she invited her mother to visit her at Hampstead (rather reluctantly), Judith wrote back that she would rather consort with the devil than with some of those people Annabella entertained. While Annabella entertained and was entertained at Hampstead, letting everyone see she was of good cheer—even those who considered it inappropriate to her situation—she had an unpleasant jolt. There was no escaping Byron's portrayal of her.

Walter Scott wrote a long, admiring, and anonymous review of the Third Canto of *Childe Harold* in the *Quarterly Review*, which Annabella read in February 1817. In it Scott referred to the enormous fame Lord Byron had achieved since the First Canto of *Childe Harold* appeared, and he questioned the Hamlet-like melancholy, the holding of the world's opinion in contempt, that was to be found in this Third Canto. He attributed the gloom in part to Byron's "recent family losses" to which the poem alluded. Scott gave the impression that his wife had left Byron for superficial reasons. He quoted the poem's opening lines to Ada, as well as quoting from the glorious crescendo of stanzas to Ada which ends the poem. The myth that Annabella was raising her daughter in "dull Hate" of an adoring, heartsick father was perpetuated.

Annabella's parents and friends were horrified. They couldn't say enough against Scott. Yet the temperate component of Annabella's nature, her striving toward cheerfulness, was once more evident. Joanna Baillie, a close friend of Scott as well as Annabella, wrote to him from London in late February:

> The amiable and candid view Lady Byron takes of your motives in reviewing as you have done . . . is not the effect of prudence and deliberation, but was the immediate fruit of her own sweet and forbearing nature. I saw her, just after she had read the *Review*, not knowing who was the writer, and she well perceived the use that will be made of it against herself. The next time we met, a few days afterwards, she told me she was informed the article was written by you (which I was not willing to believe) but added that tho' it was calculated to give an unfavourable impression of her to the world, she believed it was written from a generous desire to befriend Lord Byron, and honored you for your motives.

In a second letter she wrote to Scott, we can clearly see that Annabella, who would not defend herself in public, confided in her closest friends: "The firearms or daggers, kept at night on the table of Lord B.'s bedroom, Lady B. herself made light of, and said that she never supposed they were intended against her, tho' he once pointed a pistol at her with threats. I must not tell you the darkest part of Lord B.'s character, and if I did, you would most likely not believe it."

If Lady Byron could have "continued to live with him without becoming herself worthless and debased, she would I am confident never have left him." Scott might consider her partial to Lady Byron, but "why should I be too ready to think or believe ill of Lord Byron? After the great friendship I have on all occasions experienced from yourself, I have not from any of the modern poets received stronger proofs of a disposition to serve me than from him."

She enclosed a letter Annabella had written to her. Walter Scott suggested she left her husband because of his "irritability" and "the provocation of a casual estrangement." If that were true and if it had precluded a husband's "studied cruelty," Annabella herself couldn't uphold "the character of such a wife." Though her marital relationship "can never be restored, Mr. Scott will nevertheless believe that I shall always remember with grateful regard those who have stretched forth an arm to save Lord Byron." In her postscript she told Mrs. Joanna to use her "own judgment" about sending this on to Mr. Scott. In any case, "pray convey my thanks in warmest terms" for his positive review.

Walter Scott, receiving these words, responded directly to Lady Byron in an effusive missive. Annabella said the letter was "as long as a marriage settlement," expressing his "esteem and admiration" of her in terms too warm to repeat. Then he went on to praise Byron so highly that Annabella joked that "nothing short of taking Lord B. 'For better or worse,' would, I think, cure Walter Scott."

THAT SUMMER OF 1817, Lady Byron traveled to Scotland, leaving Ada with her grateful grandmother. Frances Carr, a lifelong friend, whose sister Sarah would later marry Dr. Lushington, traveled with her part of the way and witnessed Annabella breaking down in tears as they approached her childhood home of Seaham.

Only a few years previously she had scampered up Featherbed following Byron's lead, reaching him flushed—their playfulness, their arms interlinked, their moment of harmony. It all rushed back to her in "On Seaham—1817":

> Ada! Wilt thou by affection's law
> My thoughts from the darken'd past withdraw—
> Teach me to live in that future day
> When those hands shall wipe these tears away
> Which flow, as I think on the craggy brow
> Where I stood . . . that form is before me now!
>
> *That* eye is beholding the waters roll,
> It seems to give them a living soul;
> *That* arm by mine is trembling prest,
> I cherish the dream, he *shall* be blest!
> O yet—tho' the phantom melt in air,
> The heart's devotion may *not* despair!
>
> Again must I break from the magic bond,
> Which Memory fastens with links too fond?
> Had I been happy I might have wept,
> The resisting nerve of my soul had slept;
> But I must not soften beneath the spell,
> Nor pause o'er the spot where the vain tear fell!

Had she been happy, Byron might have been able to tempt her beyond her sense of self.

Arriving at Edinburgh on her own, and out of England for the first time, Annabella visited her friend the famed actor Sarah Siddons and Sarah's recently widowed daughter-in-law and well-known actor, Harriet Siddons, who was involved in progressive educational causes. She was introduced to George Combe, who would become the most prominent phrenologist of his time and would found the Phrenological Society three years after this visit. That one could read a person's psychological nature from the structure of one's head was considered scientifically sophisticated, and attracted Annabella, as it did other intellectuals. A high forehead was a most desirable attribute, and a *New Yorker* cartoon could be made of Annabella among her morally worthy and intellectually gifted friends who were as high-foreheaded as they were high-minded. She was also in favor of Combe's progressive ideas in areas such as penal reform. Edinburgh was a city in which the new was taking hold and, always interested in new ideas on social issues, Annabella visited, observed, and learned.

In late July, Walter Scott found out Lady Byron had been touring Scotland and wrote to "dear Friend" Joanna Baillie that he was sorry Lady Byron does not extend her tour. How he would have liked to host Lady Byron and show her his region. He was on his way there, headed toward "my poor kingdom of Abbotsford, where I hope to find my subjects rejoicing at the expected return of plenty. The pasture grass is far more plentiful than I ever observed before, so that there is a profusion of verdure upon the hills and the meadows which belongs to a better climate than poor auld Scotland." Mrs. Joanna must have sent Scott's message on to Annabella, for she did extend her tour. Scott wrote, "I have just received the honor of your Ladyship's letter and hasten to say with what pleasure we will receive you at Abbotsford and accompany you to Melrose or to any other scene in this neighbourhood which may possess any interest." He and his wife added "more apologies than I am able to express for the very humble style of accommodation which we are able to offer." Their cottage was "being rebuilt, but I have always found my house like the fairy-tent, capable of being stretched to any dimension to receive those we wish to see." He hoped her Ladyship "will overlook the inconvenience of a garret-bedroom in consideration of the warmest welcome."

Annabella visited and stayed overnight. Walking at Abbotsford with Scott, who had a pronounced limp because of a childhood bout with polio, must have recalled Byron—raised in Scotland as well. Certainly they spoke of the poet. Later critics revised history and accused Lady Byron of pursuing the popular author to gain his favor. It was Scott, a commoner three years from knighthood, who was thrilled to entertain *her*. Lady Byron was an aristocrat, a celebrity, a "catch," and Scott was vain in such matters.

A Lord Somerville heard of her arrival and became "an accidental and in some respects a self-invited guest" at dinnertime, Scott confessed to Joanna Baillie, protesting too much. His Lordship was a close neighbor and "expressed himself so anxious to pay his respects to Lady B , as an old friend of her family, that there would have been a sort of affectation" in not inviting him to dinner. There was an affectation in inviting him as well. Having, in Judith's words, "so *notorious* a person as Ldy B." at your table was indeed a coup the year after the infamous separation. Annabella was not insensitive to having been trotted out or to Scott's aristocratic pretensions. In her journals Annabella proved underwhelmed by her host: "Walter Scott appeared to me to have a pride in acting the Selkirk Laird." She found his manners unpolished and rather affected. "His love of country" was the very opposite of the poet William Cowper, whose depictions of nature she cherished. In Scott's conception of the country "Man is more of a lord," and "he is supreme over the activities of those sports from which Cowper turned with disgust. He talked of Cowper coldly. Told stories about Burns." The next day "Scott accompanied me along the Yarrow, Ettrick and Tweed." Her "curiosity was in many respects gratified and I hope not without giving some pleasure at the same time." Though Scott's lord-of-the-manor attitude did not impress Lady Byron, she certainly impressed him.

He wrote to Joanne Baillie: "Now one would suppose Lady Byron, young beautiful, with birth, and rank, and fortune, and taste, and high accomplishments, and admirable good sense, qualified to have made happy one whose talents are so high as Lord Byron's, and whose

Walter Scott after he was knighted and after the
young, separated Lady Byron visited him and
discerned his lordly aspirations.

marked propensity it is to like those who are qualified to admire and understand his talents: and yet it has proved otherwise." His heart went out to Lady Byron "all the time we were together." He found her "one of the most interesting creatures I had seen for a score of years. I am sure I should not have felt such strong kindness towards her had she been at the height of her fortune, and in the full enjoyment of all the brilliant prospects to which she seemed destined." As tragically Romantic as Lady Byron's recent separation from Lord Byron appeared to Walter Scott, it was only when Annabella returned to England from Scotland that the full force of her new life struck her. The cheerfulness she had cultivated drained away.

She had attempted her own hop, skip, and jump over grief's stages.

She had certainly been in denial: she would never accept her anger; with Augusta she had bargained. Now depression overcame her. By the autumn of 1817 the death of her marriage, and with it all her youthful dreams, had caught up with her. When it comes to profound loss, grief takes its time. "I feel as if in a desert—and do not like passing through the dark alone. Two months ago the reality of Solitude did not give me these sensations."

"At first indeed I felt relief from breathing in an atmosphere of innocence—but it was not for long. There was a burning world within, which made the external one cold. I had given up all that was congenial in youth—though imagination of what *might have been* was all that remained—in this state I had a singular degree of insensitivity to *the real*. The touch of every hand seemed cold. I could look on tears without sympathy—and I returned kindness heartlessly and mechanically. One principle was still active, tho' unaccompanied by natural feelings—to follow his example who 'went about doing good.' The poor were rather benefactors to *me* than I to them. They had a claim upon my thoughts which I could not set aside for visionary indulgences. They saved me from myself."

Her prodigious philanthropy would continue to save her from herself throughout her long and eventful life. The grief would always be there; the anger, disappointment, jealousy—swallowed whole, never digested. Romantic forgiveness, she had called it once, fearing that if she were to face her dark side she would go mad. The narcissism that occurs when one needs to mirror only the good in one's nature in order to function was her demon. Her critics have seized on this dysfunction and turned her into a monster. Granted, there was nothing Romantic about her character flaw. It was not the drunkenness of the gods, nor promiscuity, nor conscious cruelty. It was not the glorious madness of male poets. It was the flaw of many who also do great service to others. Two years after her separation Lady Byron returned from Scotland, claimed her daughter, and began the philanthropy that would distinguish her life.

———

ALTHOUGH SHE HAD RETURNED from Scotland "appalled at the desert which seemed to spread before me," she brought back with her the educational concept of "cheerfulness," which she could not feel, but which she spread among needy children. In those days, while she was still living on 500 pounds a year, she founded the first Infant School in England. It would serve the working-class children of her beloved Seaham, where she went with her daughter in 1818. The Infant School she established at Seaham was based on the original one Scottish mill owner and early British Socialist Robert Owen had set up in his industrial community of New Lanark outside of Glasgow a few years previously. She had experienced a replica of it in the Infant School her friend the actor Harriet Siddons established in Edinburgh. The crux of this new form of childhood schooling was that a humane education of the working poor would improve character and such improvement would benefit society as a whole. It wasn't book learning that a young child—any young child—should be exposed to early on, but the world around that child. The schoolroom should be decorated with bright pictures, preferably of animals.

Lady Byron would see that large colorful maps as well as other bright pictures were affixed to the walls of the Seaham schoolhouse to attract children and make them curious to learn more. Natural things from fields and woods appeared in the classroom to incite a child's curiosity. Children were children—they should dance, they should draw. Music and art were encouraged. A child's nonverbal communication was knowledge in a new key.

Much of this cheerful approach to early education is taken for granted now, but was startling and controversial in a society in which it was customary for schoolmasters to teach by rote and when necessary for order, to humiliate their students over their books. Instead, at the Infant School at Seaham no child was to be beaten or threatened by either word or action. Nor were there to be conventional "lessons." Children were naturally curious; for the young everything was a game or an "amusement," as Owen phrased it. Through pleasant environment and happy interactions these children would grow to love to learn.

Lady Byron didn't believe, as Socialist Owen did, that the child was born a blank page on which the right education would stamp out a conforming and contributing member of a harmonious, right-thinking, community. She did believe education could lead the child to develop the best rather than the worst of his or her characteristics. The educational ideas she put forth in England would be considered "progressive" today. In the early nineteenth century such ideas were radical. Lady Byron was not only pioneering, but brave. From that first Infant School at Seaham to her major accomplishments in establishing Co-Operative Schools in England, Lady Byron has received little, if any, credit. One article in the 1990s singled her out. Brian W. Taylor wrote, "What is certain is that Lady Byron was a member of that small group that includes Jeremy Bentham and Richard Lovell Edgeworth, whose work for education was considerable." In Lady Byron's case "public recognition has largely been withheld."

The reason goes beyond Lady Byron's desire to stay in the background of her projects, or as she put it, to take the criticism at the beginning of a project and allow others to take the praise when the project worked out. Her accomplishments were not acknowledged by two influential scholars and biographers in the later part of the twentieth century: Malcolm Elwin and Doris Langley Moore. They both spoke to the choir of Lord Byron's admirers as they allowed their own admiration of Lord Byron's genius to color their judgment when it came to his wife. Neither saw Lady Byron as having *one*—not even *one*—redeeming quality. Elwin could not even bear to name her in the title of his biography of her, *Lord Byron's Wife*. Disrespect is visceral in their interpretation of the wealth of letters and papers Lady Byron left behind. To both, she was nothing more than the cold monster Byron presented in *his* letters to his sister and in his poetry. Just about everything Annabella did after love was seen as another justification of Byron's treatment of her. To paraphrase what Lady Byron wrote of Walter Scott, nothing short of actually having been married to Lord Byron would "cure" either of these critics of an obsessive desire to discredit her.

Take Malcolm Elwin's description of Lady Byron's opening of the first Infant School in England. His slant on—perhaps his ignorance of—this pioneering endeavor reveals a blindness to Lady Byron's historical importance which has influenced others. At Seaham: "As some excuse for establishing herself as mistress of her parents' house and servants . . . Annabella proposed to found such a children's school" as she had seen in Scotland.

He writes as if Annabella had laid siege to her childhood home, as if her parents were still living there, not at Kirkby Mallory, and as if Seaham had nothing at all to do with their daughter, who was raised there and loved by those servants still retained. Worst of all, her Infant School was dismissed as some sort of capricious "excuse" of this woman whom he had earlier labeled "The Spoiled Child." He continued: "She did not intend to incommode herself by doing any practical work; she was the capitalist employing executives to practise under her direction."

For Elwin and those who took his word, establishing, funding, staffing a school, getting it off the ground, wasn't "practical work." Socialistic ideas were "capitalistic." Teachers employed from the Seaham area chosen through their love of children and God-given patience, often lacking book learning, were "executives." And so it goes in the bizarro world of Lady Byron–bashing. These critics reduce Lady Byron's enlightened educational theories and practices to a most simpleminded axiom—that she deplored the English public school system only because of the debilitating effects she saw Harrow as having had on Lord Byron's character—and on the encouragement of his homosexuality. Yet other reformers as well as she deplored the elite public school system: the fagging, the bullying, the competitiveness; the drunkenness; the ubiquitous "English vice," all seen somehow as eventually contributing to "manliness." Lady Byron had direct experience with its effects. However, she and these other early educators were attempting through progressive methods to allow young people of all classes to find their own path to learning. They wished to direct them humanely and individually toward finding in their own unique natures that which would inspire them toward becoming wholesome contributors to their societies. This was to be accomplished without physical force and without hectoring. It was all very exciting, and it was all very new in the merry old England of that time, and Lady Byron was instrumental in this progressive movement.

EDUCATING ADA

A month before Ada's second birthday Annabella had written to Theresa Villiers, "Ada loves me as well as I wish, and better than I expected, for I had a strange prepossession that she never would be fond of me." The next month, on Ada's second birthday, Annabella compared her more positive feelings toward her daughter with the negativity she felt on Ada's first birthday: "My heart uncloses to the kindly influence of her smiles." "Uncloses." There's emotional exactitude for you. By the age of two Ada's "intellect is so far advanced beyond her age that she is already capable of receiving impressions that might influence her—to what extent I cannot say." For that reason, she continued to keep impressionable Ada as far from Aunt Augusta as possible.

It was in the education of her precocious daughter, and in her belief that her daughter as well as any son should be well educated, that Lady Byron hit her stride as a mother. By the age of four Ada was tutored at home. Her education was a more rigorous one than that offered at the Infant Schools, and she faced it without companions. So did other intelligent girls of her class if they hadn't siblings. No child of the aristocracy was allowed to mingle freely with just anyone's children. Ada would later recall with pride than when her governess was on duty and met her own sister on the street, she would barely acknowledge her in passing. In England, girls of Ada's class who had brains had to be educated at home. They hadn't access to the public schools of the boys of their class. Loneliness was built into the system for daughters. Among affluent commoners: How Elizabeth Barrett Browning mourned when the brother closest to her in age and with whom she studied was sent off to public school and she was left behind. How Jane Welsh Carlyle, who in Scotland did attend school with other girls and boys, wanted to "be a boy" when the sexes were separated, and the boys went on to Latin. ("Let me be a boy!" She pleaded, darting out from under her dining room table. Her startled parents did hire a tutor and Jane did learn Latin.) The isolated situation of intelligent girls was endemic, not limited to Lady Byron's only child.

Ada's weekdays were filled by her lessons, dipped into about a quarter of an hour at a time, and broken by rest or "reclining" on a board intended to ease her restlessness. There was music, French, arithmetic, exercise, drawing, geography, outside play. She was given "tickets" when she was good and had some taken back when she wasn't. This was a continuation of Owen's system of rewards and punishments, replacing verbal and physical punishments with "tickets" the children would strive to earn. The system led to the gold stars given out in kindergarten, to the beads and feathers at a summer camp's bonfire.

Ada's early tutor, Miss Lamont, seemed unable to channel the child's high spirits or that fidgeting that seemed excessive. When the tickets didn't work, Miss Lamont put Ada in a corner—and Ada bit at the cornice. There was "a room above," apparently a closet, where she was confined for a half an hour. All this in Miss Lamont's notebook. Lady Byron fired her soon after: "Miss Lamont appears quite unable to gain the necessary ascendancy over so masterly a mind as Ada's." As a result "I now give as much of my time to the schoolroom as if I were teacher."

Lady Byron observed that "the only motive to be inculcated with a character like Ada's is a sense of duty, combined with the hope of approbation from those she loves."

There is little doubt Ada strove to please her mother to win her "approbation," a motivation Lady Byron encouraged. At five Ada wrote: "The lessons have not been done as well as they might have been done—and I am sorry for that because I want very much to get another 12 [tickets].—I want to please Mamma very much, that she and I may be happy together."

What Lady Byron failed to realize was that by strongly motivating the natural desire of her child to please her, Ada might be led to secrecy about things that would not make her mother happy. Ada's tendency toward fabrication, telling her mother and others what she thought they would want to hear in order to get what she wanted, was often thought a trait from her father. It grew more from Lady Byron's small passive acts aimed at curbing disobedience by withholding affection. For example, one day when Miss Lamont could not control her charge, Lady Byron left the house without saying goodbye to the child. Through her lifetime, many friends and acquaintances seemed to *need* Lady Byron's approbation and would do much—some anything—to be held in her esteem. Psychologically, rebellious or not, Ada was one of them.

The more sensitive the child, the stronger her intuition of the mother's needs. Lady Byron calmly reported that once Ada had asked if her grandfather Sir Ralph and her father were the same person, and she replied that Ada had a Grand Papa and he was *not* her Papa. As an adult, Ada recalled her innocent question turning her mother furious and causing her to fear her mother for the rest of her life. Which account is correct? No doubt Ada's question underscored her mother's vulnerability—Ada was "not in a father's arms," in fact was confused about who and what a father was. But did Lady Byron, a master of the passive response, explode in anger? She very well might have, as her child made a direct hit on her sorest spot. It is also possible that Ada intuited the pent-up rage beneath Lady Byron's answer and felt significant guilt, fear, and shame for having asked the question. Whatever the facts, the emotional outcome was the same; it didn't curb Ada's habit of hiding certain things from her mother.

Lord Byron heard from visitors to Italy that Ada took after him. He told Shelley's cousin Thomas Medwin, "I was a wayward youth and gave my mother a world of trouble,—as I fear Ada will hers." That Ada was fascinated by the mechanical working of things delighted Lord Byron, as did her absence of interest in poetry. He was the same as a child, interested in the mechanical, not the poetical. Lady Byron did not keep Ada from her father's poetry. In fact, she read poems with her when her daughter reached her teens. Ada was simply more interested in science as a child.

As Ada began her education, the first cantos of Byron's comic masterpiece, *Don Juan*, appeared, full of sex, cross-dressing, and cannibalism. Every conventional virtue was turned on its head and cracked open with the lightest touch, with the most delicious wit. Who could resist the brilliant parody he made of his marriage? Lady Byron appeared as Don Juan's mother, Donna Inez—an interesting transformation, as the poet had told his wife at times she was like a mother to him.

Donna Inez was "a learned lady, famed / For every branch of every science known:"

> Her favorite science was the mathematical
>> Her noblest virtue was her magnanimity
> Her wit (she sometimes tried at wit) was Attic all,
>> Her serious sayings darken'd to sublimity;
> In short, in all things she was fairly what I call
>> A prodigy—. . . .

However she had, with all her merits, "a great opinion of her own good qualities," and "a devil of a spirit," which "sometimes mix'd up fancies with realities." For some time the couple lived respectably as man and wife, which meant in polite society: "Wishing each other, not divorced, but dead." Then, Donna Inez acted. She called in the physicians:

And tried to prove her loving lord was *mad*,
  But as he had some lucid intermissions,
She next decided he was only bad.

Poor beleaguered Don Jóse was an honorable man, no fault his that he had "been ill brought up," and was "bilious" to boot—or that he was quite unfaithful. When Donna Inez had enough of her husband's "plucking fruit without her leave," she brought in the civilian lawyers. It was then that the beleaguered husband realized

No choice was left his feelings or his pride,
  Save death or Doctors' Commons—so he died.

"I am very much relieved," Lady Byron wrote to Theresa Villiers. Goodness knows what she had expected to follow the venomous *Childe Harold*. *Don Juan* "was not so disagreeable as I expected." The satire did not unnerve her. She knew Byron knew she had not been a sexually inhibited wife. No fig leafs east of *their* Eden. Neither did she consider herself pedantic (she wrote rather pedantically), and was "very sure" neither did Byron. Byron's ribbing of her "in one or two passages was so good as to make me smile at myself—therefore others are heartily welcome to laugh." More and more Lady Byron seemed able to separate herself from the world's opinion, as she went about her philanthropy and her life maintaining public silence. Her sense of humor might be "Attic all," but she had one. She might have enjoyed that Byron mitigated the "perfection" he and his sister constantly damned her with, by admitting his wife had "a devil of a spirit." Still, her favorite science was "the mathematical," and not only had she been, but Ada was, "a prodigy."

Just as his wife excelled when she directed her energies to educating the laboring class, Byron, in Italy, was admired for taking up the cause of freedom for the common man. He wanted to see the unification of Italy, of Greece; he thought of travel to America, to Argentina. The political life that did not work out for him in the House of Lords was something he yearned after, and through his connection with his mistress, the married Contessa Teresa Guiccioli, and her brother, the Italian patriot Count Gamba, it took flight. Lord Byron raised a band of men to fight for Greek independence from Turkish domination—and outfitted them with a flourish, of course. Lady Byron was pleased to hear of this, felt that Byron was doing something admirable, that he was turning toward the good in his nature.

Byron had aged prematurely, physically and psychologically. In Italy he constantly looked for himself in the eyes of beautiful young boy pages who no longer fell in love with him. His yearning was not unlike that of the much older writer seeking an unattainable youth in Thomas Mann's *Death in Venice*. If Lady Byron's friends thought she enjoyed hearing reports as they returned from the Continent to tell her Lord Byron had grown fat, they were mistaken. It saddened her; she knew what looks meant to him.

The poet had arrived in Greece in time to celebrate—if that is the word—his birthday in the bleak marshes of Missolonghi on January 22, 1823: "Yet though I cannot be beloved, / Still let me love!" he wrote in "On This Day I Complete My Thirty-Sixth Year":

> My days are in the yellow-leaf;
> > The flowers and fruits of Love are gone;
> The worm, the canker, and the grief
> > Are mine alone!

Greece is awake, but not his spirit:

> If thou regret'st thy youth, *why live?*
> > The land of honourable Death
> Is here. . . .
> . . . .
> Seek out—less often sought than found—
> > A Soldier's Grave, for thee the best;
> Then look around and choose thy ground
> > And take thy Rest.

Lord Byron did not take his Rest in battle. His end came less than nine years after leaving his wife and daughter, in that swamp-plagued town of Missolonghi, feverish, disoriented, prostrate. Incredulous, frantic men were in attendance; no woman there who could face the mess of illness and the approach of death without the panic and desperation that was evident in that bleak, disorganized household. Byron himself was the most clearheaded at first. As sick as he was, he held out against the leeches, till he finally gave in, was bled by his doctors, and died— for liberty, for the people!

Cousin George Byron came to break the news to Lady Byron in 1824. She had had a premonition, and when she saw George arrive, she anticipated the worst. She was devastated, as George knew she would be. He let her know that Byron had talked of her in his final feverish delirium. Later, she found out through Fletcher himself that Byron's last words had been "Go to Lady Byron, and say . . ." On Byron went for close to twenty minutes, but Fletcher could not understand what his Lordship was saying. Try, try! Lady Byron exclaimed. She was beside herself. He tried, he couldn't. She would regret this for the rest of her life. She and Byron were separated once again, this time from what he wanted to tell her on his deathbed. Cruel the history of their dysfunction. It was a waking dream of running, running, getting nowhere.

Who knows what Byron meant to tell her? It may have been, as he had in one of the three letters he actually sent her, after writing many others which he showed to friends but never sent: Be "kind still to Augusta."

He had talked often of wishing to reconcile with his wife to people who would record and posthumously publish his words—Thomas Medwin, Lady Blessington. He vacillated between the fantasy of reconciliation and the belief it was too late. He repeated till the end that he had no idea of why Lady Byron left him (beyond the interference of her parents and Mrs. Clermont, that is). When he wasn't damning his wife's desertion, he was speaking highly of her, or, as she might have it, damning her with perfection. He hoped their daughter Ada would take after her mother in all ways. His daughter. He thought of sending an eight-year-old Turkish girl he had taken under his wing to England to be Ada's playmate. (Byron had an eight-year-old under his wing?) There was enough published ambiguity in Byron up to his dying day to allow his widow to entertain the belief that he may have had a deathbed conversion of sorts, a feverish reaching out to Pip for forgiveness.

Judith was gone, having died two years before Lord Byron, so her son-in-law had received half of the income from the estate. Because of the terms of inheritance, Byron added "Noel" before his last name, which, to his pleasure, gave him the initials of his hero Napoleon Bonaparte—and the money for his Greek expedition. Annabella became Lady Anne Isabella Noel Byron (AINB, she often signed her letters), her income rising from 500 pounds a year to 4,000. With Byron dead, her income doubled. Because Byron left his personal worth, around 100,000 pounds, to his sister and her children, cousin Colonel George Byron inherited nothing but a title. Without batting an eye, Lady Byron turned her 2,000-a-year marriage jointure over to him. The seventh Lord Byron and his family would have been left out in the cold had it not been for Lady Byron's spontaneous gift, but even that gift would not keep on giving after her own death. "ADA!" didn't receive a pence or a keepsake. Lady Byron, of course, became extremely wealthy, but now begrudged not that Augusta Leigh inherited, but the single-mindedness of Byron's bequest, leaving nothing to his legitimate daughter. She found out (as Philip Roth in his memoir of his father) that it is one thing to assent to receiving nothing because one was not in need, and quite another being bequeathed nothing and finding out one has needs.

There were compensations. For her aged father, Lord Byron's death was a relief. Sir Ralph in his late seventies, infirm, in debt, after the death of his wife, lived with his daughter, who supported him. He knew he had little time left to protect his only child. Now this sweet ineffectual Don Quixote could stop fighting windmills. For Lady Byron, Byron's death signified something that could be said of few women at the time: "With respect to all pecuniary arrangements I am now completely independent—and I trust that years of comparative privation will have taught me how to do more good to others." One resists the temptation to underscore that sentence by printing it in boldface.

Lady Byron had become a completely independent woman who had the power to do things her own way. She had no desire to hand that power or that money over to any new husband. Being Byron's widow suited her in more than one way.

Ada had her own reaction to her father's death: The eight-year-old cried. Annabella, less psychologically astute than usual when it came to her own flesh and blood, assumed she was crying for her mother's grief, as the child had never known her father.

Byron's body was returned to England: "The misfortune that has befallen us is terrible and irreparable," Count Gamba wrote to Signor Hobhouse from Missolonghi. "I scarcely have words to describe it. Lord Byron is dead! Your friend, my friend and father, the light of this century, the boast of your country, the savior of Greece is dead."

Count Gamba had Lord Byron embalmed. His innards remained in Missolonghi, now incased and enclosed under his statue there. His body was pickled in alcohol for its month's sea voyage home. In England the coffin was opened, Augusta Leigh in attendance. His right foot was amputated in order to be examined, his brains were removed for the same purpose, though this dissembling was closely held. The world mourned Lord Byron in an outpouring of shocked disbelief and grief. Easter festivities were canceled in Greece; shops closed for three days; there was a gun salute lasting over half an hour. Harriet Beecher Stowe remembered at the age of thirteen, climbing to the top of a neighboring Litchfield hill in order to grieve in silence.

When the *Florida* arrived bringing Byron's body back to his homeland, crowds greeted the hero poet, the hero liberator. More crowds joined as the funeral procession of *forty-seven* carriages wended its way through London. His friends had wanted Byron to be buried at Westminster Abbey, but enormous popularity did not erase notoriety, and Byron was crowded into the vault among the disarrayed remains of his ancestors in the Church of Hucknall Torkard outside of Newstead Abbey.

A grieving Lady Byron went to visit Sophy, Lady Tamworth, the big "sister" of her childhood, and then on to the home of the new Lord Byron and his family. Ada wrote a joint letter to her mother and to the Seventh Lord Byron's young son, George—whom Ada called her "dearest brother"—on the freshly minted black-bordered stationery of mourning. The *Florida* that carried her father's body stayed at port for a month. Ada confided she had been taken by her governess to see "Papa's ship and liked it very much." Viewing the ship made her realize "what a great misfortune it is for me not to have brothers and Sisters." When young George dies "I shall have none that are so well suited to my age to talk." His death was going to be "a very severe blow of grief." Even though she liked "Papa's ship," how much better she would have liked it "if my brother George had been there." The only child asked "you my sweetest mother" if George could live with her while his parents traveled. She was sure that her mother would see "the comfort" it would be to have one "suited to my age that I can look upon as a brother." Ada did not need logical connections to experience bereavement over her father's death or over her own existential situation.

Sir Ralph, the only father/grandfather Ada knew, died two years later. Lady Byron had stayed with her beloved father during his decline. Now she and her ten-year-old could leave England. They were to travel with an entourage of friends and servants and be away from England for more than fifteen months. It would be Lady Byron's first trip to the Continent. She had wished to travel there while Byron was alive, but Lord Byron threatened legal trouble should she bring Ada with her.

It was during this trip that young Ada became even closer to her much older cousin, Robert Noel. Ada's "dear cousin" was a son of the Reverend Thomas Noel, who married the Byrons and would have inherited all that devolved to Lady Byron had his birth been legitimate. Thomas was a bitter man (who could blame him?), but his animosity— and his failed lawsuit against her mother—did not discourage

Annabella. As soon as she inherited and added "Noel" to her name, she called Robert Noel and his three brothers "my children" and made them her financial responsibility. Thomas was the oldest, then came Robert. Charles, who would manage Lady Byron's estates, was third, and then Edward of a poetic nature and her favorite. She saw to their education—the youngest two at Hofwyl School in Switzerland. She tended to their needs and helped each of them to establish a living. It is easy to say Lady Byron could afford her largesse or that she owed the Noels something. Thoughts about doing the right thing are legion; doing it, something else indeed—particularly when it comes to wills and inherited money. Read any of Jane Austen's novels.

Robert Noel was born in 1803. He remembered Lady Byron's return from London with infant Ada and later the first time Annabella took notice of him. He was sixteen by then and she was visiting her parents at Kirkby: "Her little daughter Ada, seemed to like me much, and we frequently played together. She was fond of taking me by the hand and leading me about. This appeared to please and amuse Lady Byron for she often encouraged us in our gambols, and jestingly called me 'Dandy Bob.'"

His father called Robert "Dandy Bob" as well—he was a fashionable boy, always would be. He also had a natural aptitude for billiards. However, at Kirkby, when he played with Lady Byron, she invariably won. "During this visit, which certainly lasted more than a fortnight, I felt greatly attracted to Lady Byron. She was always very kind to me and I felt no longer anything approaching to timidity in her presence."

Then, in his early twenties, tall and handsome, somewhat dilettantish by nature—it's interesting how early such a trait shows— Robert studied medicine in Edinburgh and was, through Lady Byron, closely acquainted with the Siddons family and phrenologist George Combe. Both Mrs. Siddons and Lady Byron influenced him to change course. They both thought the Church a better (higher?) livelihood for him than medicine, and Lady Byron would have rectories at Kirkby within her gift for him. Lady Byron proposed he enter Cambridge and volunteered a "handsome allowance for the purpose."

"I never doubted the soundness, I may say wisdom, of whatever Lady Noel Byron said. I looked up to her with admiration, and in a spirit of veneration, and I found a peculiar fascination in her beautiful diction and in the calm earnest way she had of expressing her sentiments and opinions. Her views on practical subjects especially those relating to the characters of others and what might be expected from them in the future, always impressed me as spoken by an oracle."

Before attending to theology at Cambridge, he met up with Lady Byron and Ada in Milan and traveled along with them and their entourage to Genoa, where they spent the winter. For the next three months Lady Byron tutored Robert every day in mathematics and Latin. They went through five books of Euclid and the whole of Virgil's *Aeneid* together. Then he was sent off to Cambridge with the liberal allowance she supplied. However, in the long run he found, like others influenced by the progressive theological ideas coming from Germany, that he could not in good conscience pledge to the Thirty-Nine Articles of his church and so gave up the thought of a clerical life. Bob did find his way—it led to Germany, the source of all that was forward-thinking in theology, in literature, in culture, at the time. It also led, through the influence of Scottish George Combe, to Dandy Bob becoming Germany's foremost phrenologist.

Ada turned eleven while on this fifteen-month tour. Views of the Alps fascinated her and she drew pastel sketches of the scenery as she and her mother headed north. Arriving in Switzerland, Lady Byron said the country reminded her of Seaham. It was a less naïve remark than it appeared; it meant she felt at home. Her main object was to visit Hofwyl School outside of Berne and to meet the great educator Emanuel de Fellenberg. In a sense, while her young daughter painted pastels, experiencing progressive Hofwyl for the first time was Lady Byron's view of the Alps.

BUT BEFORE she put her experiences at Hofwyl to use—to be discussed later—she had an exceptionally gifted young daughter to raise and educate. Returning to England, Lady Byron leased a house in Bifrons, near Canterbury. In the winter of 1828, Lady Byron was away at a health cure, most probably suffering from her chronic bronchitis. The day after her mother left for Devon in early January, Ada, just turned twelve, wrote to her, detailing the antics of her cat Puff. She missed her mother, but she was also attached to her governess, Miss Stamp, whom she called her "Guardian Angel" for she would not allow Ada to overeat. They danced the quadrille together and on a rainy night Ada taught "Miss Stamp chess, and find her a very apt scholar indeed." She signed her letters "Carrier Pigeon." "I wish that supposing I fly well by the time you come back you would, if you are satisfied with my performance, present me with a crown of laurels, but it must only be on condition that I *fly* well."

Ada's imagination soared in these months her mother was away. No doubt "she played with the idea of flying" as a metaphorical way of reaching her mother. However, she also made her idea concrete. In *Don Juan* her father had written, "Steam-engines will convey him to the moon." His far-sight was satiric and poetic. Ada did not stop by imagining flight; she was going to make use of the steam engine. At first she made wings in exact proportion of bird's wings to their bodies. To study the issue of navigation carefully she asked her mother to send her all sorts of books about the anatomy of birds. Then she brought her scheme to "perfection," she wrote to her mother. It came to her that she should make a machine that resembled a horse, not a bird, and a steam engine should be placed in its belly. The steam engine would move an immense pair of wings, proportionate to the *horse's* body and placed outside it. She imagined this fifteen years before William Henson designed his very similar aerial steam carriage in 1842–1843, according to Ada's biographer Betty A. Toole. Flying would be quicker than any "terrestrial" means," to get to her mother, but there was the practical matter of going in the right direction: "To make the thing quite complete," the twelve-year-old wrote, "a part of the flying accouterment shall be a letter bag, a small compass and a map which the last two articles will enable me to cut across the coun-

By the time precocious Ada Byron was twelve, she had conceptualized a flying machine run by steam, predating Henson's aerial steam carriage (bottom) *by fourteen years.*

try by the most direct road without minding either mountains, hills, valleys, rivers, lakes, etc, etc, etc." Ada saw to the details.

Since Lady Byron came from a line of women who believed in educating their daughters, Ada's brilliance was to be cultivated. What concerned Lady Byron was the intensity of Ada's single-minded preoccupation with flight, her limitless confidence in her own ability, bordering on the grandiose—years before the kick of laudanum added to her vision of greatness. Her mother urged her to get on with her other studies as well.

The next year as Ada was going through puberty, she developed measles. Her health was often precarious; when she was seven or so she had bad headaches that affected her vision. Now, the measles led to paralytical episodes. In the summer of 1830 when she was fifteen, twenty-seven-year-old cousin Dandy Bob wrote to her from Germany in German and Lady Byron insisted she answer him in German as well, which Ada did while claiming it difficult.

In Ada's German letter she told her old playmate and later travel companion Dandy Bob that she was now over five feet tall, and "getting stronger step by step, and with the help of crutches I can go for walks." She had lost her taste for riding and flying, she continued, but she was well enough to play some piano, which gave her pleasure, and she told Bob that if he sent her some light pieces of German music she would be very happy: "I especially like the waltz."

So it was that Ada slowly regained her strength and studied her German as her mother urged. Not that she always listened; in fact, as a teenager, Ada was a defiant, uncoordinated, ugly duckling of a girl. People would try to find Byron in her looks, and she would sense their disappointment. In his journals Hobhouse, meeting her for the first time during her awkward years, wrote there was nothing of Byron except for her broad chin. At sixteen a rebellious Ada was up and around, though still using a cane at times. She wouldn't sleep in her bed, but tended to wrap a rug or blanket around her and sleep on the floor or on a sofa. She wouldn't kiss anyone but her mother, but that kiss was not "a loving, hearty kiss," according to her mother's friends. She had many whims about food and ate too much, tendencies Lady Byron attributed to Lord Byron, forgetting all that Milbanke mutton she chomped down through her life, and at times threw back up. Eating disorders came to Ada from both sides of the family, and there was no longer a Miss Stamp to stand as "Guardian Angel," arms crossed in front of her appetites.

By seventeen Ada was attracted to her tutor. In Tom Stoppard's play *Arcadia*, that is the age when his young prodigy of a heroine died in her bedroom during a fire at the mansion after having a "waltzing" lesson with her tutor. Thomasina's feelings for the young man and his conflicted feelings for her are subtly evident, their conversations brimming with her theories, which she writes out, leaving behind her a wealth of perceptivity on scientific matters that would not be understood until the following century. This scientific gift to the future would be true of Ada as well.

Ada did live a life close to Stoppard's protégé, brought up in a mansion (in Ada's case, mansions) surrounded by adults and tutors, having few friends her own age, though Stoppard too might have romanticized that loneliness. It had its advantages. She formed a passion for her tutor—the real Ada, that is. Rather than burning to death at seventeen, Ada had a thrilling love affair, sneaking around the big place when Lady Byron was elsewhere, meeting in the gardens, making love where and when they could. According to Ada, who was sexually adventurous and bolder than Stoppard's Thomasina, they did everything except what Ada called having "connection." How were they found out? Three of Lady Byron's friends were constantly snooping around, according to Ada, who called them "The Three Furies": Dr. Lushington's sister-in-law Miss Frances Carr; good old MM of the bad back, still alive and kicking; and Selina Doyle. Selina was raising Ada's friend Fanny Smith, the illegitimate daughter of Selina and Frank's extraordinarily handsome brother, the military man General Carlo Doyle. Even if Lady Byron wasn't in residence, at least one of these women would be hovering, keeping an eye on things. Nothing was safe from the scrutiny of "The Three Furies"; nothing was kept from Lady Byron. In this case it was Selina Doyle who saw Ada's being rather familiar with her tutor and blew the whistle.

The tutor, probably a Mr. Turner, was fired. Little is known of him—a lot of Ada's reaction. Ada was beside herself, furious at her mother. Distraught, she ran after Turner but was soon returned to Fordhook, the mansion they were living in at the time. According to biographer Betty A. Toole, she was watched even more carefully after that, professing eventually to seeing the error of her ways. More and more back to physical health, she began riding her beloved horses again with "wild passion."

In order to clear a stable path for her wild daughter, Lady Byron turned her mind from good works to high fashion. In the spring of 1833, Ada was presented at Court. Her walking difficulties and earlier illnesses were clearing up; she was losing weight. Dressed in white tulle, to her mother's delight, Ada, by the time of the London Drawing Room, and under her mother's careful companionship, was becoming a swan.

A few weeks later in London, on June 5, 1833, at a party Ada and her mother attended, Ada met Charles Babbage. This eccentric genius, in his forties at the time, clean shaven, dapper, and outgoing, was one of the great nineteenth-century visionaries. Nothing mechanical escaped his eye. His hobbies included picking locks and cracking ciphers, and he had figured a way of speeding up the mail. "He himself neglected no vein of knowledge," according to James Gleick in his mind-opening study, *The Information*. On a trip north Babbage became an expert on manufacturing Nottingham lace, the use of gunpowder in quarrying limestone, on all the ways known in which machinery produced power and saved time. "He analyzed hydraulic presses, air pumps, gas meters and screw cutters. By the end of the tour he knew as much as anyone in England about the making of pins."

At the time, Babbage had government support to build what he called his "Difference Engine." "Computers" in those days were human beings, computing itself a cottage industry that used logarithms and other tables to navigate the seas. In France it was said many computers were former hairdressers who lost their profession when their clients lost their heads. Human computers, human mistakes. Babbage had the grand idea of a machine run by steam which could compute mathematical calculations flawlessly.

"Like the looms, forges, naileries, and glassworks he studied in his travels across northern England, Babbage's machine was designed to manufacture vast quantities of a certain commodity. The commodity was numbers. . . . Producing numbers, as Babbage conceived it, required a degree of mechanical complexity at the very limit of available technology. Pins were easy, compared with numbers."

A model of the room-sized Difference Engine he was building with government support sat on a table. Ada and Lady Byron were invited to see it, along with others. As Sophia De Morgan, the daughter of Lady Byron's earlier Cambridge tutor William Frend phrased it, these highborn others stood by gaping as if they were primitives astounded by seeing their image in a mirror for the first time. Only Ada and her mother recognized what was in front of their eyes. Seventeen-year-old Ada admired the workings and the beauty of the calculating machine Lady Byron called it a "thinking machine," while describing it to a friend. Actually it was not yet a "thinking machine," it was a counting machine. Babbage's "thinking machine," his Analytical Engine, would come later.

Something about that visit to Babbage's Difference Engine, the way both mother and daughter understood it while others stood agape, brought them closer together at this dangerous period of Ada's life. What they didn't share in temperament, they shared in mind.

LADY BYRON'S PHILANTHROPY led her to be associated with the middle class, and with workers, union members, religious dissenters. She had become a member of the Co-Operative Society in the 1820s, when it was something close to scandalous for a woman of her rank. However, like Lord Byron, Annabella had both an identification with the people and a pride of birth. Particularly after Ada's romance with her tutor, she did what she could to accustom Ada to the privileges and responsibilities of her class. It was unusual for Lady Byron to make Court appearances, yet after Ada's presentation that spring, Lady Byron accepted the invitation for her and her daughter to attend the Royal Drawing Room to be held at the fabulous Brighton Pavilion, designed by George IV.

Ada wrote to friend Fanny of how *"very pretty indeed"* her mother looked, as she gave an account of "Mama's grand exploit on Friday night, the 8th of Nov. 1833." She described her mother's figured satin gown "of a most beautiful colour something between crimson and brown." And it was low cut "like anybody's gown, and had a peak in front (a shape which by the bye becomes Mama particularly) and long sleeves. Her neck was completely covered up to the throat by means of white satin and blonde, beneath which she had her flannels as usual." The flannels attest to her bronchial condition, and her fears of the cold. Nevertheless, Ada told Fanny they stayed till midnight and couldn't have left earlier, as they both were invited to sit in the "Queen's private circle." She drew it for Fanny. "X" marked "the spot where sat my illustrious parent, and where the King was for some time, talking to her."

The king was then William IV, who came to the throne in 1830 after the death of his brother, George IV. Ada, having the pleasure of her illustrious mother's company more often, appeared delighted when Queen Adelaide showered her mother with attention. Lady Byron was more blasé: "The King and Queen were really kind to me, and I should like to see more of them: but I must not often run such risks. I had a blister on, which saved my chest." As pleasant as Queen Adelaide was, so many topics had to be excluded in the presence of royalty that the conversation was "insipid." Lady Byron quipped that apparently "it is etiquette to stultify oneself." She had put on finery and hid her flannels and advanced her daughter, now a slim and elegant young woman. That broad chin remained. Ada later remarked that "mathematics" should be written across it.

By late April of the next year, Ada appeared to have turned a corner: "One thing is undeniable—that my feelings towards Mama are very different," she wrote to her mother's friend, Sophia De Morgan, telling her, "I hope I am not deceiving myself when I say that I believe I have now a real dread of my own powers of *self* deception and of the blindness of my own heart." Sophia was not convinced.

During the summer of 1834, Lady Byron took her repentant daughter on a trip north to the industrial heart of England, to visit the burgeoning factories of the Midlands and to Manchester, the heart of what was new and where Engels, a decade later, would observe his father's mills. Lady Byron wished to see not only the advances, but the condition of the workers; she and her daughter went from industry to industry, two women who understood what they saw—Lady Byron even sketching the punched card that instructed the weaving looms. In this system invented by Joseph-Marie Jacquard, the loom was controlled by coded instructions stored in the holes punched into these cards. Punch cards could dictate patterns, colors of threads, etc. It was such a loom on display in the Strand that gave Babbage his idea that a steam-propelled machine could go beyond calculation and become what Lady Byron called a "thinking machine" and Babbage his Analytical Engine. Not only *numbers*, but *information* could be coded, he realized. So did Lady Byron. So did Ada.

On their way home, mother and daughter stopped by the "young" Lady Gosford, and Ada tutored her daughters in mathematics. At home Ada stayed in contact with Babbage and plunged into Euclid.

THE VERY NEXT YEAR, Ada met her future husband, Lord William King. She was nineteen, William twenty-nine. He fell in love with her and she seemed to fall in love with him as well. He proposed. For all of Lady Byron's relief that Ada had met a man of quality, one of whom she heartily approved, she would not allow her daughter to marry under false pretenses. Ada must tell William of her relations with her tutor. No more secrets, such as those perpetrated against Annabella before and during her marriage to Lord Byron. If her daughter and William were to marry, they would marry into truth. It was no small matter at the time. Most men of King's class and social standing would have given up a woman who had been so "ruined," actual connection or no actual connection. Not William King. He was smitten. He forgave Ada her trespasses. It was in the man's power to offer dispensations, God in his heaven, Husband and Father in his house. The Three Furies and others impressed Ada on how lucky she was to have met a man who would forgive her, how grateful she ought to be. "Gracious God," a former governess wrote, gave Ada "an opportunity of turning aside from the dangerous paths." He has provided both a friend and a guardian—who was ten years her senior. "Bid adieu to your old companion Ada Byron, with all her peculiarities, caprices, and self-seeking; determined that as Ada King you will live for others."

Lord Holland, calling himself an old friend of Lady Byron's father as well as of Ada's father, sent his congratulations to Lady Byron (presumably not one of his "old friends"), realizing that "you must have looked forward with great anxiety to the settlement of your daughter for life." He rejoiced for Lady Byron's sake that Ada had accepted the hand of one whose "character, connections and circumstances" would "contribute to your comfort and endure her happiness." Within high circles Ada's peculiarities certainly had been noted. Nothing like a socially acceptable marriage to wipe the slate clean. So it was that the *World of Fashion* reported: "The fair Augusta Ada Byron, 'Ada, sole daughter of my house and heart,' has become the wife of Lord King."

One cannot overestimate Lady Byron's relief. She loved William King as a son, and William King, who never had a loving mother, found one in her. Her relationship with Ada grew steadily; the two wrote every day. A month after the marriage Lady Byron came for a visit, afterward writing: "Whilst in your house my feelings were too excited to let me rest—this might be my excuse for the first time, and I shall learn to love the birds less—shall I?" The birds. Lady Byron became "The Hen"; Ada, "The Thrush" or variations of

Ada, putting aside her childish ways,
entering both society and matrimony.

"The Birdie"; and William, with his dark eyebrows, "The Crow." Shades of the good Goose, dearest Duck and Pip, Pip, Purray!

When the Crow was away at another of his estates, making architectural improvements (William King's obsession), his little Birdie was "as happy here as I could possibly be without *ou*." In his absence, Ada wrote, "the dear old Hen pets the Bird very much." However, if the Hen was not good, Birdie threatened to "peck" her. The Hen was as mawkish addressing her Birdie and her Crow, but the reader will be spared further barnyard baby talk. There were three in this marriage, no doubt.

But not the same three as in Lady Byron's. Her daughter was finally in a father's arms, in a father's heart, and Lady Byron was no longer a single parent raising a difficult and extraordinary child, for all geniuses, Lady Byron knew from experience, no matter their age, were children. Now she had a helpmate, more than a helpmate, a serious, stable, and high-born man, to whom she passed on the responsibility for her prodigy. The doting Hen couldn't do enough for her dear Crow, who guarded the nest, and the fragile stability, of her Birdie.

BY THE END OF 1835, Lady Byron had the best reason of all for postponing a trip abroad. Even though she had wished to spend time in Switzerland, to gain a deeper understanding of the Hofwyl system of education, she canceled. She would not have been able to return home in time for the birth of her first grandchild. How charming "he" will be, she wrote to Ada. "You see I have settled that I shall have a grand *son*." Lady Byron suggested the firstborn be named Byron, "as the name could not otherwise be preserved." Byron King, Lord Ockham, was born on May 12, 1836. Byron was quickly followed by Annabella and lastly, in 1839, by Ralph. With old names, these children were born into a new age, one in which Lady Byron had the ability to serve her Birdie and her Crow in a new way.

IN 1837, two years after Ada married, King William IV died. It is said he clung to life, realizing how important it was that he not leave this vale of tears until his niece Victoria turned eighteen. Should he die before her birthday, there would be a Regency again—another outrageous one. It would be Victoria's mother, his dead brother's calculating German wife, the Duchess of Kent, and her Irish adviser John Conroy who would rule England in their own interest. Silly Billy was William IV's nickname, but it did not apply in this case. He knew he must not leave England in his sister-in-law's hands. Nor did he. Victoria turned eighteen before the King, her remaining uncle, died.

The first thing the young Queen had to do was disentangle herself from her mother's grasp for power and any residual thought of a Regency. She was a small person, Lady Byron's height, with as strong a will. Victoria waved her magic wand, took a bedroom of her own, banished her mother to the furthest wing of the palace, and sent John Conroy packing. Rather than becoming the figurehead for her mother's political ambitions, Victoria freed herself from her mother's iron control. Still, she needed guidance. She had just become head of a considerable chunk of the world—and the world is a devious place. The eighteen-year-old found her sophisticated mentor in Lady Byron's first cousin, William Lamb, who by then was Whig Prime Minister, Lord Melbourne.

Lord Melbourne and Lady Byron hadn't seen each other for years, though the first cousins had corresponded, particularly when difficult issues concerning Lord Byron arose. Caroline Lamb was long gone. William had before the end separated from his wife, succumbing to family pressure and Caroline's increasing instability. Eventually, two women looked after her and there was a "waist jacket" waiting when needed.

Was Caroline Lamb insane, or was she insanely erratic? Paul Douglass's excellent twenty-first-century biography portrays her as an individual, not as some frivolous aspect of Lord Byron's life, a joke of a woman to be dismissed by Byron's oft-quoted: Some women play the devil and then write a novel. Douglass pointed out the alcoholism that helped to kill her in 1828—not before William Lamb made it back to Brocket to be at her side. With the irony implicit in his nature, William noted it had been difficult to accomplish this time. Suddenly he was no longer idle, his political star was rising, and at the time Caroline needed him he was in Ireland as Chief Secretary to the Lord Lieutenant. His reward on return was that his wife gained lucidity on his arrival and they had last words, their son present, before Caroline Lamb died.

With Caroline gone, the family also wanted William to put away his hulking, mentally retarded eighteen-year-old. Augustus had little sense and much strength. His elderly Nanny would lock him in the drawing room at times when he'd run around half dressed, often pushing her over and sitting on her. When the Lambs went to a performance of *Frankenstein*, sister Emily (generations in advance of political correctness) reported that "the huge creature without sense put us all in mind of Augustus." Leaving his son in the hands of keepers—institutionalizing him—was something William would refuse to do. Five months after his wife passed, William's father in name only passed as well, and William Lamb became Lord Melbourne.

Augustus would live until the age of twenty-nine, which says something about the power of parental love. In November 1836, William was doing paperwork at Parliament while ill son Augustus lay on the couch in his office. "I thought he had dropped asleep," Lord Melbourne recalled. "Suddenly he said to me in a quiet and reflective tone: 'I wish you would give me some franks [stamps] that I may write and thank people who have been kind in their inquiries.' The pen dropt from my hand as if I had been struck; for the words and manner were as clear and thoughtful as if no cloud had ever hung heavily over him. I cannot give any notion of what I felt; for I felt it to be, as it proved, the summons they call lightning before death. In a few hours he was gone."

They were all gone—mother, wife, son. Much of his reputation as well. Lord Melbourne had scandal attached to his name early in his ministry through his close friendship with Caroline Norton. Her husband demanded money not to name Melbourne as his wife's lover. Melbourne, true to his nature, refused to be blackmailed. As a result, Norton brought a court case against the Prime Minister.

The case against Melbourne was thrown out in a little more than a week, and he survived the scandal politically. Caroline Norton, however, left her husband—against Melbourne's advice—and lost access to her children. Her subsequent writing and championing of women's rights was instrumental in the Custody of Infants Act of 1839, and the Matrimonial Causes Act of 1857. Artist Daniel Maclise chose Mrs. Norton as model for his fresco of *Justice* in the House of Lords, because for many she was not only beautiful, but had become the symbol of the injustice suffered by women.

Melbourne was a lonely man, who after the Norton scandal of 1836 had to curtail his intimate friendship with the woman he had visited at the end of each day, with whom he could relax, talk, enjoy companionship—be himself. On Victoria's ascension the next year, Melbourne quickly became more than the Whig Prime Minister the young Queen was bound to see formally. He became Victoria's mentor, her adviser every step of the tricky road. Another younger—much younger—woman, a girl still, Victoria could use a father's arm, a father who knew so much about the world and affairs of state, who had such an eye for the inane, the treacherous, the ridiculous, and who knew men and could tell such stories of a bygone era. So it was that Lady Melbourne's favorite son, born and bred of the Regency, became instrumental in ushering in the Victorian age. "Life is a comedy to those who think and a tragedy to those who feel," was Lord Melbourne's favorite saying, as it had once been his mother's. Melbourne's sister-in-law Caro George confided to her close friend Lady Byron that Melbourne regarded Victoria "as his child—this is not for the public."

The new Queen's principal residence was Windsor. At the time of Ada's marriage, Lady Byron wintered there usually, "imprisoned" as she called it, by her bronchitis and missing out on the festivities accompanying the new Queen's reign. It was at Windsor, in January 1838, that Lord Melbourne came to call on his first cousin, whom he had not seen in person since the Byron days.

Melbourne, on entering, could not control his emotions on seeing slim, blue-eyed Annabella, who certainly didn't look her forty-five years. He was in tears and beyond caring that two of Lady Byron's friends were in attendance and witnessed this. Annabella's emotions were stirred as deeply, but she was able to control them though she had just received the most unexpected jolt. Her initial turmoil had nothing to do with shared memories of Byron or with the pain of their past. It was the lightning flash of the unexpected. When Melbourne entered her drawing room at the age of sixty, Annabella saw her father

William Lamb, 2nd Viscount Melbourne, Prime Minister of England and trusted mentor of the young Queen Victoria.

walk toward her. It was "like a resurrection," she wrote. Melbourne had aged to look so much like his uncle, Sir Ralph, that they could have been twins. The apparition of her adored father rising from his grave stunned her, yet Lady Byron, with that outward control of hers, kept her balance though many circumstances they shared in the past excited her feelings. It turned out to be a long visit. Sporadically, Melbourne broke down. She wrote that she hoped their next meeting would be calmer.

Her cousin brought with him an invitation from the Queen, who expressed a wish to meet her. It has been suggested that Lady Byron declined the invitation because the age difference between herself and the new Queen dampened her interest. In fact, Lady Byron would have opportunities in the future to meet with the Queen, and rather than being confined to the decorum of "insipid" royal conversation, she would have the opportunity to discuss educational plans for the working classes with Victoria. It could have been the cold weather and the "blister" she needed to keep bronchitis and other chest complaints at bay that made her miss yet another festive evening at Windsor Castle. However, she had also refused the Queen's subsequent offer to meet her during the day. She may have had her reasons.

An obviously lonely Melbourne had been so caught up in the reunion and all the memories it recalled, Lady Byron wrote to her son-in-law, that "he never asked of you and Ada!" It may well be she did not want to see the Queen until after her cousin controlled his emotions and focused on her children. Apparently, Melbourne did focus shortly after. For in the same year that he and cousin Annabella reunited, Queen Victoria declared William King the First Earl of Lovelace, and Ada Byron King became the Countess of Lovelace.

That July, 1838, Queen Victoria, who would have an abiding interest both in poets and their marriages, met "ADA! sole daughter of my house and heart." The Countess had such a dreadful period, she wrote to her mother, that her increasingly freakish "Black Dwarf" almost caused a blunder. At the ball, the Countess of Lovelace did her bow and curtsey in front of Victoria, and planned to pass when the Queen "made a kind of motion" which Lord Lovelace understood. He told Ada to go up to the Queen. "Other wise I should never have dreamt of such a thing. . . . She looked very kind and gracious and immediately held out her hand, which of course I had sense enough to take.—But I thought it very good natured in her to notice such an *ugly nasty* little bird at all."

The little bird had been pleased at being made a Countess. But "'Lovelace'" ? The Hen went to lengths to prove to her chick that the name had roots in the family and was not a frivolous, but a dignified, designation. With that explanation, Ada made peace with her title. And the Crow? For the first time in his life, the first Earl of Lovelace opened his bill to the full-bodied flavor of motherly love. That love had such force, such commitment, that he took it to be unconditional.

8

EDUCATING ENGLAND

The richness of her family ties—a son-in-law to whom she was devoted and whom she was able to advance; a daughter, now a countess, with whom she had grown closer; three grandchildren to carry on her and Lord Byron's line—Annabella had become a respected matriarch, the dowager Lady Byron. Her response to the loss of first passion had not been to rush into other arms, but to claim independence, family, and meaningful work. In 1837, at the age of forty-five and by then twice a grandmother—when her granddaughter and namesake Anne Isabella was born, she cried with joy—Lady Byron completed her most ambitious educational project.

Today it is called the Ealing School of Art, memorable for being part of the sixties musical scene, attended by rockers such as Pete Townshend and Ronnie Wood and by the newly emigrated Freddie Mercury. On the red brick wall of one of the buildings at Ealing, however, there is an oval of robin's-egg blue in excellent condition. The inscription reads:

LADY BYRON
1792–1860
Founded the Renowned
Co-Operative School
Within these
environs
1834–1850

The well-kept plaque, as blue as her eyes, commemorates Lady Byron as the founder of the Ealing Grove School, the first Co-Operative School in England. It is such a rare public acknowledgment of her work that coming across it—beyond the humor of connecting Lady Byron with rock 'n' roll; was she never to escape the bad boys?—is satisfying. "LADY BYRON," it reads. Lady Byron on her own.

EALING GROVE SCHOOL'S educational ideals had Romantic roots that stemmed from Switzerland and branched out from the earlier work of Henry Pestalozzi, a follower of Jean-Jacques Rousseau, to Emanuel de Fellenberg, who established Hofwyl School, on which Ealing was based. Somehow in the first half of the nineteenth century, an atheist such as socialist Robert Owen, a bohemian Romantic such as Pestalozzi, and progressive social thinkers and Christian humanists such as de Fellenberg and Lady Byron met in the belief that a person's character is formed during the early years through absorbing the lessons Nature teaches. The operative word in all of their writings is "cheerfulness." One does not stuff the adult into the child. De Fellenberg considered punishments and awards equally objectionable. Fear makes slaves and "love of distinction" leads to the bullying and the aggressive passions encouraged in England's elite public school system.

In *A History of the Industrial Schools* Lady Byron wrote of how these Co-Operative Schools began. Though she had "printed" privately before, this is the only work she ever published. "It's out," Lady Byron wrote to Ada, "price 4d."

Pestalozzi had planned to be a theologian but broke down giving his probationary sermon. Instead, he set up a school for the homeless orphans of war-torn Switzerland in 1798: "The path of Theology was closed to him, but not that of practical Christianity," Lady Byron wrote. "He converted his little property into money, tied up his bundle, and set off for the Canton Unterwalden, to become the guardian of the poor deserted children there. It was an inclement season, but with the help of some kind-hearted friends he succeeded in raising a shelter for his new family amid the ruins of the village of Stans, and here he fed, clothed and housed the homeless little ones and formed them into a school." More and more children flocked to him, she wrote: "He was obliged to consider how he could bring them under some kind of discipline. The only help he could obtain was from the children themselves, and he took care to select those who showed most intelligence, and exercised most influence over their companions. These he made his assistants in giving lessons, as well as in the necessary occupations of the little household, such as keeping the place in order, mending the clothes, preparing the food, collecting wood, etc. He soon added the cultivation of a piece of land. The little colony then assumed the character of an orderly community."

After peace was restored and people returned, lack of funds forced his school to close. Pestalozzi's reputation grew, however, and he attracted another class of followers, many belonging to wealthy and influential families. He could carry on part of his educational system "teaching through touch, sight, smell, through the senses rather than through words on a page." However, he couldn't put his method of industrial training into practice, for these students wouldn't need to support themselves through manual labor. They wished to teach, but they didn't comprehend Pestalozzi's *great* idea, and that for Lady Byron was "making labour, and more especially agricultural labour, a principal means in the education of youth." It was the more practical and the wealthy Emanuel de Fellenberg who was able to carry out this idea. "For while Pestalozzi built his system of education on *the perception of the senses*," it was de Fellenberg who added "*action*" to "*perception*."

De Fellenberg recorded his first impression of Pestalozzi when he was a boy of twelve and outside his family castle of Wildenstein, "under a large linden tree," conversing with his old aunt. "We suddenly saw a man, clothed in a singular manner, with a thick beard and long black hair, ascending with rapid steps the avenue to the castle. My aunt, alarmed at this apparition, sought in her pocket for something to give him, to induce him to withdraw. At the same time, I saw my father who, in meanwhile had left the castle, hastening with great eagerness to embrace him. My aunt was astonished, and I could hardly wait for a convenient moment to ask my father for an explanation of what seemed so enigmatical in the apparition that had excited my curiosity. I learned, after the departure of this man, equally singular in his conversation and appearance, that, notwithstanding his then repulsive aspect, he was highly distinguished for his benevolent temper and devotedness to the best interests of humanity. It was upon this occasion that I heard for the first time the name *Pestalozzi*."

De Fellenberg himself was forced to flee to Germany after French troops occupied Berne. He went to the States for a while and came back to diplomatic service in Paris, which "confirmed his disgust for political life." His own experiences led him "to the same conviction, that the *only* resource for ameliorating the state of his own and other countries," and preventing the horrors of war that he witnessed, "was to be found in *early education*." He had a large fortune and resolved "to form on his own estate, and on an independent basis, a model institution, in which it should be proved what education could accomplish for the benefit of humanity."

De Fellenberg opened his school at Hofwyl on the first of May, 1806: "In a little wood beneath great linden trees, he had a cottage built on twelve posts and a shingle roof." Upstairs, there were sleeping quarters for teachers in training when they came to attend courses. Downstairs in the classrooms, the teachers studied, and they also worked in the fields and gardens. Through daily guidance De Fellenberg got them to see the connection between education and agriculture. "He led his pupil-teachers to do their work with a *full* knowledge of its use, to take pleasure in it, and to recognize how advantageous to themselves would be knowledge of the means of making the soil more productive, as the greater number of schoolmasters in Switzerland depend chiefly on a few acres of public ground for their substance."

Three years later the "Great House" was built, allowing young gentleman to board and to be educated. They had "a kind of independent community" from the sons of farmers being educated, but they were also sent "for a time to field-labour with the lower school." This was "a wholesome medicine," learning the pleasure of earning a breakfast before dawn after thrashing the fields. "The sons of the wealthy thus learnt to respect labour in the persons of the poor school; whilst on the other hand the poor learnt to view their richer companions, not as enemies, but as sympathising friends." (Charles Noel, educated there, became the manager of Lady Byron's estates.)

The requirements of farm life at Hofwyl also allowed the poor boys to become artisans if they had the desire and aptitude, since wheelwrights, carpenters, joiners, mechanics, were needed, as were shoemakers and tailors for those who lived in the Great House. Goethe's pedagogical ideal in *Wilhelm Meister* was based on Hofwyl.

By the time Lady Byron met de Fellenberg on that first trip to Europe with Ada, he was a middle-aged man with a well-born wife and twelve children to boot. His son Frederick had already met Lady Byron's youngest cousin, Edward Noel, being educated there. Edward and Frederick would eventually attempt to spread the Hofwyl farming methods in Greece. De Fellenberg was just short of six feet, with "a broad high forehead," which would have immediately impressed the phrenologist in Lady Byron. He was bald, but had long silver hair at the back of his head. Thoughtful and benevolent in his speech, he spoke of girls' education as well as boys'. One of his daughters conducted a girls' school on the property.

At Hofwyl, Lady Byron's ideal of what education could be was in plain sight. The estate itself was beautiful, with its Great House and many outbuildings and barns. Situated on "a slight undulating plain," the higher ground was cultivated by the students, the lower was meadowland. A water fountain flowed continuously and there was a bathing pool as well. The upper-class boys used the fencing room, while the "Rural Scholars" could be seen "breaking stones for the repair of the roads." The Great House itself was large enough to contain sixty heated apartments, and commanding on one side views of the Alps, on the other views of the Jura. Just as she had established Infant Schools in England when Ada was a child, Lady Byron slowly developed plans for establishing Co-Operative Schools that would follow the example of Hofwyl. (They would not be called "industrial schools," as that had a different meaning in England.)

Her extensive plans for Ealing Grove were drawn up close to final shape on an overlarge sheet that remains in her archives. Reading her plans in that clear handwriting of hers, one feels in direct contact with the clarity of her mind. So many who knew her wrote of the clear and penetrating power of Lady Byron's intellect. But how does one *experience* the mind of someone in the past who, as she once said to a friend, was not a "word monger"?

Of course Lady Byron wrote poetry throughout her life, poems built on special occasions or the sudden force of feeling, often psychologically revealing and not half bad. Among her papers and myriad drafts of poems, there is a collection she had selected and thought might be published after her death, with proceeds given to charity. When she wrote of Ada or of Byron or of the spray of sea at Seaham, she at times revealed her heart and was even able to touch on her darker emotions without reserve. When the prose she wrote was close to her heart, and she was not attempting to allude to what she felt rather than to speak out, one can glimpse her mood, her thoughts, a specific feeling on a specific day. Later, during Ada's illness, one reads in her letter journal her emotions in the round.

However, it is in her plans for her Co-Operative School that one finds oneself in actual contact with Lady Byron's mind, experiencing its breadth and liberalism, its no-nonsense practicality, its forward-reaching vision. It is here that her own genius lay, an intelligence that went beyond her personal cares and the dark emotions she sublimated. So many others in her times were served through a philanthropy based on that wide intellect. In her plans for Ealing Grove, a prototype as well for her other Co-Operative Schools, one finds in that scope of her mind and the realism embedded in her philanthropy the most endearing qualities of a complex and difficult woman.

Ealing Grove wasn't built in a day. There was plenty of experimentation of methods and false starts. However, by 1837, Lady Byron described a general co-operative scheme that was both in effect and effective. Thirty-one years after de Fellenberg founded Hofwyl, Lady Byron founded Ealing Grove School, translating the Swiss model to English soil. The first Co-Operative School in the British Isles, it was mainly devoted to the lower classes. It would have been impossible to mix the classes in British society to the extent done in the Alps.

Boarders were admitted when at least twelve years old, Day Scholars when at least seven. Boarders had a one-month trial period, and if approved, were educated either as village teachers, or fitted for other useful trades or situations. Those who had ability lived in the rooms above the school as they did at Hofwyl, but they were not young gentleman living in the "Great House"—though there were some of rank who followed her educational system. The boarders were charged 14 pounds per annum; day scholars 2 shillings a week. Payment was an essential part of Lady Byron's plan. This was no dole turning the poor to psychological dependency on a mighty benefactor.

It was a collaborative effort between the school, hardworking parents, and children who wished to learn. Payment of a small sum—and on time—went a long way on the road to self-realization.

"Indoors," as she expressed it, the children learned to read and spell, the younger ones under a monitor, the older under the master. Grammar was taught by question and answer, the boys parsing the sentences and giving examples of parts of speech. In teaching arithmetic, care was given to impart practical knowledge and to apply mathematics to day-to-day transactions. Geography and natural history were geared as much as possible to subjects of natural interest to boys. Whenever questions were asked that required consideration, the students raised their hands when ready and the master attended to each in turn, answering, correcting errors—and as much as possible letting them "set each other right." They learned from each other. Besides common instruction, any boy who showed a particular talent for arts or trades not generally taught—mechanics, drawing, carpentry—was to be so instructed. Lessons were given occasionally in the evening to the best-conducted scholars.

These indoor pursuits were rotated with those out of doors. "Boys who are strong enough to work in the garden will go out twice a day to do so. Care will be taken not to expose them to bad weather, nor to task them beyond their strength. Where employed in tilling the land of which the produce goes to the support of the School, they will receive fair wages. But a piece of ground will be set apart to be allotted to such boarders or Day Scholars as are able to cultivate it on their own accord, and whose conduct renders them deserving of that advantage. (They will have to pay a low rent, once a month, *punctually*.) They may either take the produce of their allotments to their Parents, or sell it to the School."

This was the allotment system developed by co-operative societies, of which Lady Byron was often a silent organizer and funder since the 1820s. *Urban* allotments made it across the pond nearly two centuries later. Lady Byron, for all her own eating disorders, was quite aware of the need for fresh produce to ensure healthy nutrition.

Twice a day the students left their well-ventilated classroom with its high ceiling, good desks, and large windows. The school, a restored, converted stable, was mainly designed and fully paid for by Lady Byron. Reading Lady Byron's words, one can intuit the excitement of these boys getting up from their desks, picking out their farm implements in the cloakroom. Then they walked in procession to the garden, singing together, "with their spades or other implements upon their shoulders." Sometimes they sang useful information, chanting the multiplication tables for example, sometimes ditties. Whatever the selection, they "cheerfully" greeted the open air, their spot of land, the brisk day. In bad weather, they could spend time browsing the collection of "pleasing and instructive books" that could be read then or could be borrowed and taken to room or home to read. One of them was appointed to keep a list of books with names of borrowers and when taken out and returned. Time could also be spent in the gymnasium. The only punishments allowed at Ealing Grove were a suspension from their "little garden" for a time or an occasional separation from their compeers. Corporal punishment was prohibited. "Influence of mutual good will, when combined with steady and affectionate treatment by the Master, is found to be more effectual in doing right than fear or a wish to excel one another." By banishing "fear," Lady Byron wrote, "several sources of falsehood are thus removed." By banishing competition: "Boys are in every way encouraged to assist each other both in their learning and labours," the younger being helped, not bullied, by the older. At Ealing Grove, awards for good conduct consisted in exchanges of the numbered badge each boy wore—numbers rather than names being called out in assigning tasks in the field. At ten o'clock every boy who had behaved well the previous day received a red badge to replace white. Those who misbehaved—a black badge, though black was rarely required.

The Christian spirit of brotherly love and kindness "should pervade the whole community," as it did at Hofwyl, but Ealing School was more liberal. The day did begin with a reading from Scripture, but the boys were not allowed to use the Bible as a lesson book. No sect was excluded from the school, and if any objected to the morning Scriptural reading, they need not attend. The boarders accompanied the Master to church on Sunday, unless it was objected to by parents. Some years later Lady Byron would write to a friend who disagreed: "In regards to religious opinions I am a Communist—my Neighbor's good as mine. If he be right, under whatever name, it is so much gain for me. I call this 'Christian,' you do not." The religious liberality at Ealing Grove was Lady Byron's stamp.

She summed up the school's objectives: "To cultivate industry and morality as well as instructions—employment arranged to leave no time vacant. Indoor and outdoor succeed each other through the day. Constant activity promotes health and cheerfulness and excludes possibility of gossiping [changed to 'idleness'] or any of the ills of a number of boys together unamused or unemployed." Lady Byron couldn't presume her aims fully accomplished, "but the results gratifying so far as to demonstrate the perfect efficiency of the principle and turning entirely to its efficiency, we look forward to future improvement with hope and confidence."

Annual expenditure since first outlay had gradually diminished and the year before amounted only to 70 pounds. Lady Byron calculated that in a short time the school would support itself. The ability to become economically viable was the last of the four reasons she listed in her own hand for not turning Ealing Grove over to the English government to run. The first reason was that religion would then have to have a "more formal doctrinal aspect to satisfy Church." The second was that the government would insist on a fixed plan, which would mean "less experimental variation putting restraint on Master's judgment." And the third was that enrollment would increase "to an extent I think incompatible with due attention to individual character." At Ealing Grove there were around 70 students at a time.

Ealing Grove School was an outstanding achievement, and the prototype for others Lady Byron set up, including one on her son-in-law's property at Ockham. Lady Byron combined the ideas inherent in the Co-Operative Society, in Socialist Robert Owen, in Henry Pestalozzi influenced by Jean-Jacques Rousseau, and in philanthropist and educator Emanuel de Fellenberg. However, it was the addition of her own clear mind, liberal values, and her steadfast commitment to the education and betterment of the working classes that allowed her to bring these new educational goals to England, to spread the value of the allotment system for increasing healthy nourishment, and to make her schools such viable accomplishments.

When James Anthony Froude, the great biographer of Thomas Carlyle, was sent to Winchester much too young, he was woken up at night to the pain of having the lit cigars of older students burned into his cheeks. Terrorized, he had to give all his pocket money, and most of his meals, to the upper classmen. When home on vacation, undernourished, his clothes in rags, the small boy did not snitch and tell of his victimization (that would not have been approved). He was beaten once more, this time by the archdeacon, his father, for his ragged appearance and his truculent silence. It was not through mutual help but through fear, competitiveness, and brute strength that one flourished or floundered. Lady Byron's educational ideals put in practice were a direct rebuttal to the elite public school system. Though Lady Byron was dealing with the children of workers, not the ruling class, she, by example, was giving the status quo a bloody nose.

However, no Socialist she, though. Robert Owen admired her. In a letter to her at the Bodleian Library, he hoped she would soon be well enough to see him, so that together they could "persevere in promoting practical means by which poverty and crime may be prevented and society at large permanently benefited." Her assessment of Owen is interesting. He found religion inconsistent with human nature, she wrote, yet he would govern mankind by his laws. "In short he would be the Messiah!"

Still, "I respect his honesty and courage, and like his kind temper. Had he met with charitable treatment he might have been less inclined to impute all the evils of Society to Religion—I feel it my duty, little as *I* can do, to show him at least as much kindness as if he were of the same fold." Of course, her little was a lot. One wonders if showing kindness meant Lady Byron would, as Owen put it, find "sufficient health to converse" with him on education and penal reform tête-à-tête. Or did her health hold him at arm's length?

With the marriage of her daughter, the birth of grandchildren, and the flourishing of Ealing Grove School, happiness was apparently at Lady Byron's feet. She had for long believed she could only be loved by strangers. Had she been wrong?

9

THE HALF SISTERS

hen Ada became engaged to William King in 1835, Augusta Leigh wrote to Annabella asking if she could *now* be allowed to speak with her niece when they were "out in the world" together. In town, Augusta had kept her distance from Ada in respect for what she considered Lady Byron's wishes. She confined herself to trips to Ada's full-length portrait by Margaret Carpenter on exhibition in London—"I went twice." Ada stood erect in her well-structured, low-necked gown. Her dark hair was pulled back tightly, her head turned, exposing her right profile and the line of Byron's broad chin. The deceptively solid strength of the figure was balanced by her stately attire's softly billowing full sleeves and her contemplative gaze. Could Augusta now be permitted to speak with the seemingly strong, composed eighteen-year-old? If she received no answer to her question, Augusta would consider Lady Byron's silence permission to reintroduce herself to Ada. Lady Byron was thus forced into what she called the "exquisitely painful" position of having to speak. If Augusta hadn't been allowed intercourse for the last five years while Ada was under mother's supervision, Lady Byron asked, why would Augusta suppose she'd sanction any intercourse now that Ada was out on her own in London?

THE STRAW that broke the camel's back of the sister-in-laws' relationship came in 1830 after Lord Byron's friend Douglas Kinnaird withdrew as a trustee of the Byrons' marriage settlement because of ill health and Augusta's inextricably muddled finances. Annabella appointed Dr. Lushington in his place. When informed, Augusta replied she did not know Lushington and she more or less demanded to name a trustee in his place. When Lady Byron demurred, Augusta countered that Lady Byron already had one trustee to champion her interests and Augusta needed one to champion hers. (There was a mortgage in question.) To understand Annabella's shocked anger over this demand, one has only to repeat a variation on the old saw that disrupts many an unbalanced relationship: "After all I have done for you and yours, this is the thanks I get? You don't trust me?" Annabella had had three in her marriage, but she refused to have three in a marriage settlement that was legally hers.

Dr. Lushington was as incensed and as personally insulted as Lady Byron. Augusta had questioned his well-established reputation for veracity by demanding someone else in his place. Augusta might not know him personally—he made sure of that—but he remained a liberal Whig Member of Parliament, fiercely opposed to the slave trade and to capital punishment. He supported Catholic emancipation and the civil liberties of Jews. He was at the time on the Consistory Court in London and a decade later he'd be made judge of the High Court of Admiralty. When he died in the 1870s at the age of ninety-two, the *Times* remembered him as the last of a great generation of honorable men. One did not trifle with his reputation. Still, he saw quite a bright side to this insult. If Augusta's distrust in Lady Byron's fair dealings finally prevented Lady Byron from any further contact with her sister-in-law—a relationship he had always considered a "degradation" to Lady Byron—well then, "All the anxiety you had will be repaid by the cessation of such intercourse."

Lady Byron had taken her pledge to Byron to "be kind to Augusta still" quite seriously, and had an open purse when it came to Augusta's children. She helped niece Georgiana who, as a child, had lived with the ménage at 13 Piccadilly. In her late teens Georgey wished to marry her distant cousin on the Byron side Henry Trevanion. Everyone except her mother advised against it. Georgey's remote father, Colonel Leigh, was so incensed he wouldn't attend the wedding; neither would Trevanion's family. Augusta Leigh and twelve-year-old Medora, who was bridesmaid, were the only family on either side attending the wedding. Lady Byron and young Ada were at the time on that first trip to the Continent and to the Hofwyl School. Annabella knew little of Henry, Augusta informing her he was of fine character and planning to enter the law. Being kind to Augusta still, and always protective of Georgiana, Lady Byron paid for the wedding.

Georgiana had her first child while Lady Byron and Ada were traveling and two more in the next two years. After the birth of Georgey's third, Lady Byron decided to clear out of her home Bifrons, near Canterbury, and go on to her home at Fordhook in order to give Georgey's family a suitable place to live. Bifrons was never her favorite residence. Even so, the move was costing her some trouble, and Bob Noel would have to find other lodging when he visited England with his new wife, a sweet German baroness. (Dandy Bob had lived for some years in a castle with a baron—eyebrows lifted at the change of venue.) Clearing the house was worth it though, she wrote to Bob. As she put it, the Trevanions were as poor as "church mice."

Besides giving Georgey, Henry, and their three children a large place to live rent-free, she continued to help the family financially in other ways. There's a mention of 300 pounds on one occasion in her archives, a 1,000-pound bond in Henry Trevanion's name on another. There were probably gifts for the children, and other money to Georgiana as well. In the days of her own marriage, Lady Byron and Augusta protected the eight-year-old from the foul language and the sexual insinuations of her uncle. Now Lady Byron was able to protect her from need.

However, no good deed to a Byron—the Seventh Lord Byron excluded—went unpunished. In fact, it was George Byron who had to tell Annabella that there were scandalous goings-on under her roof at Bifrons. Medora had been sent by Augusta to live with Georgey and Henry on and off since she was twelve years old. By the time she was fifteen, she was pregnant by her brother-in-law. There were rumors, as well, that Augusta had once been Henry Trevanion's lover and had promised him each of her daughters in turn. Annabella consulted the neighboring cleric, her family friend, the Honorable Reverend William Eden, who confirmed the ménage à trois. Whatever had happened to that protective mother who had united with Lady Byron to protect Georgey from Byron's advances? Augusta, pregnant herself at 13 Piccadilly, had made Annabella promise to take Georgey should she die in childbirth, and protect the child from her uncle. The poet's wild disrespect and sexual allusions were no secrets kept from Judith or Dr. Lushington. Lord Byron's treatment of his niece was thought of in terms of the libel. Then, after the separation, in the years when Augusta was showing Annabella Lord Byron's letters to her, Annabella was surprised to find that Byron thanked his sister for sending Georgey's letter on to him in Italy. She was allowing Georgey continued contact with her uncle?

Oh, it was just a "*scrawl*," Augusta assured Sis. Her brother had written to his niece, and expected to hear back. What else could she do? There was not harm to it, just a *scrawl* to keep everybody happy.

By the end of 1829 the Trevanions had cleared out of Bifrons, and in January 1830 a pregnant Medora traveled with the family to Calais. Out of concern for Medora's health, Lady Byron had anonymously contributed to the voyage. A month after they arrived in France, the fifteen-year-old gave birth and was convinced to leave her newborn son behind. The family returned to London in the spring, to find their own lodgings. Henry Trevanion wrote smarmy, obsequious letters to Lady Byron—they still slither in her archives—but Lady Byron's increasingly iron-laden curtain of silence fell on both him and Georgey.

Medora's baby boy left in France died there after a few months. It seems that so many of these unacknowledged children of the mist died shortly after being given up. Lack of care? Lack of love? Conscious neglect? Medora was not told of the death of her son till much later, and for a long time after thought the boy might still be alive. She fantasized Lord George Byron had come for the child and Lady Byron was raising him. Who knows the true fate of these children abandoned by their blood? It is no wonder rediscovered heirs became such a plot element in opera and theater.

Medora was sent back to live with her mother at St. James's Palace, but Augusta allowed Henry Trevanion to be alone with Medora during the two or three nights a week when she was out past midnight, performing her courtly duties. She turned a blind eye, even though Henry had given hints of what had transpired and was transpiring—for soon Medora was pregnant again. Henry sent Augusta a "strange note," saying Medora had "half" consent to tell her mother the cause of *his* "fatal misery." In a second note he apologized to Augusta for the first, saying he had taken laudanum. "I promise you not to do so again." By the time the girl's second pregnancy showed, truth surfaced with it, and Augusta went into one of her fits of nervous hysteria. The distraught mother attempted to persuade Medora to abort. After Medora refused, Augusta allowed her pregnant sixteen-year-old daughter to go back to Henry and live with him and Georgey and the children outside of Bath. Medora said she'd kill herself if she couldn't go, and Augusta lived in fear of her husband finding out the truth during one of his stays at home.

Of course, Colonel Leigh did find out and traveled to Bath, where Georgey was creating scandal as well. Through George Byron, Lady Byron learned Georgey had a reputation at the resort. It was said she went to bed not with one but with "any one." Colonel Leigh could be violent, but when he arrived at the Trevanions' cottage outside of Bath, he wasn't, though he hated Henry and had been right in opposing the marriage. Strangely enough, Medora was his favorite child and she wrote she was the only one who could arrest his temper. His calm might have masked determination. As Medora would write in her fragmented "Autobiography" a decade later, Colonel Leigh pretended he was taking Medora to live with *him*, not her mother, till she gave birth. Instead, back in London at midnight, he brought her to a home for wayward girls of good family near Regent's Park and forced her to enter.

The place was locked down, a fortress, though Colonel Leigh visited three times, her mother once, and an aunt, she didn't recall which one, sent religious books. Henry lurked about the neighborhood. They communicated. Georgey sewed notes from her husband into the hems of her sister's returned laundry. These notes informed Medora of what Henry's gestures meant as she watched him through the bars in her window.

Mrs. Pollen, the proprietor, was aware that Augusta wished Medora to abort and feared that her servants might be bribed to put certain remedial poisons in her food. Should Medora die or should the birth appear quickened, Mrs. Pollen, not the perpetrator, would be brought to court, and she would summarily be convicted and sentenced to death. These laws on her mind, Mrs. Pollen showed Medora how to unchain the front door. Medora didn't hesitate, put on her bonnet, unlocked the front door and left. Henry was waiting for her exactly where her linen had informed her he would be. It surprised the girl no one blocked them as they hurried away.

They fled England. Georgey and her three children were abandoned, left with nothing, and took refuge in Augusta's rooms at St. James's Palace. Henry and Medora set up in France, in Brittany, going by the names Monsieur and Madame Aubin. Their second child was stillborn. After that disappointment, by the end of 1831, Medora converted to Roman Catholicism. At the time of Ada's marriage, Medora was leading a wretched existence, writing to her mother, to her aunt Lady Chichester, to her godmother Lady Anne Wilmot-Horton, and to Lady Byron for aid.

By the late thirties, as Ada was becoming a countess, Lady Byron anonymously sent Medora 20 pounds—four times more than Lady Chichester, Augusta's half sister, sent. She would not refuse help to Byron's daughter. The disparity between Medora's fate and Ada's gave her pause, even after Lady Byron's curtain of silence fell on Augusta Leigh. By the time she received imploring letters from her long-lost niece in the late 1830s, she was looking forward to meeting with the famed Félix Voisin in France. He was both phrenologist and psychologist, and ran a famed asylum for the insane. He believed, as she would later write to a friend in a letter not for her daughter's eyes, that Voisin and his eminent partner who was *not* a phrenologist had come to the same conclusion: Not only was insanity inherited, but one's moral nature was inherited as well.

THE SUMMER OF 1840, her three grandchildren all safely born and flourishing and her daughter intent on new mathematical study, Lady Byron traveled to France. On shipboard Annabella composed a poem, "written under affliction":

> I will to be but clay
>   Beneath thy forming hand.
> To take what shape I may
>   If true to thy command.
>
> Yes—break and break again
>   The too imperfect cast—
> I'll bless thy mercy, when
>   It makes me *thine* at last!

She never prayed for a change of circumstance, she wrote; she only wished "to conform to the directing Will."

This ill health of hers, ridiculed by later biographers, was real enough, though her physical illness and her sagging spirits were most probably compounded by anemia. Unlike Lord Byron, she was a devotee of bloodletting as a cure—leeches, cuppings (which brought blood to the surface to be drained), eventually a state-of-the-art stent in her arm to keep blood flowing. When one couples this with her episodes of overeating and heaving it would seem that she was sporadically at war with her whisper of a body. Her underlying constitution must have been unusually strong—it was so in her youth—to have survived such constant drains.

Frank Doyle's death eight months previously contributed to her malaise on shipboard. She had witnessed her dear friend's sharp decline to utter helplessness—to die of "old age" while only in his late fifties. What had Lady Byron to look forward to once she got to France? Visits to friends, visits to French institutions to gather information that would help her work on prison reform, visits to the phrenologist Felix Voisin's "establishment for the Insane." Her life after love was all about progressive causes. "I have a vision before me of you in your bed covered with letters," one friend would write a few years later. These letters were "about all sorts of grave matters—agriculture—allotments—prison discipline—church building—to say nothing of the thousand and one calls upon your heart for help and sympathy—and upon your understanding and your conscience for the right direction of both." Her philanthropy gave much to England, but as the song says: Is that all there is?

There would soon be a full summer moon at sea, she wrote. "How much I lose by not being able to remain on deck at night." At the age of forty-eight, sailing to France, Lady Byron was finding herself deprived of moonlight.

She brought with her to the Continent a letter that had been forwarded to her. It was from niece Medora Leigh.

After the first three years of cohabiting with Henry Trevanion in Brittany as Madame Elizabeth Aubin, and after many miscarriages, Medora's health deteriorated. Once Henry realized there would not be a living child, he loosened his grip on her and she had a chance to leave him. The Roman Catholic convert wrote to Augusta telling her mother she wished to enter a convent in Lower Brittany as a boarder. It took Augusta much coaxing from her half sister Lady Chichester and her nephew Lord Chichester to finally do something: "After much delay and difficulty I left Trevanion and entered a convent, my mother engaging to allow me £60 a year." Augusta had delayed too long in sending the money that allowed the separation. For within a month of convent life, Medora realized she was once more pregnant. Forced back into the world, "I did not feel I was doing wrong," for she and Henry now lived as brother and sister.

When news of this reached Lady Byron, she took it with a grain of salt. But it may have been true, for a cessation of sexual intercourse could account for Medora's not miscarrying as she often had. In 1834 she gave birth to a live child, her daughter Marie. This apparently was a great joy to Henry. For a while he gave himself over "to religion and shooting, I to my child." They never met alone. Poverty forced Henry back to England for six weeks and he returned with money. It was then that he wanted to bed her again. Medora's response is revealing: "But I was no longer a child. I was twenty-one; and two years experience had enabled me to know how to resist. I pass over three years of misery."

During them, Henry found a new mistress and Medora was treated by him and his mistress as their indentured servant. They worked her to the bone. By the spring of 1838 she was so ill that she was mistakenly declared consumptive and was considered within months of death. Her mind was set to have her last days free of Henry and his mistress's control: The French medical man, Monsieur Victor Carrel "who attended me was very kind," and "at his solicitation" Medora confided her true history. "I asked his aid to free me from the cruelty of one whom I had never really loved, and by his conduct every day convinced me more and more of his worthlessness. My greatest wish was to die away from him."

Lady Byron knew of all this through her good friend Lady Wilmot-Horton who was Medora's godmother—whatever that meant in these days, Lady Wilmot-Horton remarked. A softspoken woman of sense whom Annabella admired, the Lady had years before been the inspiration of Byron's "She Walks in Beauty." Through her, Annabella once more sent Medora 20 pounds anonymously "to be followed by more if she lives." She told Lady Wilmot-Horton that no one must suspect from whom the money came, but that she couldn't get the girl's wretched condition out of her mind. These funds allowed Medora to leave with her child to a neighboring town.

To maintain herself and her daughter, by the end of 1838, Medora also wrote directly to her godmother's husband: Sir Robert Wilmot-Horton (formerly Robert Wilmot), who had stepped down as Governor of Ceylon the year before. Though a cousin on Byron's side, Wilmot-Horton, having found out about the incestuous affair between Lord Byron and his sister, became a staunch friend of Lady Byron during the separation procedures. Medora wrote to him that her mother had promised to make out a deed of appointment to her for a portion of the money that would come to her through Lord Byron's will, but Augusta kept delaying. Medora needed it to live. Deeds of appointment were viable from the 1820s until close to the twenty-first century. They were based on an heir's future expectations, cost nothing beyond legal fees to write, yet one could raise money on them or hold tight. The issuer of said deed would be resting in peace before claims, complications, confusion, additional lawyers' fees, and wrangles ensued. Like many complicated fiscal dealings today, they were based on expectations and plenty of hot air.

Augusta could base her deed on Lady Byron's jointure of 66,000. The interest on the jointure would stop going to Lord George Byron, and the 66,000 devolve to Augusta after Lady Byron's death, as per Lord Byron's will. It was assumed, given her fragile health, that Lady Byron would predecease her sister-in-law—an assumption one finds to be the surest way of insuring longevity. Medora begged Wilmot-Horton to use his influence with Augusta, which he did, and her mother eventually sent Medora a copy of a deed made out to her for 3,000 pounds. However, Augusta would not send her the original of the deed, which Medora needed to raise money on it. Finally, Medora wrote to Sir George Stephen, the well-respected lawyer who had previously raised money on the 11,000-pound deed Augusta had willingly assigned to Henry Trevanion. A desperate Medora had Sir George initiate a Chancery suit against her own mother in order to procure the deed.

It was in her letter to Sir George that Medora enclosed another to be forwarded. She was sure, "my aunt, Lady Noel Byron, would use any influence she might possess with my mother, to induce her to give up to me that which was my right." That Medora was so convinced indicates both that she found out Lady Byron was her benefactor and that Sir Robert Wilmot-Horton, who handled these transactions, let her know. Though Lady Byron's answer to Medora had been kind and she had enclosed money, she was skeptical. She assumed it had actually been Henry who had deserted Medora and their child, not the other way around, and that if Henry wanted her back, Medora would be at his beck and call. Still, debarking in France, a dispirited Lady Byron took a gamble. She wrote directly to the girl. Would her niece like to see her? If so she'd arrange a meeting, proposing to come part of the way to Pontivy, where Medora and Marie were living on their own.

Medora responded that she wanted to leave Pontivy forever, as it was only four miles from Henry. She wished only quiet and seclusion for her and her child and some peace before she died. Surprised by and impressed with Medora's earnest desire to get beyond Henry's control, that it indeed *was* Medora who initiated the break up, Lady Byron wrote back asking her niece "to trust herself to me." She sent her own medical man to accompany Medora and the child to her at Tours, where they met on August 21, 1840.

Lady Byron hadn't seen the girl since she was little more than a child. Medora had grown into an unusually tall reed, with long dark hair and wild eyes. Her aunt was shocked by her gaunt appearance, by ragged clothes that hung from her frame as her little seven-year-old clung to—was able to encircle—the remains of a waist. Medora was so ill, so painfully thin, and in such a confused state of mind. At times the young woman seemed to be in a stupor, at times in too great an excitement, talking in a disconnected way about the past. Lady Byron realized that "several of my previous suppositions were contrary to facts."

One of them might have been that Medora took on other lovers or that she prostituted herself in order to survive. Men did seem to be drawn to this mysterious young Englishwoman, this damsel of the upper class who had converted to Roman Catholicism and fallen on hard times in France. Dr. Carrel had gone far out of his way for her, as other men had and would as well. From the goodness of their hearts? It would seem, in many cases, so. She was one of those women who appealed to men's protective instincts.

Convinced now that Medora sincerely wanted nothing more than to be saved from Trevanion, Lady Byron planned to resettle her and Marie there at Tours, where she had friends. However, "The more I considered her distress of mind and her desolate situation and that of her little girl, the more reluctant I felt to leave her at the time." Medora and the child could travel with Lady Byron, they could remain together, that is if Medora and Marie assumed "another name." By Lady Byron's request, Elizabeth Medora (Libby) Leigh once more became Madame Elizabeth Aubin, but this time Mme. Aubin appeared to be a widow with a young daughter traveling with an older, quite famous, widow.

By early September, they were at Fontainebleau. In the late summer heat, as they traveled, Lady Byron's condition worsened, her heart acted up and she experienced stabbing pains in her chest. Perhaps she believed her own days were numbered as well as Medora's. Resting at Fontainebleau, she reminisced. It was as if Lord Byron had returned to her in a new form. Medora's resemblance to the poet was uncanny. The mannerisms, the way she looked sideways when another entered without her knowledge, her very face, the bottom half a twin to Ada's. The mood shifts were like Byron's as well—the daring, the playfulness, the sudden plunges into darkness. One distinction, that height of hers—"my lanky doodle," Lady Byron called her.

Lady Byron was not blind to the fact that living hand to mouth had made Medora not only mercurial, but shrewd. The story Medora had to tell of her mistreatment by Augusta was so outrageous that it is doubtful Lady Byron—or anyone else—would have believed her. However, like Lord Byron, Medora saved letters. At Fontainebleau as aunt and niece attempted to shut out the heat and heal, Medora opened her own version of Byron's "red portfolio" and let her aunt read Augusta Leigh's responses in first finding out, in February 1831, that her sixteen-year-old daughter was pregnant—and for a second time. Augusta immediately wrote—to *Henry*:

> It would be impossible in the *first* instance to speak to you my dearest—without such emotion as would be painful to us both. I therefore take up my pen, but only to break the ice.

How I have loved and regarded you . . . I can never cease to do so! To the last moment of my existence you will find in me the tenderness, the indulgence of a Mother—can I say more? If I could, tell me so! Show me only how I can comfort and support you—confide in me dearest. . . .

I am convinced, dearest, that as I have opened my heart and feelings to you, you will comfort me! I need not point out to you the means! your own heart will dictate them—as you are dear! MOST dear! **much** is in your power! Heaven bless, comfort and guide you!

She wrote Henry a second letter as well: "*Dearest*—I wish I *could* comfort you!" He was not to "make yourself out *what you are NOT*!" For: "*Remember I* do 'depend on your Love'—and oh! How I *have* loved you!—how I will always love you and God bless you! dearest."

To Medora, her sixteen-year-old, Augusta wrote that her daughter had "committed *two* of the most deadly crimes! recollect who you have injured." She must think of how she has harmed her sisters, her brothers, her poor father, her "wretched" mother. Augusta went down on her knees, she wrote, imploring Medora to "cope with those temptations" that assaulted her. "This DREADFUL affair" is either going to "*upset my reason or break my heart.*"

Augusta had her heart set on the sixteen-year-old being confirmed that Easter Sunday. She was so looking forward to it, she wrote. Knowing what she now knew, she could not instruct Medora herself, but a clergyman could, one who would only have to know what was necessary for the ceremony. Augusta, in effect, was begging Medora to abort—perhaps the better infinitive would be to erase—and to be confirmed. "Pardon me if I inflict pain on you—I must in this case 'be cruel to be kind.'" At times Augusta's words channel, centuries ahead of its time, the outlandish mother of *Absolutely Fabulous*: "Dearest Darling! Speak to me, confide in me!" she implored Medora: "Spare! oh spare me, Dearest! Spare yourself and all you hold most dear!"

In the cool shadows of the high-ceilinged bedroom at

Fontainebleau, doctor and nurses in attendance, shutters closed, resting against soft pillows, and, of course, being bled, Lady Byron put these three letters down beside her on the bed: "Moral idiocy!" she exclaimed.

Lady Byron had always blamed Byron for seducing his older sister. After reading Augusta's severe letters to Medora, and loving letters to Trevanion (all of which still exist in her archives at the Bodleian), she wondered for the first time if it had been his older sister who had seduced the younger Lord Byron. Visiting Félix Voisin's asylum for the insane later that season, she would have no ready evidence to offer against his theory that not only was insanity inherited, but so was moral nature.

One could make a case for the years without Augusta, at least since Ada's marriage, having been the best of Lady Byron's life. She had established her Co-Operative School at Ealing Grove. Her beloved son-in-law was setting up one at his Ockham estate as well. She bragged he could teach *her* new methods of advanced farming techniques. Her daughter had given her three grandchildren and at the same time as Lady Byron sailed for France, Ada had returned to her mathematical studies with great intensity. By bringing Medora into her life, not only were the best moments of Lady Byron's life with Byron recalled—and most likely enlarged—but she had a project that revived her.

"I am particularly happy at present, feelings that have long lain, like buried forests, beneath the moss of years, are called forth and seem to give happiness to one for whom I have something like a Mother's affection." She wrote this to Edward Noel, the youngest and most artistic of her Noel cousins: "I must not attempt to justify by reasoning only the affection I feel for her—other sentiments strengthened by a decided resemblance have endeared her to me and made her my adopted child." The feelings that sprouted into fresh bloom were romantic, in the sense that youth was recalled, Spring returned. Suddenly there was hope, the perfume of flowers. She was alive again. She had a destitute daughter to whom she could be of help—whom she could save! She had Byron again.

That she told Medora much about her marriage is evident. With the playful audacity of Lord Byron, Medora began to call her aunt "Pip." Lady Byron did not protest; in fact, she enjoyed that endearment from her "baby Porpoise." Pet names had taken an aquatic turn. She told Medora of the beautiful look on Byron's face when he gazed at her as an infant. How was it possible that Augusta could deny their child the deed that would have kept her from starving at Pontivy or being forced to return to Henry Trevanion?

At Fontainebleau, she told Medora that if her mother refused to be reasonable and insisted on allowing this Chancery suit to progress rather than handing the deed over to Medora, Lady Byron would tell the truth of her birth to the court and Medora would receive what was rightfully hers. As Medora underscored in her autobiography, three years later, Lady Byron revealed *"the cause of the deep interest she felt, and must ever feel, for me. Her husband had been my father."*

Both her sister Georgey and Henry Trevanion had told Medora the same thing. They of course had been trying to separate her from Colonel Leigh, the father who she knew loved her. She had not believed them. Now she did. She was Lord Byron's daughter. Lady Byron went further in her righteous indignation. Byron had told her in Augusta's presence that he planned to do *more* for Medora than for her other children. And here was Augusta refusing her a deed for such a modest share of her birthright. Since Lady Byron's moral compass pointed exclusively in the direction of the Good, she was unconscious that in going after Medora's love she was once more in competition with Augusta, who had been left to flounder in the dark.

Five months of silence until Augusta was frantic enough to petition her sister-in-law "reluctantly," at the beginning of 1841. She hoped she'd be "forgiven," she jabbed. Not hearing from her daughter had become "most perplexing, if not bewildering," and she didn't know how much longer she could keep quiet. She had always considered Medora "a free agent" and had confidence in all her daughter said, but there "are those who view them differently and variously" and consider Augusta the "*Dupe!*" of her daughter. "God knows, I have been

too often and cruelly deceived, to be in a position to give a very sat-
isfactory answer to such suspicions." There were "good people" who
had a natural right to know what was going on.

Augusta was threatening to disclose Medora's identity as an unwed
mother traveling with Lady Byron. Lady Byron responded coldly that
she was not aware of any communication about Medora being "confidential." If Augusta thought it was a threat to reveal who Mme. Aubin
really was, she was mistaken. Augusta was free to disclose Lady
Byron's share in the business as she wished, but then "I am prepared,
in justice to Medora and myself, to explain fully the reasons of my thus
interesting myself in her welfare."

If Augusta had "a Mother's affection" for Medora, she would not
have to be asking after her child. The facts, however, were "glaringly"
in another direction. After Medora freed herself of the "tyranny" of
Trevanion without any help from her mother, Augusta left her in poverty and without protection, alarmingly ill and vulnerable to every
temptation. The little bit of money she sent her daughter was in the
eyes of the most respectable people of Pontivy not sufficient to maintain her life or the life of her child. Augusta left her daughter with only
two alternatives: the "vice" of returning to Trevanion, or starvation.
According to Lady Byron's physicians, Medora's malady, a combination of physical and mental suffering, could be retarded, through
extreme care and eliminations of all upsetting excitements. Lady Byron
could secure Medora's physical care, but not her freedom from mental
distress. She told Augusta, "I would save you if it be not too late, from
adding the guilt of her death to that of her birth. Leave her in peace!"

Augusta was mortified by her sister-in-law's strong words.
She sent Lady Byron "Statements" attested to by her half sister and
nephew, Lady and Lord Chichester, to prove that she had done what
she could for Medora financially. Lady Byron returned the packet
unopened. Augusta did not then nor did she ever argue against "the
guilt" of Medora's birth.

Once Augusta got the packet back, their mutual friend Theresa
Villiers wrote to Lady Byron—who did open her letters—to explain

that she hadn't seen Mrs. Leigh since "the year 1831, *because* I thought her conduct towards *you* in some financial arrangements was ungrateful and improper." Still, it was an old friendship and she had maintained an interest in what she termed Augusta's "disasters."

She had to confess that she felt Augusta had done more for Medora in the "*confined*" area of "*pecuniary matters*" than was warranted. Augusta's own means were scanty. She was now living on 900 pounds a year. Queen Victoria had not renewed Colonel Leigh's per annum. Because of Medora's running off with Trevanion "Georgiana with *her* three children" were left abandoned and penniless and had far greater claims on Augusta than errant Medora. Georgey and her brood were living with Augusta, who deprived herself not only of luxuries but of many necessities of life to be their sole support. She also had to provide bed and board to her husband when he came around. Lady Byron should remember that Augusta had five adult children besides Medora, all but one, the youngest, Emily, "disasters." That word again. Emily refused to go out in society, as she would not buy new clothes when she saw her sister and nieces in dire need. (Almost every large dysfunctional family appears to have an Emily weighed down by issues not of her own making.)

Augusta had sent Theresa a note asking to see her as soon as possible, and she could not deny her childhood friend. She went to the palace, where Augusta showed her the letter Lady Byron had sent. "She was in the deepest distress." Augusta wanted to express her gratitude for Lady Byron's taking her unfortunate daughter and child under her protection, but also to let her know that "Mrs. L's conduct to her daughter on *pecuniary matters* had been misrepresented to you."

Two times in the same letter Mrs. Villiers underscored the limitation of her defense of Augusta to that of money matters. She offered not one word, in any of the many letters and statements that followed, about Lady Byron's accusation of the "guilt" of Medora's birth. Nor did Augusta. No usual flurry of capital letters, underscoring and exclamation marks disputing it.

Certainly it is a wise child who knows her own father, and Hebraic wisdom has it that one can only be sure of one's mother. Byron claimed he was Medora's father to Lady Melbourne, Caroline Lamb, and to his wife. Lady Byron thought Medora was his daughter. So did Lady Melbourne, Hobhouse, Georgey, Henry Trevanion, the Wilmot-Hortons, Mrs. Villiers, Dr. Lushington, the Doyles, the DeMorgans. . . . and Augusta. But why are we back to all this again? That is just the point. Lady Byron was.

After a decade of freeing herself from Augusta Leigh, Lady Byron was in a psychological tug of war with her sister-in-law once more. Like the buried personal animosities that can flare to savagery in political arguments, something of the sort happened here. Annabella had extricated herself from the Byron orbit, made a life for her and her daughter, and turned her philanthropic impulses to concrete and significant results. A few years previously she even boarded a ship "incog" to find herself a popular person in her own right. Once she brought Medora back into her life, the past became prologue. To Edward Noel, she wrote from Paris, explaining her unique situation. She was presently divided "between a Daughter in the most prosperous circumstances and one who has become dependant on me for the means of existence and of moral existence too."

THE DAUGHTER in the best of circumstances had returned to her scientific studies the year before Lady Byron traveled to France and four months after the birth of her third child, Ralph. Ada Lovelace was not yet twenty-four and was being tutored in mathematics by one of the most renowned logicians of his day, Augustus De Morgan, of the University of London. He had married Lady Byron's friend Sophia Frend, daughter of Lady Byron's old Cambridge tutor. "Calculus," Ada wrote to her mother, had become "King." Mathematics might very well have taken precedence over husband William King. At approximately the same time as Lady Byron leased that house in Paris on 24 Rue de Rivoli for the 1840–41 season, Ada was finding her calling. She had already told Charles Babbage she thought there was a way of programming games:

*Charles Babbage, precursor of the information age
and friend and mentor to Ada, Countess of Lovelace.*

"My Dear Mr Babbbage," she wrote. "Have you ever seen a game, or rather a puzzle called Solitaire?" The idea is that pegs jump each other at right angles till only one peg is left on the board. "People may try thousands of times, and not succeed. . . . I *have* done it by trying and observation and can now do it at any time, but I want to know if the problem admits of being put into a mathematical Formula." Ada was convinced: "There must be a definite principle, a compound I imagine of numerical and geometrical properties, on which the solution depends, and which can be put into symbolic language." Was she "too imaginative" for Babbage? She thought not.

"Mathematics flourish on famously," Ada wrote to Lady Byron in late September 1840 and signed the letter "A Mathematical Avis." The carrier pigeon was becoming a new kind of bird.

A month later, Ada pronounced herself "wonderfully altered as to courage," after riding a horse of wild spirits. "I never was so bold and full of nerve at any time in my life." When Lady Byron and her entourage settled in Paris, she sent Ada what her daughter termed very interesting letters about her long-lost cousin. "We shall certainly go to Paris, if you remain there," Ada responded to her mother in late November, telling her how they would miss her when they moved on to Ockham for the holidays. In mid-December, from Ockham, Ada became "anxious to hear more of your wishes about our going to Paris."

The first week of the new year, 1841, Ada wrote to her mother asking her to thank Medora for the pincushion she made for her. She complimented the Hen, revered her for not shunning but taking in her unfortunate cousin and couldn't wait to visit. However, her mother still hadn't sent her the traveling schedules she'd need. Not until the end of February 1841, with Ada planning to arrive in Paris for Easter, did Lady Byron, an only child herself, let *her* only child know she had a half sister not a "cousin." She might have decided the timing was right, for it would also act to divert her daughter, not from scientific study, of which she approved, but of the obsessiveness that attended those studies. Ada was no different in spirit and intensity than when she was twelve years old and obsessed by flight.

As her scientific acumen advanced, Ada wrote to her mother she believed herself "to possess a most singular combination of qualities exactly fitted to make me *pre-eminently* a discover of the *hidden realities* of nature." Her mother of all people would not mistake this assertion either as wild enthusiasm or "*self exaltation.*" In another letter Ada told her mother the mountain she was climbing was enough to frighten anyone who hadn't "the most insatiable and restless energy, which from my babyhood has been the plague of your life and my own."

"My sun is rising," she wrote. "He" would gradually run its course and "set amidst rosy, golden dazzling clouds, that may show to *me* something of the Spirit Land." He will tell her "to leave for mankind in my footsteps a little of that brightness from *Beyond,*" a glimpse of "the Great Future." Lady Byron replied that Ada appeared to be "under the dominion of electricity."

"There was some truth in it," Ada responded, amused, for "the King of my mind is rather *electrical* in his attributes certainly right

William King, the Earl of Lovelace, Ada's husband
and Lady Byron's helpmate.

now." Again, the William King she married seemed replaced. At this
juncture Lady Byron informed her daughter she had a half sister.

"You merely *confirm* what I have for *years and years* felt scarcely
a doubt about," Ada replied on February 27, 1841. Not that she had
imagined a half sister; after all, her aunt was a "married woman." One
can almost hear husband William in the background asking Ada:
How can your mother be so sure? That aside, somehow she knew her
father and his sister had been lovers. The last year she told William so!
When William questioned how she could come up with "so *monstrous*
and *hideous*" a supposition without having tangible evidence, she felt
ashamed.

However, her intuition having been proved correct, Ada took a
moment to reflect on the empirical evidence of her fabulousness. This
awe at her own perceptivity, a trait since childhood, was heightened
by her advanced mathematical studies and by the use of laudanum
necessitated perhaps by the increasing misery caused by her Black

Dwarf. "I wish hereafter, as you know, to apply a little of my sometimes strange *penetration* and *tact* to the reading of the many mysterious things in Nature's World around us.—Yes—I think the time will come for that!"

Now that Ada knew her cousin was her half sister, Lady Byron hoped Ada's "imaginary" feelings for her father would be charitable. In his "purified state," Lord Byron might even prefer Ada knowing the truth. No more secrets! she proclaimed. Her daughter could now become the friend of her mother's past as well as her present life, *"without reserve."*

But how did her mother come to realize Medora was her half sister, Ada asked. She had too pure a mind to have such a thought herself. "I cannot help fancying that *he* himself must have given you some very clear hints of it. He too well liked to taunt you with his crimes. Alas!"

Yes, he had, Lady Byron answered: "Medora was born Ap.15, 1814. I was married Jan. 2. 1815." When she and Byron "visited Mrs Leigh in the Spring, I found the child still nursed by her. It was the loveliest Infant I ever saw—so smiling and intelligent—the only creature there who was not miserable!—I heard him claim it was *his*," but attributed such outbursts to other causes such as his "malignant feelings" and delight in tormenting Lady Byron "without foundation."

She confided in Ada that she had always blamed Byron exclusively for imposing himself on his older sister, but the way Augusta had mistreated her own daughter, handing her over when a mere child to Henry Trevanion, made Lady Byron think otherwise: "One who could, *as she clearly did*, connive at the ruin of a daughter, must have been capable of injuring a brother in the same way."

BY THE TIME Ada arrived at 24 Rue de Rivoli, Medora and her child were comfortably set up in their own quarters. For all her years in France, Medora had never been to Paris. She was not the first to fall in love at first sight. She had a new life, a new mother, new clothes, help for daughter Marie. Paris was at her beck and call. It all added up to a slow and steady return of vitality in a country whose language she spoke well. Ada and Medora got along famously. Ada, who as a child called her cousin George her brother and wished him to live with her, was delighted to have a half sister. It couldn't cause the jealous rivalry such news might provoke in different siblings. For Ada would help her mother care for this unfortunate sister, so would William. The idea of competition was meaningless. The Countess of Lovelace lived in the upper stratosphere. The only one who could possibly conceive that having Lord Byron for a father made the Countess and Medora equals was Medora.

To William, who had not yet arrived in Paris, Ada wrote: "I see a good deal of Medora; by my *own desire and choice* I mean, for so scrupulous is the Hen that she has placed her in an apartment quite in a separate wing of the house, in order that she may in no way be *forced* either on myself or any other of the Hen's visitors. I therefore go there whenever I choose, and she does not come into the other apartments." Did Medora even understand the implications of Lady Byron's partitioning of 24 Rue de Rivoli? In their hours of intimacy, Medora told her sister she had hated Trevanion. Her rape was "by the *united efforts* of the Mother, the Sister, and Mr Trevanion himself," Ada wrote to William. The girl had been drugged and "found herself ruined on coming to her senses." Medora was "absolutely guiltless."

BEYOND THE SORDID DETAILS of the past, Ada witnessed her mother's return of vitality. Lady Byron planned to be in England for the summer months, but would spend the next winter, perhaps all winters, abroad—in France. "There is no doubt how very materially better in health she is out of England." Ada had "never seen her so well; and she shines most brightly on the Avis." And obviously on her Porpoise as well.

Lady Byron wrote gaily to her close friend Lady Olivia Acheson, Lady Gosford's daughter. She wasn't going to have any time for Olivia and her three children when she returned to England "for the year

1842," she wrote joyously. She had her own child, her own tall "Lanky Doodle," to occupy her. Perhaps she already knew of Olivia's conversion to Roman Catholicism in the years when Oxford clergyman John Henry Newman and many others were "going over" to Rome. However, this was before a deathly ill Olivia joined the converted Cardinal Newman in Birmingham, where Lady Byron would meet him and be skeptical, phrenologically, of the value of his skull. Her notable ecumenicalism did not extend to the "Scarlet Woman," as she exhibited in her witty, trenchant analysis of her adopted Roman Catholic daughter's psychology.

She had a Lanky Doodle who refused to take the "sugar basin," from under Lady Byron's chin. Instead, Medora made "*conscientious lumps of sugar*" out of it. She knew the "throat" of her aunt's "conscience is small," and she was adept at fitting the "sweet sin" to the size of it with "wonderful precision." She wished to describe the "morality" of all this to Olivia, and since it "comes from a Roman Catholic you will be the more disposed to adopt it."

In a clever satire of Newman's justification of theological "economy"—i.e., equivocating to reach religious truth—she wrote: "If a Sin would choke you, break it in two—for instance if a Man should ask you to run away with him, and you can't make up your mind to so decided a step, refuse, and go somewhere from whence he may run away with you. Again, if you want the contents of your neighbor's pocket, don't steal, but borrow them, and add to the first little *lump* a second—the failure of payment. One more edifying instance—if you can't tell a downright falsehood, tell that half of it which will convey the other half inaudibly to the mind of the receiver."

Signing this wicked and cheerful missive "Your personified Bon-bon," she was under few illusions about the manipulative nature of her adopted daughter as she sailed back to England, her confectioner in tow.

10

INTERMEZZO: LADY BYRON
TIME-TRAVELS ON THE
BROWNINGS' *MOON*

Thirty years after Lady Byron's contentious separation proceedings, two poets married with more harmonious—if no less mythic—results. Elizabeth Barrett at the age of thirty-nine, a world-famous and until then invalid poet, secretly married Robert Browning, six years her junior. Soon after, she left England with her new husband, secretly again, with the hopes her father would forgive her. This flight from Wimpole Street was necessary, as Elizabeth's father would not allow any of his nine adult children, male or female, to marry—and could be physically violent if opposed. Edward Barrett's silent torment was that his mixed blood, Creole blood, would show in a grandchild. With a growing irrationality based on guilt and isolation, he attempted to end his line.

Edward Barrett's grandfather had been the biggest landowner and slave owner in the northern part of Jamaica, and Edward, by birth a master early used to command, lived on his grandfather's estates. His own father had long disappeared, when, at the age of seven the boy was parted from his mother and sent with his younger siblings to England for his education. He never returned to the West Indies— though his livelihood in trade was made on the backs of slaves. Slavery ended in England in the 1830s, but the stigma of being a planter and an outsider in English society remained.

There is a monumental painting by Benjamin Haydon of the World Anti-Slavery Society Convention held in London in 1840. In it, Haydon (Elizabeth Barrett's friend) painted portraits of a third of the 500 delegates visible. It was an overwhelmingly male audience, as women were kept behind a curtain and not allowed to speak. One of the few women in the assembly is Lady Byron, pictured seated in the second row. After the meeting Annabella asked to be introduced to the American delegates Elizabeth Cady Stanton and Lucretia Mott, who traveled all that way only to be pushed aside. It would take the two another eight years before they called out for women's rights loud and clear, at Seneca Falls, New York. In London, on the issue of slavery, they were silenced.

Mixed blood was common in Jamaica, the planters often preferring the slave women to their wives. Some of the illegitimate children of these unions were sent to England to be educated—not abandoned by their fathers as was the case in the American South. Edward Barrett was legitimate, but his dark skin, obvious in portraits, showed his mixed racial heritage, probably through his reprobate father. Elizabeth's complexion and her broad, exotic features showed her racial mix as well in later photographs, not in earlier portraits. She was the first Barrett to be born in England, not Jamaica, in over two hundred years. One wonders, had there been photography before he died, what Byron really looked like, with his pronounced chin, inherited by his daughter Ada, his one eye smaller than the other, and his "little" leg. Thomas Medwin said of Byron's bust by the renowned neoclassical sculptor Bertel Thorvaldsen, that it was far "too thin-necked and young" for the out-of-shape Byron he knew in Italy. When Lady Byron, later in life, saw the posthumous full-length statue of her husband by the same sculptor, she remarked, "It is very beautiful, but not half beautiful enough for my dear Byron."

Whether or not they captured the living Byron, portraits in the nineteenth century aimed at the ideal of beauty society held dear. For example: Edward Barrett's young sister Sarah, the poet's aunt, was immortalized in a famous portrait by Thomas Lawrence often called

Pinkie and paired with Gainsborough's *Blue Boy*. Actually, Pinkie was Sarah's nickname in the West Indies. To the Jamaicans a "Pinkie" was a light-colored black who passed. In England, people assumed "Pinkie" referred to the color of the child's sash, hat, and to the tones in her dress. Quite understandable, considering that Pinkie herself was painted blush white.

Elizabeth Barrett, her father's eldest, famous, and most obedient adult child, with whom he read the Bible each night, knew as an adult Christian woman she had the right to marry—she was close to forty for goodness sake—but this didn't alleviate the guilt she felt at disobeying and disappointing her father. She knew his motives—to end his line. Such racial concerns made her passionately antislavery in poetry and in her life. Joining Robert and leaving England in secrecy, she insisted on a mad rush to Italy, far, far away from her guilt and with the hope of reconciliation with her father by post along the way (it never happened).

Robert Browning, a complex thinker and lesser-known poet at the time, was simply madly in love, an indifferent organizer of trips abroad, and sublimely unaware of the responsibility his doting parents understood: In his hands was the life of a physically fragile and famous woman with whom he had begun a long and difficult voyage to the land she dreamed of but might not live to see. Indeed, Elizabeth was exhausted, depleted, by the time they arrived in Paris, yet she was insisting that they move on immediately—or as soon as they could, since Robert hadn't procured proper papers.

Robert Browning knew that a good friend of theirs was in Paris at the time—Anna Jameson. Mrs. Jameson was a well-known writer, an early feminist, and the first art historian, who opened the eyes of a burgeoning middle class to the treasures awaiting them in the museums and galleries of Europe. As the nineteenth century progressed, prosperity widened; the invention of the steam engine and the ensuing industrial revolution moved things along. One needn't be to the manor born to go on the grand tour. With leisure time, how big the world, how much to learn. The newly rich as well as the aesthete were lucky to have as perceptive and as good a writer as Mrs. Jameson to guide them.

Born in Dublin to an Irish father and an English mother, Anna Brownell Murphy emigrated to England with her parents in 1798, when she, the oldest of a growing brood of girls, was four. Her father, Denis Murphy, was a fashionable painter of miniatures. Like many an artist, popularity didn't insure financial stability. There were payments due—the higher the title, the slower the payment. George IV's only daughter, Princess Charlotte, whom Denis Murphy considered his patroness, hinted at buying the series of historical *Court Beauties* he was painting. He based the family's future prosperity on the completion of this ambitious set of miniatures. After the Princess died before her time, her husband, Prince Leopold of Saxe-Coburg (later the first King of the Belgians), sent his secretary down to tell Denis Murphy he wouldn't buy the completed series, but out of curiosity, how much had he wanted for them?

Anna Jameson adored her impractical artist of a father. From an early age she took on financial responsibility for her parents and sisters, first through her work as a governess to the high-born and then through her writings. Though Browning hadn't breathed a word to her of his coming marriage, he knew she was leaving London about the same time as he, on her way to Rome to write what would become her most renowned work, the two-volumed *Sacred and Legendary Art*. With her, her seventeen-year-old niece, Gerardine Bate.

Anna planned to train her sister's daughter as her assistant and as an art engraver. "Geddie" would be able to make her own living, not have to marry a rich man or become a governess to survive. In Paris, Mrs. Jameson was exposing her niece to a wider world opening for women, encouraging her toward an independence which could be won through meaningful work. Geddie would need to work; her father, another impractical artist, had recently gone bankrupt.

Robert Browning arrived at Anna Jameson's hotel in Paris while aunt and niece were visiting galleries and left a cryptic note: "Come to see your friend & my wife EBB . . . RB."

Who? What? Mrs. Jameson puzzled over the handwriting, the initials. The desk clerk described the bearer simply as a gentleman. What the initials indicated simply couldn't be. While she pondered, night fell.

It was Elizabeth who insisted Robert go to a separate room in their hotel that night where he would not be disturbed and could get some sleep. He had spent the last three weeks planning and executing the secret marriage, and in his own poetic way making botched travel plans. He hardly ate at all. They had arrived first at Rouen to find their visas weren't adequate, and though they could stay the night, their luggage had to leave immediately. So of course they picked themselves up and went along with their cases. Elizabeth wrote to her favorite sister, Arabel, that she would have been startled at the scene of Robert picking her up and carrying her in and out of travelers' restrooms, as Robert "in his infinite kindness" wended his way with her in his arms through crowds of curious foreigners carrying her to their train: "& so we rolled on towards Paris."

Unconsciously, Browning's note to Anna Jameson, his breaking of secrecy, was a call for help. Though Browning had spent time abroad, Mrs. Jameson was a practical, seasoned, intrepid traveler. At the age of sixteen, as governess to children of Regency aristocrats, she had been on the grand tour. In her twenties, after the breaking of her engagement with Robert Jameson, she accompanied yet another high-born family abroad and wrote a novel based on her travel diaries. *Diary of an Ennuyée* brought with it her first fame and launched her writing career. She did not die of illness caused by a broken love affair, as did her heroine. In fact, Robert Jameson himself urged her to publish the book and through his connections helped her to do so. He was a handsome lawyer connected to the literati, a member of Basil Montagu's circle, and a good friend—or more than good friend— of Coleridge's son Hartley. A few years later, in her early thirties, she did marry him, though he was often referred to as "strange." So was the marriage, which took place in 1825. The couple soon went their separate ways, he to Dominica, then to Canada, where he rose to become the first Vice-Chancellor of the Upper and Lower Canadas and slowly drank himself to death; she to rise among the literary elite of her times. Lively, witty, empathetic, intelligent—a peerless storyteller and conversationalist—she became sought after in literary circles not only in England, but in Germany, the United States, and Canada.

Elizabeth was so worried about her husband's exhaustion that though Anna Jameson would be the first person to be privy to the secret marriage, Elizabeth would face her alone if she had to. It would be rather embarrassing, as on a visit to Elizabeth in her invalid's bed-sitting room on Wimpole Street, Jameson herself had offered to bring Elizabeth to Italy, along with niece Geddie, to keep the fragile poet from the perils of yet another English winter. Elizabeth's father would not allow it. Well, then, there is nothing for you but elopement, Jameson had quipped. She had no idea that Elizabeth and Robert were planning just that. Chagrin to the side, the poet assured her new husband she was up to greeting Mrs. Jameson by herself, should she arrive. Which Mrs. Jameson certainly did. She came in, Elizabeth recorded, with eyes as wide as those of Flush, Elizabeth's spaniel, who witnessed all from his mistress's lap.

"Can it be possible? Is it possible? You wild dear creature."

Mrs. Jameson, plump and energetic at fifty-two, motherly yet without children of her own, was as open-hearted as she was gifted. Why, they were poets; each should have married a good provider to keep them reasonable. Hadn't she attempted, back on Wimpole Street, to convince the incredulous Elizabeth Barrett that all artists were temperamentally like children? All she had succeeded in doing was upsetting her. Well, never mind, Robert was a wise man and she a wise woman. Let the world say what it will, "I shall dance for joy both on earth and in heaven my dear friends." Elizabeth found Anna "the kindest, the most cordial, the most astonished, the most out of breath with *wonder*—and I could scarcely speak." When Mrs. Jameson caught her breath, she took over, insisting the Brownings stay in Paris for a week. Elizabeth was in no condition to rush on. She was so fragile a carriage ride itself bruised her. She moved the poets to her hotel, where she could be of further assistance.

"I really believe I have saved her life by persuading her to rest," Anna Jameson wrote to a woman she adored—Lady Byron.

It was the first of five letters Anna Jameson wrote to Lady Byron in 1846 as she traveled on from Paris to Pisa with the newlywed poets, who planned a long honeymoon in Pisa following the path Lord Byron forged twenty-five years previously. The Brownings were not traveling in the style of the poet they admired. Lord Byron had hit the road with five carriages, nine horses, seven servants, an extensive library, elaborate furniture, a monkey, two dogs, two cats, three peafowls, and some hens. The Brownings traveled light. A faithful servant, a dog, their cases, a portable writing desk . . .

Mrs. Jameson had agreed to accompany this modest entourage, not without silent reservations, given the impressionable age of her niece and the circumstances of the Brownings' secret marriage. The poets' characters, however, were so fine, their need of practical guidance so evident, that she overcame her scruples. Still, "I have not faith in the poetical temperament as a means of permanent happiness," Anna wrote to her friend, in essence preaching to the choir.

The truism that the Victorians' admiration for the Romantic poets paled the more they learned about their private lives has been used as an example of the prudishness of a later generation—a reaction against the freewheeling days of the Regency. However, what the next generation was having difficulty absorbing was more than surface indiscretions. Victorians really weren't that easy to "shock." Much of what they found out about Byron, about Shelley, came word of mouth from those who had witnessed—and experienced. For more than fifteen years Anna Jameson would be an intimate witness, as well as a main actor, in the unfolding drama of Lady Byron's life after love. She was nothing if not dramatic when involved in the affairs of her women friends, and she could gossip as vividly as she could write. Anna Jameson became the Typhoid Mary of Lady Byron's private story.

THE ART HISTORIAN had originally met Lady Byron after an extended stay in Germany in 1834. "The English and French tend to imitate one another," Anna Jameson told her readers. "There is something uniform in their dress and behaviour; they are afraid to swerve from a given fashion, to make themselves peculiar or ridiculous. But in Germany every man follows his humour, without troubling himself about others . . . for in each man lives the idea of personal and individual freedom, from which proceeds much that is excellent, and also much that is absurd." Such was the bohemian, free-spirited Germany of the early nineteenth century. Diversity and abandoned eccentricity aided an expatriate such as Lady Byron's cousin Bob Noel. It was there that he rose to fame as a phrenologist. He made casts of the heads he wished to study—not only of Countess Hahn-Hahn and her aristocratic circle, but of professional men, cretins, prostitutes, clerks, and murderers. Apparently, Dandy Bob knew everyone, and it was through him that Anna Jameson returned to England with a letter of introduction to his eminent cousin. Previously he had introduced her to Ottilie von Goethe, the great writer's daughter-in-law.

Ottilie von Goethe was more attached to world-famous Goethe— "Close thy Byron, open thy Goethe"—as Thomas Carlyle would proclaim—than to Goethe's son, whom she had married reluctantly and who died an alcoholic in Rome in 1830. Two years younger than Jameson, Ottilie was oval-faced, blue-eyed, sensual, and free-living. She ran an advanced literary magazine, *chaos*, to which Goethe submitted work. She had seen her failing father-in-law through the second part of *Faust*. Many say she was the inspiration for his "Eternal Feminine." Goethe died in her arms, shortly before she met Anna Jameson.

Jameson was immediately attracted to Ottilie. In the following years she drenched herself in Ottilie's life. She would spend as much time as she could in Germany—learning the language, absorbing the culture in the land where so much advanced thought on religion,

*Ottilie von Goethe, the great poet's
daughter-in-law and Anna Jameson's great love.*

ethics, and literature originated. When Ottilie became pregnant by an English lover some years after her husband's death, Jameson devoted herself to Ottilie's predicament. Bob Noel was of help as well. Anna traveled with Ottilie away from prying eyes, gave her good advice about accepting the reality of her situation, and saw her through her pregnancy and the birth of her daughter—named after Jameson. The old story: Little Anna was given to others to raise—and died soon after. Jameson had dreams of living with Ottilie, saving her from her "malady," her "madness"—what we'd call her sexual addiction.

Living with Ottilie hadn't worked out: "Always my first wish is to be near you, but it is true that sometimes I *fear* it too, for it is like being bound on a wheel of fire, which whirls me round with its restlessness and consumes me with its feverish glow," Jameson wrote from Dresden on her way home. "Forgive me, forgive me, my own O. But when I read your letter in which I find not one word of any of your children [Ottilie had three legitimate children], and a great deal about those horrid men who have destroyed your happiness and mine—I see there is no hope—what pain, what fear, what shame overpowers me!"

Back in England in 1834 with Bob Noel's letter of introduction, Mrs. Jameson's first impression of Lady Byron was the common one which even loquacious Anna with her Irish gift of gab summed up in a word: "Implacability." Annabella never did conquer what she knew to be an initial reserve.

"I wish I could give you a photograph of her," George MacDonald would write in his later novel *The Vicar's Daughter*, where Lady Byron is portrayed as philanthropist Lady Bernard. "She was slight, and appeared taller than she was, being rather stately than graceful, with a commanding forehead and still blue eyes." When newly met she appeared cold, "with a touch of haughtiness." For Anna Jameson that impression lasted no longer than it did for MacDonald. Just as he portrayed, the moment the Lady's eyes lit up and the conversation began, Jameson became as captivated as the characters in his novel.

"I have seen a great deal of Lady Byron, who is certainly one of the most excellent beings in the world," Jameson wrote to Ottilie von Goethe soon after, as she breathlessly rushed from "Implacability" to the opposite extreme, speaking of Lady Byron being blasted by life and love and saving for herself "a wreck of happiness," by devoting herself to good works and the education of her daughter. Not only was Lady Byron captivating but "Ada Byron is a singular girl, and one whom I could love exceedingly if we were more together."

LADY BYRON was a woman who had many close female friends, a loyal band, actually, including such variety as north country childhood friend, plainspoken Selina Doyle. It included sharp-tongued Sophia De Morgan, daughter of her girlhood tutor. There was the aristocratic Caro George, wife of Lady Melbourne's son George, the Honorable and letter-writing Theresa Villiers, the calm, well-spoken

Lady Anne Wilmot-Horton, and the physical scientist and mathematician Mary Somerville, the first woman to be elected to the Royal Astronomical Society. . . . This a random sampling of *close* friends; the list goes on.

There were many men in her life as well, but as friends, lawyers, advisers, relations, not as lovers. Basically, like many women of her time, Lady Byron remained more or less true to her wedding vows. She wore widow's weeds in the first years after Byron's death, a delicately crafted, quasi-see-through widow's cap thereafter, and her response to Lord Byron's "Fare Thee Well" may very well have remained constant through the years:

> Never can the heart forget thee
>   Which has felt a love like mine

On the other hand, there is an intriguing poem, written when she was thirty-five, titled "'You are Silent' (said to me on an occasion of deep feeling)":

> I *may* not speak—the tears would flow
>   Were ever softer thought recall'd
> No—let the stream run deep below,
>   From all but friendship's eye conceal'd!
>
> I *may* not speak, when "auld lang syne"
>   Link'd with each vision now no more,
> Is rous'd again by strains like thine
>   A phantom, darkly clouded on.

Bernard Henkels, a Belgian, and it would appear, a waiter, arrived on the scene and became "the comfort of my life"—that according to Joan Pierson in a biography that does not document the source. One assumes him to have been a political refugee. Lady Byron often traveled in Belgium. It is possible there was some sort of romantic interest, the latter assumption resting on the sound basis that the relationship appears not to have lasted—or at least the records pertaining to it. Friendship appeared to be Lady Byron's comfort, not wishing, or fearful of, the passion she once felt being rekindled.

There were talented women whom Lady Byron knew—aristocrats, sculptors, and actors—who had outrageously high times making love with women under the guise of spinsterhood and total dedication to art or to social work. The word "homosexual" was not coined until the very end of the century. When Queen Victoria was asked at the time of Oscar Wilde's trial why the laws against such behavior weren't applicable to woman as well, she reputedly replied that women didn't do such things. However, they certainly did do such things and long before the word "lesbian" became standard. They were women who loved women. For better or worse, Lady Byron was not one of them.

Some biographers have spoken of Lady Byron having "lesbian tendencies," sprinkling the term about as if it were used at the time or as if one couldn't have close, loving female friendships without falling in love the way, say, Anna Jameson fell in love. Anna Jameson for all her intellectual acumen and sharp eye, fell into female friendship trembling, a lover manqué wishing to possess the other while at the same time anticipating loss. She had very few true friends, she wrote dramatically, and was doomed to live separated from them. She considered this her "fate." Married to a man a continent away, she was emotionally a woman who loved women. However, unlike American actor Charlotte Cushman, famed for her Romeo, sculptor Harriet Hosmer or her lover the second Lady Ashburton, with whom both Jameson and Lady Byron were acquainted, one doubts Jameson was having sexual high times with women behind the mask, not of virtuous spinsterhood, but of marriage.

"I have never mistaken the amount of your affection for me," Anna Jameson would write to Lady Byron one Thursday night looking back on their friendship. "Never overestimated it or accepted anything from it or through it—and have endeavoured to make my strong affection

JULIA MARKUS

for you a happiness for us both." Anna Jameson's sexuality was a long-ing that turned at times into an almost slavish devotion to the other: "I must not let my feelings and affections stray towards those, whom I must lose.—With you, dear Ottilie, the mischief is *done*—I must needs love you far or near, and would to God I could do any thing for your happiness! Why have you let it escape from your own keeping?"

Not only did her love of Ottilie von Goethe torture her, there was a distant husband who offered her no material support. To that husband she wrote: "My dear Robert, jesting apart. . . . You might perhaps be happy with another woman—a union such as ours is, and has ever been, a real mockery of the laws of God and man. You have the power to dispose of our fate as far as it depends on each other." His "vague letters," his inability to act "in a decided manly spirit, whether to unite or to part us," has left her dangling. If he wanted her to come to Canada and try to make "another trial for happiness" just tell her so distinctly and tell her when to come and what to bring. She would attempt to make his existence and hers as "pleasant as possible." Even an early feminist such as Jameson who worked for female edu-cation and the franchise, who first investigated the role of women in Shakespeare and the role of the Madonna in Italian painting, thought herself able to go against all her inclinations—politically, intellectu-ally, emotionally, sexually—and should her husband wish it, do her first duty as a wife.

An outsider's view of a marriage can be more blunt. Mrs. Jameson wanted a legal separation from her husband, and Mr. Jameson wanted her in Toronto, needing a wife—old or new—to insure his promotion to first Vice Chancellor of the newly created Chancery Court of the Upper Canadas—a position of political as well as judicial power in those days. Anna delayed the inevitable as long as she could, but in 1837 she arrived in the frozen north, taking the last boat from New York able to plow through ice early that winter. She was in Toronto on loan, a wife in name only, needed by her husband in order to advance his career. A celebrity to boot, whom everyone wanted to meet. Not that she often left the house he provided for her while a new one was

208

being built. Her letters to Ottilie are filled with her loneliness, stuck in a barren house so cold that even though a fire blazed day and night, she'd awake to find her glass of water frozen. (In *Winter Studies* she described cattle frozen where they stood.) She made constant references to the lifesaving qualities of the quilt Ottilie's mother had made her. Ottilie hinted that Bob Noel was smitten with Anna; Anna replied nonsense—it was Ottilie he cared for. Hadn't he too seen her through her pregnancy? With Dandy Bob sandwiched between them, the women flirted. Kiss your children, Anna wrote, their lips are closer than mine.

Jameson did travel, once the ice thawed. Saw Niagara Falls, but also traveled to remote Indian villages where no white woman had been before. She wanted to experience firsthand how "savage" Indian women lived. From her experiences she wrote the three volumes of *Winter Studies and Summer Rambles in Canada*, recently reissued by Clara Thomas. As popular a writer as Jameson was in Canada and the States, she said she'd die rather than live in either place. She ached for home. "I have left Canada," she wrote to Lady Byron from Philadelphia, "with the *hope* at least of never seeing it more.—which God grant Amen!"

Robert Jameson was "finally" granted his promotion, including a handsome pay hike, and after some difficulty she got her legal separation of bed and board and 300 per annum. Because of delays—she was not leaving without legal paper—she had to spend extra time in New York. This insured her a dreadfully difficult winter sea voyage home.

Back in England in 1839 she was able to see Lady Byron frequently. Anna realized how much she could love this woman who had such "a rare heart and mind." Lady Byron, however, was male-identified, and had a more conservative view of the defined role of the sexes than her feminist friend. She upheld women's education and need for meaningful work. However, why would a woman need or want a vote? Lady Byron enquired of Jameson. It was a privilege not to have one. Lady Byron was a woman who was thankful to work behind the scenes, and who took pleasure in anonymity. At times she would ask cousin Bob Noel to sign his name to her written views, particularly her paper against the gambling she found encouraged on her travels—gambling used as a temptation for wealthy English tourists at the spas of Germany.

She told Jameson that few women were made for the man's world, if any. Perhaps someone like their ailing friend, the feminist Harriet Martineau, whose informative *Illustrations of Political Economy*—sociology set as narratives—changed the minds of those in Parliament without her having the franchise. Of course, deaf as she was, Martineau spoke up in a loud voice, and when she was younger and in good health, stood on the stairs of Parliament and lobbied the politicians toward social action as they went inside to vote. She was the exception that proved the rule. A woman's influence was felt through the home, through her positive effect on her husband. Underneath the sexual politics, the vulnerability. That Lady Byron failed as a "Wife" had lasting significance for her. All her life she believed she had been deprived of her primary role.

BRINGING MEDORA back to England as her adopted child redeemed something deep within her. However, Medora had spent her entire adult life in France, and brought with her to England a confused French-speaking daughter with whom Medora did not get along. The two stayed at the Lovelace townhouse on St. James's Square, while Lady Byron went house hunting for them all. During this time Lady Byron's friend Sophia De Morgan saw Medora every day, and said Medora spread rumors, caused trouble between her and her husband; she had a wild, mischievous streak. "Lady B's intense love for her husband's child" did not allow her to see this clearly. Mrs. Jameson, introduced to the girl in London as well, said it was impossible to know Medora and not love her—an impossibility she would eventually regret.

The relationship between the half sisters remained strong. Lady Byron found a grand home for Medora and herself in the suburb of Esher, and was given a key to the Queen's gardens that abutted her property. The location was intentionally chosen as close to the

Ada, Countess of Lovelace, in fashionable attire.

Lovelaces' Ockham Park estate, and on some of the harmonious nights the family spent together, Ada, a talented musician (mathematics and music often join hands), would pick up her violin or play her harp, while Medora accompanied her, singing and playing Ada's piano. Seeing them together, Sophia De Morgan marveled at the similarity of their looks. Why wouldn't Medora's expectations grow at Ockham, as, in the elegant drawing room, she sang, Ada fiddled, and Lady Byron smiled?

In France, a widowed expatriate Englishwoman well bred and with a gift for language had been appreciated. To an extent, "Madame Aubin" had been relatively classless and free. Lady Byron's "Lanky Doodle" was striking in appearance and men noticed her on the boulevards and in the cafés. Even Sophia De Morgan noted that "tall, slender and *lithe*" body, and Ada spoke of

Medora Leigh's "Spanish" look. Though attributed
as a portrait of her mother Augusta Leigh,
it is more likely daughter Medora.

"that great tall childish figure of hers." Though Lady Byron called them both her daughters, in England the difference in class stuck out like a long thin exclamation mark! That dark beauty of Medora's—Sophia De Morgan labeled it "Spanish"—wasn't as admired in London's world of fair ladies as it had been on the Continent.

Did it matter? Medora had been offered the peace and quiet she had asked for in surroundings far above her imagining. Not only that, at Moore Place, the estate in Esher, Medora was relieved of all responsibilities. Daughter Marie was not with her. Everyone thought separation between mother and daughter beneficial to both, as there had been many scenes. Early on, Lady Byron had written to Edward Noel from France that "her little girl of seven is with me too, and alas! not likely from disposition to prove a comfort to her." At times mother and daughter appeared "to hate" each other. Sophia De Morgan found the child hateful, but this wasn't a woman who had many kind words. Medora, in one of her black moods, wrote to Lady Byron asking how she could possibly provide the "comfort" her aunt asked of her? She knew of no grief she could administer to except at a person's deathbed. In fact, she was thankful that her insane and institutionalized oldest sister Augusta was dead, and though it might shock her aunt, "would my little Marie were too." That Lady Byron longed for comfort from her adopted daughter is as revealing as Medora's dark moods.

Luckily for Medora's uprooted child, Anna Jameson was able to provide a solution. Marie was entrusted to the fond care of her spinster sisters, Charlotte and Eliza Murphy, who were running a school around Notting Hill that just about squeaked by. Anna was, as usual, supporting them in their shaky endeavor, though her own earnings were hardly princely.

Early in their friendship Lady Byron admired her new friend, a commoner who had made a big life for herself through her writing. Anna showed her the miniature her artist father had painted of her when she was a slim, forward-gazing, and fiery-haired sixteen-year-old, not the middle-aged woman Lady Byron knew. That gaze inspired Lady Byron's sonnet:

> In those young eyes, so keenly, bravely bent
> To search the mysteries of the future hour,
> There shines the will to conquer, and the pow'r
>   Which makes that conquest sure—a gift heaven sent.
>
> The radiance of the Beautiful was blent
> Ev'n with thine earliest dreams; and towards that star
> Of thy first faith, oft dimm'd and always far
>   Still has thou journey'd on, where'er thy tent.
>
> O never yet in vain such pilgrimage
> Witness the poet-souls of every age:

Miniature of Anna Jameson at sixteen,
by her father, the painter Denis Murphy.
Lady Byron admired the girl's heroic aspirations.

Long ere the Magi hail'd the prophet-beam,
　　Or Worship own'd an altar and a shrine;

The few who felt how real the dream
Thus gaz'd and thus imbib'd the 'etheral stream.'

Anna was thrilled and sent Lady Byron's sonnet on to Ottilie.

Still, Jameson was an honest critic of Lady Byron's writing: "Your sonnets contain some of the best—the most nervous and poetical lines of yours I have seen," though "the weakest lines in yours are precisely those which ought to be the strongest"—the ending couplet. She compared Lady Byron's sonnets with those of her friend Elizabeth

Barrett Browning. The *Sonnets from the Portuguese* "remind me of some of yours—because the beauty of the thought is greater than the force of the expression and she ends the thing carelessly and with an anticlimax."

She also told Lady Byron that though her ideas are "beautiful and practical," her verses suffer because "you almost strangle the thought in the expression." Two years after they met, while developing her own schools, Lady Byron asked the writer what readings had been beneficial to her as a child: "Shakespeare I stole and took to bed with me, that I might read it in the morning as soon as it was light. . . . Hamlet the most unforgettable because of that ghost which haunted me for years, and followed me up the stairs in the dark!" After reading the *Iliad* and *Odyssey* she too left home, "with a bundle under my arm to be shipwrecked somewhere or other—and was brought back and whipped accordingly." She had "great hatred of tyrants and Kings," and in a large hand wrote "a threatening letter to Buonaparte, which I put in the post myself. After eight years old I read Milton, and most certainly all my sympathies were with Satan." Jameson's prose sparkled in her unpublished letters to Lady Byron, just as it does in her published writings. She could—and did—take her reader anywhere she traveled.

By the time Anna Jameson returned from Canada in 1839, Ada Byron, the remarkable girl she could have loved, was a young married woman about to have her third child, and Anna Jameson was succumbing to friendship yet again, dazzled by both Lady Byron and the Countess of Lovelace. Ada, who did not have a history of enjoying *any* of her mother's friends, became an intimate friend of Anna Jameson. The two saw each other once a week when they were both in town. The twenty-four-year-old could talk with Anna about things she believed she dare not broach with her mother. The fear of Lady Byron's disapproval remained strong. These confidences, perhaps confessions, might have reminded Jameson of Ottilie, another strikingly attractive, intensely intellectual woman, who tested sexual boundaries, and whom Jameson both adored and counseled to no avail.

Jameson couldn't council Lady Byron, who had no need of advice.

Not only had she the best of lawyers, but that full stable of old and trusted female friends. There are unpublished letters through the years in Lady Byron's archives in which Anna despairs of not having been told her friend was within traveling distance visiting others. Returned from Canada, Jameson had either to get in line behind these older friends or find her own pathway up to the front. The erotic in her nature channeled down a new stream.

Jameson might have fared better had she kept her place in line and wooed with an eye to Lady Byron's literary improvement. However, she tended toward dramatic sacrifice when it came to the women in her life—not only those she desired, but the mother and sisters and niece who depended on her as well. Though the friendship between Mrs. Jameson and Lady Byron would be quite strong and prevail through the next decade, Jameson's approach to it was not the wisest course for establishing a balanced relationship with an aristocrat: "Find something for me to do," she implored Lady Byron. "Think of me as being literally *yours* to command."

What do they say? Be careful what you wish for. Anna Jameson wrote this in 1840, the year Medora Leigh reentered Lady Byron's life. When Lady Byron returned to England with her Lanky Doodle, she found plenty for Anna to do.

Medora had nothing but time on her hands at Esher, as she focused her hopes on winning her Chancery suit against her own mother, who still held on to the deed of appointment. Both Theresa and Augusta were sure Augusta had the legal right to do so, though Lady Byron, who had a lawyer's instinct, as well as a willingness to fuel the fire if this went to court, was convinced Augusta would lose and warned her through Theresa.

Medora's moods were flipping and sputtering with frightening regularity at Moore Place, as she waited for her day in court. Lady Byron, in ill health again, found reason to be away from the erratic eruptions of her adopted daughter. Could Jameson be a help to her "baby Porpoise?" Could she be a model for the girl, pointing her towards useful endeavors? Anna Jameson gave up many of her own interests to spend much of her time at Moore Place as chaperon to Medora. True to her words, she was Lady Byron's to command.

Biographer Clara Thomas regretted Anna Jameson's willingness to sacrifice her own needs to be Lady Byron's "agent." Yet this was the way Jameson loved. Mrs. Jameson soon reported to Lady Byron that "the monotony of her life—the want of all usefulness," was at the root of Medora's malaise. It led to a state of mind in which Medora couldn't understand reasoning of any kind; it was absurd to attempt to reason with her. On the other hand, to pamper her by flattery and acquiescence was wrong as well as absurd. "There must be some change—some remedy, but what?" she asked her equally perplexed aristocratic friend as Medora roamed the estate and the Queen's gardens, her moods shifting and intensifying.

There would be more hope if there were some "definite and immediate cause for this feverish temper—but it has been gathering long." Though Lady Byron instructed Jameson to think only of Medora's interests, never of her adoptive mother's, Jameson would do "whatever it is possible to do for your aid or comfort in this mischief and misery."

Mischief and misery it had indeed become. Lady Byron, hoping to alleviate it, did something out of character. She purchased a puppy for Medora, a tiny spaniel named Fairy. Unlike her daughter Ada and her granddaughter Lady Anne, who would one day save the Arabian steed from extinction, Lady Byron was hardly an animal lover. Horses to her were close to being a mechanical means of transportation. In her worldview they hadn't souls. Her son-in-law's only complaint of her was that she drove them too hard. And she hadn't given a thought to dogs since that early morning on leaving 13 Piccadilly when she wished to be one of Byron's.

Lady Byron couldn't understand why the puppy didn't take to her, she wrote to Medora. She treated Fairy just like a person! Pip might have misjudged Fairy's lack of concern for her, Medora replied, for she "jumped up and looked wildly about her when I told her Grandmama was ill." The puppy was a pleasure, if not having the ability to calm

Medora's fluctuating moods. My "dear Pip" she wrote, informing Lady Byron that her mother, Augusta Leigh, would be sixty years old the next day. "I believe the reason my Mother's conduct affects me so much is the very, very deep love and attachment my imagination has borne for long after I *could* not love *her*." This imagined affection which Medora substituted for actual affection "will not do and must be broken." Medora knew Theresa Villiers had informed Lady Byron of the affectionate letters Medora had sent her mother from Pontivy. So Medora made excuses for loving her mother, as if loving one's mother is based on worth and needed to be excused. In another letter to Pip she spoke about spying her mother unobserved from Lovelace's carriage in London, and of how shockingly ugly and evil Augusta appeared. Necessity itself had taught Medora how to manipulate. She aimed at her aunt's weak spot, not realizing Lady Byron understood this picture of Augusta was another one of those "sweets" her niece was attempting to feed her.

Whatever Medora's authentic feelings for her mother, she certainly favored her adoptive mother over Mrs. Jameson: "She understands and admires nature only through art. We make a sad clash—but she means kindly—poor old Aunt Twaddle as I have christened her. She is very busy with her book and it amuses me the little help I can give her." There is a photograph of Mrs. Jameson in her mature years, seated on her ample rump looking as if her large soft bosom barely escaped dissolving into the billow of her paunch by the feeble efforts of the waistband round her middle. Lady Byron might have gotten some wicked enjoyment reading Medora's characterization: While Mrs. Jameson dozed off in her chair, Medora was tempted to take a few long hair pins out of her own hair and slowly, gently insert them into the "pincushion" of Jameson's body. That would wake her!

"But I am a sweet amiable creature," she informed dear Pip. She resisted the temptation, allowing her pen to sing lullabies to "poor old Aunt Twaddle." That nickname was far from the Brownings' loving one. To them Mrs. Jameson had become Aunt Nina.

Aunt Twaddle and Medora "harmonize better" while on a long walk. "But anything is better than sitting still in this fine weather." Her verdict of Jameson's work? "She has too much warmth and coloring as an artist." (And one assumes as a companion.) Medora's dispirited letters to Pip are signed "Emedora" or "E Medora," less often "EM." Cheerful letters are often signed "Ever your Picaninny"— Ever your small black child—which in a sense Elizabeth Medora might have considered herself.

Jameson's hunt for and desire to eradicate moral and psychological characteristics assumed to be inherited from generations of wicked Byrons was not lost on Medora. She was tired of people comparing her to ancestors of "eccentric habits." She wished she was descended from famous "*Cannibals*," she wrote Pip, so the people "who so clearly 'see' the family characteristics" in her would "learn that I might by chance some day feel the inherited love of human flesh." On occasion, it appears, Medora might have loved boiling up a plate of well-larded Aunt Twaddle.

What Medora particularly resented was "that grandmother shallow reasoning of hers" about "truth to one self." Medora found herself wishing "truth to the Devil fifty times a day." Aunt Twaddle constantly lecturing Medora was driving the girl to distraction. Jameson was away for a time and requested Medora to write to her, "But I am not well nor in the humor to do so and if I did I might be 'true to myself.' What nonsense people do talk to be sure—when they set about it—clever ones the same as fools—only they look as if they were saying something clever and so impose—on the world."

The gift of gab that charmed society was lost on Ada's half sister. If Jameson had been her governess, she would have driven her mad. "She's the last person on this earth I should like to live with. She distracts me and I do not believe any man could have been *happy* with her. When she is quiet and natural I like her *very* much but otherwise she means good and irritates me—meaning to by *very* kind and do me good." Jameson's absence allowed Medora breathing room from "the

The middle-aged Mrs. Jameson,
Medora Leigh's "Aunt Twaddle."

quagmire of self she had plagued me into—but she is a good old Aunt Twaddle or means to be."

Both Aunt Twaddle and Lady Byron were of a certain age and had certain expectations of their charge: "Do not expect more of me than I can give," Medora warned Lady Byron. "I am as open as I can be and never can be more than I have been. I am and shall for long suffer—to say what I suffer I cannot and then it is thought I keep something back. Is it necessary to say all the ridiculous things that occur to one, I who keep the greatest control over my thoughts and am continually fighting them? I should gain little ground if I indulged them."

The many undated and unpublished letters between Lady Byron and Medora during this period tell their own story. Medora was happiest when Jameson was away, looked forward to Lady Byron's more and more infrequent visits to Moore Place. She kept up close ties with Ada and William nearby. Her mood swings were violent, her headaches severe and debilitating. She could write of fearsome thunder-storms or on brighter days of Fairy digging holes in the garden.

In May 1842, on the day Medora was to bring her mother to court, Augusta relented. The deed was surrendered and turned over to Medora, who gave it to brother Lovelace for temporary safekeeping. One would think Medora would consider this a victory; she had her deed for 3,000 pounds. Far from it. She complained bitterly and constantly that she had not been consulted.

Leading up to the day at court, Lady Byron had shared letters and journals with Medora, showing her evidence of her birth. So Medora had looked forward to court. Whatever scenario played out in her head as she sat at Moore Place being sketched and instructed on self-hood by Mrs. Jameson, one needn't be a phrenologist to read she had unrealistic expectations, bolstered by Lady Byron's confidences. She thought her lawyer could apply for more money, since Lady Byron could testify to her birthright as Lord Byron's daughter. She came dangerously close to opening another suit against her mother. Lady Byron realized herself culpable. Her confidences had given the unstable young woman the ammunition to harm Augusta Leigh by initiating another lawsuit or resorting to blackmail.

It might become Lady Byron's duty to protect "the mother," she wrote curtly in her journals. In this instance, the only "good" Annabella could find in herself was her willingness to do so if necessary. She had foolishly fueled Medora's great expectations. Her moral compass leaped from what was right for Byron's daughter directly to what was right for "the mother," without stopping midpoint to examine the dark complexities of her own feelings concerning Augusta.

It was Ada who came to the rescue. She recommended a French maid as companion for Medora. She was of the highest order, previously serving only the best families. She would be much more suitable for a young woman than Mrs. Jameson, and perhaps she could moderate Medora's violent black moods. Enter Nathalie Beaurepaire—Natty.

Medora was delighted. She informed Pip that she was working "hard and agreeably having Natty for a companion in whom I have not the perpetual topic of my interesting self. She is I believe really attached to me and has the refinement common to most of even the lowest class of french servants. Ada certainly did do as she says a good thing there."

Natty couldn't stem the flow of Medora's invective. When a bitter mood hit her, she castigated Lady Byron over the Chancery suit. There were times she was completely out of control. Lady Byron had her examined by competent medical men. History repeated itself. Despite mad and bad ancestors galore to prod her reckless behavior, Medora was proclaimed sane.

It was decided Medora and Marie would return to France, as Medora wished, for her health, for a while, forever, who knows? Lady Byron was willing to allow her 150 per annum, plus Natty's wages, the tuition for Natty's child in an English school, travel expenses, and finally consented to allowing Natty's husband Victor to join the band, paying him as well. These allowances now seemed paltry sums to Medora, not enough for Continental life. Add to that, Lady Byron had restrictions. She did not want Medora to pass through Paris, and she was to be informed of and agree with Medora's expenditures abroad. Lady Byron would continue to be her benefactor under the original stipulation—that she be her only one. The deed, which Medora no longer needed to mortgage, was to be left for her in England, at the law firm of Wharton & Ford.

In the weeks before she left England, Medora turned against Lady Byron with vituperation so violent that Lady Byron left Moore Place for the entire time Medora remained. Not only was Lady Byron deeply hurt, she appeared shaken. She hadn't been verbally assaulted in that way since her marriage. It was a torrent of erratic abuse. She felt herself a victim of her love, and she responded to Medora sounding as such:

"Do you remember my asking you not to use affectionate expressions—I then felt the possibility of a change in your feelings." She "ought not to have let you deceive yourself and me—(much pain would then have been spared) and I should not have accepted your expressions of entire confidence and affection. I will endeavour to forget them. It is enough for me to be your friend. I have never exacted anything in return."

When Medora responded saying she wished to see her aunt before she left, Lady Byron told the girl they had already said their goodbyes.

Mrs. Jameson traveled with Medora to London, put up with her tantrums, and helped secure her a passport when Medora's impatience was such that she wished to leave without one. When she explained to the girl that she would be given travel money, but the first quarter of her allowance of 150 pounds wouldn't be made until she arrived at Marseilles, "the suppressed rage which had been swelling into a tempest for the last hour burst out." She lavished on her absent aunt and Jameson "every term of unmeasured abuse." The next morning she apologized, but learning she would get "only" 40 pounds for travel, "she burst into another rage and at first refused the money." She asked for the money a few hours later. When Mrs. Jameson counted out the pounds in bank notes and handed them over, Medora clutched them "with a sort of contemptuous eagerness and impatient haughtiness." She said there were things she *would* have and she'd *make* Lady Byron pay for them.

Yet that afternoon, July 19, 1842, Medora wrote to Lady Byron as "dearest Pip." She had come to London a day earlier than she had planned to sit for a daguerreotype as a parting gift to her aunt. "I have heard you say it would please you to have one." It was a cloudy day, but she did the best she could. Perhaps if she loved Lady Byron less, she would appear to love her more, she told her protector. She had no more wish than Lady Byron for this to be "farewell." They would meet again "when I am merry and well." The photograph she sent was a profile of her head, quite splendid, her long dark locks, and her strong good looks. In more than the features, in its aura as well, this memento was eerily reminiscent of Lord Byron. An inherited quality shone through: undaunted pride.

JAMESON TOLD the Brownings about young Medora's seduction by her brother-in-law during their pilgrimage to Pisa, spinning her own version of Lady Byron's travails as they traveled. Not only did Jameson, a peerless raconteur, know a lot; she had witnessed a lot. On the road, when Geddie was out of ear range, she spoke of the Medora she had tended, of Byron as a husband, of the "guilt" of Medora's birth. Lady Byron had written to Jameson from France in 1840, soon after reading Augusta's loving letters to the man who raped her child and had impregnated the girl twice by the time she was sixteen. Could she believe her eyes? Anna Jameson responded, before burning Lady Byron's letter because of Lady Byron's "absolute" demand that she do so. Was Lady Byron saying that Mrs. Leigh conspired against the chastity of her own child? Had she corrupted the one daughter and "sold" the other?

Jameson was doubly motivated in removing the scales from Elizabeth Barrett Browning's eyes. The poet was a passionate admirer of Lord Byron (as she was of Napoleon) and had until the wedding trip abhorred Lady Byron. Three years previously she wrote to her epistolary friend, the artist Benjamin Haydon, that Lady Byron was a "false wife," for all her supposed virtues. Haydon, who painted Lady Byron into his group portrait of the Anti-Slavery Convention, had met her twice "and we quarreled without hope, the second time," he wrote to Elizabeth. "The first day, I thought Byron a brute—the second day I was convinced *she* was—a Mathematician. . . . By Heaven I should have liked to have seen the Woman who would have refused me in the flush of youth—*because it was proper.*"

GOSSIP IS an unacknowledged mover of culture, and often both the raw truth and the pain it contains inspires one to make sense of it in art. Call it oral history, if you prefer. Elizabeth was mistaken about Lady Byron's character, Jameson insisted. Lord Byron's emotional cruelty to the wife who loved him passionately was a cautionary tale for these dear, innocent poets, as they slowly wended their way to the Italy they envisioned—Lord Byron's "magnet," the Brownings' "Siren's call."

*Medora Leigh, leaving England and Lady Byron
behind, sent her "adoptive mother" this
daguerreotype sat for on a cloudy day.*

That Jameson told the Brownings of Augusta Leigh's role in corrupting her young daughter can be seen in certain sections of Elizabeth Barrett Browning's late and great novel-in-verse, *Aurora Leigh* (1856): "If there's room for poets in this world," Aurora tells us:

> Their sole work is to represent the age,
>   Their age, not Charlemagne's—this live, throbbing age,
>   That brawls, cheats, maddens, calculates, aspires,
>   . . . .
>   The full-veined, heaving, double-breasted Age:
>   . . . .
>   . . . this is living art
> Which thus presents and thus records true life.

In Barrett Browning's feminist masterpiece, hailed by Virginia Woolf, the mean streets as well as the salons of London are cracked open. A depraved, poverty-stricken slum mother attempts to sell her daughter into sexual slavery for financial gain. Marian Erle cries out:

> My mother sold me to a man last month,
> And so my mother's lost, 'tis manifest.
> And I, who fled from her for miles and miles,
> As if I had caught sight of the fire of hell
> It seems I shall be lost too, presently. . . .

In Barrett Browning's poem the poor girl's mother is not an upper-class woman selling her daughter out to prove to an ex-lover how much she cares, but an abusive, poverty-stricken woman. However, Marian Erle escapes her birth mother, and in the long run, it *is* an upper-class woman, Lady Waldemar, who intentionally has the girl sexually enslaved. Marian had been deceived into considering Lady Waldemar her "spiritual mother." However, this fine Lady was in love with the man who was to marry Marian, so she sent the unsuspecting Marian off to be raped and pimped out. The ruined girl is left desolate and pregnant in the streets. The poet cries out: "When mothers fail us, can we help ourselves?"

Not only in Barrett Browning's portrayal of "real life," but in the confident feminism of *Aurora Leigh* one finds the influence of Anna Jameson and the shades of Medora's rape.

Politically, Elizabeth's views remained close to Lord Byron's— her uncritical admiration for Napoleon, her political commitment to Italian liberty, her criticism of England, her preference for life abroad. Her husband came to consider Byron a poet who shouted out fine sentiments on mountaintops. Aesthetically, however, both Elizabeth Barrett and Robert Browning created poetry in reaction to the Romantics. They wrote to cut through to the heart of humanity, not rise above it. The title of Robert Browning's masterpiece, the collection of poetry written in Italy during the marriage, underlines their intentions: *Men and Women*.

———

ROMANTICS SUCH AS Byron's friend and biographer Thomas Moore did not exalt the humanity but the necessary inhumanity of Genius. Byron's deep flaws were *necessary* fodder for Art. In Moore's 1830 biography of the poet, he wrote that Byron's capitalized "Imagination" took him so far beyond the bonds of humanity, that it was close to a necessity for his marriage to fail. The "entire man" must be *sacrificed* to his poetry. A great poet cannot be happy or bring happiness to others. Moore even made the assumption that Byron had a happy childhood, hadn't been a tortured soul until he became a poet. As he put it a "tamed and domesticated" poet may be popular, may be loved, but he will never achieve greatness. "The marks by which Fame has always separated her great martyrs from the rest of mankind are not upon him and the crown cannot be his."

Geniuses are better off not marrying, Moore wrote, but when they do, their very Imaginations lead them to unlucky choices: "On the list of married poets who have been unhappy in their homes," he listed Dante, Milton, Shakespeare, and Dryden. "We should now have to add, as a partner in their destiny, a name worthy of being placed beside the greatest of them—Lord Byron." The bad marriage of Genius is turned into a rite of passage, a sort of graduation into Greatness.

Moore was such a believer in the lack of human constancy necessary for Genius to flourish that he had to explain that Byron's love of his sister could never have been sustained. Brother and sister had been separated in youth. "There is little doubt his love for his sister owed much of its devotedness and fervour" to its newness. He assures the reader Byron's love would not have lasted. For a Romantic such as Moore, "Genius" must flourish beyond human values. Perhaps one reason Lady Byron's genius in the area of education and philanthropy has never been acknowledged is because her efforts were directed away from the Romantic sense of self.

In truth, the Romantic imagination allowed a poet such as Byron to break through the settled barriers of tradition in order to pierce through to nature—human and divine—in thrilling new ways. The organic "Imagination" was in service of an intense and perhaps at that time unique form of utter self-absorption that could find its objective correlative in the art it created, the drugs it used, the brandy it drank, and the conquests it bedded. All of this was exciting, daring, inventive, new. Byronists today—who would probably lock their daughters (and their young sons) up should a real Byron appear in their living room—extol the importance of Byron's art and either downplay the importance of or, like Moore, turn to myth the cruelty to others—mostly women—Byron displayed throughout his life. Like Moore, they cast blame on a stereotypical rendition of Annabella. They are almost forced, given their belief in the Sublimity of Genius, to believe the purposely distorted pictures the great poet painted of his wife.

What matters the man when there remains the Art? It is a Romantic view, a modernist view as well.

Elizabeth Barrett and Robert Browning didn't see it that way. The disparity between Byron's life and his art, something they were acutely aware of through those who had witnessed it, weighed on them. How could God-given artistic truth and beauty coexist with the human destruction caused by a Byron, by a Shelley? They came to believe that the moral flaws of an artist impeded the art that person created. They found evidence for this in artists of former times and in artists they knew. We call this a Victorian view and turn our faces from the human wreckage on which it was built—just as Dorian Gray turned from his portrait.

Byron's cruelty to his wife, Augusta's cruelty to their daughter, appalled the Brownings. In terms of the incest, Robert Browning heard that gossip years before the wedding trip. When the Byrons' grandson Ralph, by then Baron Wentworth, sought out the truth of his grandmother's marriage in the 1880s, Robert Browning was long a widower returned to London. He told Ralph that as a boy, his first voice teacher had been Isaac Nathan who earlier supplied the music for Byron's *Hebrew Melodies*. Ralph recorded: "Browning repeated to me more than once what he had heard from Nathan, the singer, who had sung to Byron and Augusta, no one else being present. When Nathan was supposed to be entirely absorbed by his singing, he observed distinctly what passed between them, which left no doubt in his mind of the most intimate relations. Nathan was an enthusiastic admirer of Byron and thought him above common morality. He was not horrified by what he saw and suspected, but spoke of it many years afterward to Browning as quite right in this marvelous being. Browning had heard something similar from another quarter. . . . It was therefore no surprise to him when in 1846, or 1847, and in Italy, he heard about it again "from a friend of Lady Byron's."

Anna Jameson's cautionary tales of an earlier generation seemed to have been rewarded. When the Brownings' wedding party arrived at Pisa, the poets convinced Aunt Nina to stay with them for another three weeks. Lady Byron was sent news of the poets settling themselves into comfortable lodgings: "As sensible as if they had never spoken anything but prose in their lives." Elizabeth and Robert Browning were "so happy and the *quality* of the happiness is so rare and so fine." Mrs. Jameson described Robert Browning "carrying his wife up and down two flights of stairs—hanging over her as if she were something spared to him for a while out of heaven!"

"Oh!" Jameson exclaimed, as if suddenly recalling to whom she was writing: "If it may but last!"

POSTSCRIPT

THE FAILURE of her relationship with Medora underscored Lady Byron's thinking it her fate only to be loved by "strangers"—by the common people she benefited through her schools and her philanthropy.

Medora did everything her aunt warned her against once in France, including rejecting, after many misunderstandings, Lady Byron's offer of 300 pounds a year. "Take it you fool!" Lady Byron's emissary called out. She wouldn't. It wasn't enough. She expected a house too. She returned to England for her deed, but was shunned by all her relatives. Not one of them would give her a pence, except Lady Byron who, after Medora returned to France with her deed, anonymously set up a fund for 120 pounds a year, her niece's original request.

Back in England, Natty's husband, Victor Beaurepaire demanded money or said he would sue Lady Byron. She led him and his wife to believe they were serving a highly respectable widow, Madame Aubin, and her legitimate child. They were hired under false pretenses; who would hire them again? Refusing to be extorted, Lady Byron planned to go to court. Dr. Lushington told her it was a case she could not win, though it took a lot of correspondence to convince her to pay Victor off—which she finally did. The affair thus ended, Lady Byron wrote to Selina Doyle, to count it as "one more in the self-incurred sorrows of your friend."

WAS MEDORA a great fool when she declined 300 pounds a year? After this second trip to England, she and Marie settled outside Paris, lodging at a pension at Saint-Germain-en-Laye.

Medora was thirty years old and living without servants, relatives, or friends. It was then that she took her life into her own hands. She placed Marie in a convent in Saint-Germain where she would be educated and then did something extraordinary for a woman of her class. She went to work at the pension where she lodged. Did she tend the desk, did she cook, did she wash linen? Who knows? She served others, she made her own way. She *worked*!

At the pension she met a new boarder, a thirty-four-year-old soldier, Jean-Louis Taillefer, who was an orderly to the famous author of the "Grammont Law" dealing with the humane treatment of animals. Jean-Louis fell in love with Medora—madly in love, it would seem—and two years later, on January 27, 1847, Medora gave birth to a healthy boy. Jean-Louis could not marry her until his term of service was completed, but he recognized the son and also adopted Marie. Since the time Medora was six months pregnant she had left employment and gone to live in Saint-Affrique, in southern France close to Jean-Louis's village of Lapaeyre, losing contact by then with Lady Byron's representatives and the 120 pounds per annum.

She married Jean-Louis on August 28, 1848, and she lived from then on as a farmer's wife. She once complained to Lady Byron that the only education she ever received was in gardening. Apparently she put it to good use on the farm. The villagers accepted her. She was different, of course, mysterious and foreign, and considered quite beautiful in that rugged, untourist-ridden area. She had a *piano* in her house and played. She apparently did not pretend to be a peasant, but somewhat in the spirit of Hofwyl simply joined in to farming life and the community. She was a devout Roman Catholic like her neighbors, which helped, and she seemed a good wife and mother. In her short "Autobiography," she wrote of her "most strange and dreadful history." But back in France a few years later, she had a husband who loved her, a daughter who had a name, and a healthy son, Elie. Her new life lasted for another year and a day after her marriage. Some say she developed small pox, others cholera, but on August 23, 1849, she wrote out her short will: "I bequeath all my worldly goods to my husband Jean-Louis Taillefer including the Deed of Appointment under the will of the late Lord Byron, to my husband and children. I also declare here that I forgive my mother and all those who have so cruelly persecuted me, as I hope myself to be forgiven."

Her heirs never received a shilling from that deed of appointment, though lawyers attempted to right the situation, both in France and England, for many years to come. That fine piece of parchment might as well have been buried with her on August 29, 1849, when at the age of thirty-five and four months she died. Her gravestone marks her married name on a second line.

The first line reads: Elizabeth Medora Leigh Byron.

Impetuous, proud, foolish, betrayed by almost everyone by the time she was thirteen, young, manipulative, unhappy, Medora Leigh made her own mistakes, suffered most her life from her thoughts, her violent temper, from her early rape. Yet, after she left England that second time, she appeared not to have looked back. Having been renounced, she renounced, and found her own life. It might have been a humble life, but it was hers. Her biographer Catherine Turney wrote in 1975 that the French villagers did not forget her, that she had been greatly respected, her grave tended for years after she was gone. Perhaps future biographers will delve deeper into the life Medora led after she rejected the only kind of love Lady Byron had to give her.

With what the records tell us at this time, it would appear that in the last five years of her too-short life, Medora saw her way out of the quagmire of illusions concerning who she should be and what was owed her. She stuck those long hairpins of hers into her own airy expectations and faced the truth of her singular situation. Aunt Twaddle might have been of use to Medora after all. In France with husband, children, and meaningful work, Medora, though she once cursed it to the devil fifty times a day, was true to her self.

11

ATTEMPTING AMENDS
AT THE WHITE HART

T he year of Medora's marriage, 1848, was one in which all England shook with fear that the revolutions raging throughout the Continent would land on its shores as well. Lady Byron was forced to recall grandson Ralph, whom she was raising, back from Hofwyl School. That same year Lord Melbourne died. He had suffered a slow and demented death as did his mother before him. "A heartless Public saw the light grow dim," Lady Byron began her long elegiac poem on the "falling star" of her cousin's life, for he had died during the nadir of his popularity.

"Biographers should know the world in which Lord Melbourne moved—should understand how its malaise could poison or neutralize Nature's best gifts—how Nature thus poisoned could 'mock itself,'" she wrote to Anna Jameson. Melbourne "was not forgiven by some very near him for remembering and upholding" a higher standard. "His Memory must rest with the Queen. She only can 'render to Caesar, etc' at some future day."

Biographers should know! But a new generation did not know how corrosive the morality of the Regency had been. They didn't know how it affected not only brilliant Melbourne, but a sensitive young Byron. And all the public knew of Byron's marriage was what Thomas Moore told them in a biography that demonized Lord Byron's wife. Moore had made no bones about his own opinion of Lady Byron. He quoted himself telling Lord Byron "After all, your choice was your misfortune. I never liked———"

"*You* think her too straight-laced for me." Byron to Tom.

Moore had proved his dislike of Lady Byron in person right after Lord Byron's death. He returned to England in 1824 with the dead poet's unpublished memoirs of his marriage. During the separation procedure Byron had offered to let his wife read what he had to say, but she wisely refused. He had added to his memoirs while abroad and the few who read them considered them scandalous, X-rated. Murray bought them from Moore for 2,000 pounds and offered them to Lady Byron, who planned to do what she always did with such documents, seal the memoirs up and leave them for her executors to decide how they were to be handled after her death. She told Frank Doyle this, but by the time Doyle reached London as her emissary, Moore had regained possession of the memoirs and Lady Byron planned to buy them from Moore instead of from Murray. Doyle arrived at his London townhouse to find Moore already waiting for him in his drawing room. Moore appeared to take pleasure in telling Doyle that he could not sell them to Lady Byron, as Byron only wished them to go to his *family*. And Lord Byron's family was his sister Augusta Leigh.

Thus, with a fine flourish. Moore handed the memoirs over to Augusta Leigh, who appeared flustered and said she couldn't imagine what was in them, had never read them and that she hadn't the money to pay and whatever should she do? Hobhouse came to her greatly agitated by her hesitation and while the Seventh Lord Byron sat in her outer chambers, Hobhouse asked her how foolish could she be, she had them in her hands, she must burn them. There appear to have been two copies, one handwritten, one printed. It is quite possible Augusta burned one copy herself and it was the other copy so famously burned in John Murray's fireplace with only men attending. Myth after myth has grown up around this lost autobiographical account, but it was Augusta and Augusta alone, as she wrote in her own hand, who had the authority and did order the manuscripts burned.

When Lady Byron was informed the memoirs had been destroyed she admitted that perhaps that was for the best, though she would have had them sealed up. How Lady Byron felt about being told through Thomas Moore that she was not part of her husband's family, that Augusta alone was family, can only be imagined. By extension that meant daughter Ada was not part of her father's family either. It was a deep insult followed eight years later by the publication of Moore's *Letters and Journals of Lord Byron: With Notices of His Life*.

In Moore's pages, a sanitized version of the burned memoirs and the incestuous relationship between Augusta and Lord Byron remains. Lady Byron learned that Augusta, referred to by Moore as Byron's sex-undefined "friend," never wanted Byron to marry her and had tried to marry him off to others first. She read Byron's true reaction when receiving the letter in which Annabella shed all pretensions and spilled over with love. Byron handed her letter to his "friend," saying "It never rains but it pours."

When her sister-in-law *was* named, she appeared as her brother's "sole consolation" through the "bitter" trial of his marriage. All one had to do was strip away any reference to incest and the love between brother and sister became a heroic idyll, as melodic as one of Tom Moore's melodies. ("Believe me, if all those endearing young charms . . .") The two met last on the brink of Byron's leaving England. Moore portrayed the parting of Platonic lovers, quoting the stirring poem Byron wrote on the occasion. Far from the ambiguities of "Fair Thee Well," his poem to his sister ended in the exquisite:

> In the desert a fountain is springing
>> In the wide waste there still is a tree,
> And a bird in the solitude singing
>> Which speaks to my spirit of *thee*.

So there it was. At the age of thirty-eight, in Moore's *Life*, Lady Byron read in black and white that Augusta and Byron had actively conspired together to marry him off, she his last chance that particular year. He and his "friend" had shared her love letters as they determined his course. Lord Byron married Anne Isabella Milbanke *because* he was deeply in love with his sister. The aristocratic and intellectually gifted woman read that she "would have made the home of a more ordinary man happy." Her cold mediocrity unfit her to understand or minister to male genius.

Later critics accepted Moore's interpretation of Lady Byron, based on Byron's journals and poetry. However, those who were closer to the situation at the time could plainly see the use Byron made of his glorious words. Caro George was quick to ask Annabella, tongue in cheek, what did she think of Byron "making a peeress"?

In his journal of Monday, March 7, 1814, which Moore published, Byron noted he brought John Hanson's "eldest daughter Mary Anne (a good girl)" to church and gave her away in marriage to the Earl of Portsmouth. Three days later he received the kindest thanks from Portsmouth's parents for the matchmaking he had accomplished for their son. Byron didn't regret this, he told his journal, for Mary Anne "looks the countess well." In fact, he complimented himself: "I had no idea that I could make so good a peeress."

The Portsmouths had reason to thank Byron for helping them to marry off their deformed and mentally incompetent son to Hanson's daughter. That Hanson was held in disrespect by the civilian lawyers who handled Lady Byron's separation had much to do with knowing Hanson had forced an unwilling daughter into this unholy alliance. As Byron would tell Annabella once he and she were wed, while walking Mary Anne down the aisle, he kept reminding "the very good girl" of the sex she had had with *him*. When Byron wrote "I had no idea that I could make so good a peeress," he was punning. Moore printed the pun as gospel, while society snickered and some fully understood genial Moore's gullibility. Mary Anne, by the way, was eventually able to have the marriage dissolved on the basis of her husband being incapable of knowing what a marriage was or what was expected in one.

There were sinister undertones in another journal entry Moore printed innocently that would not have escaped Lady Byron's notice. It underscored Byron's sexual attraction to children: "Today Henry Byron called on me with my little cousin Eliza. She will grow up a beauty and a plague; but, in the meantime, it is the prettiest child! Dark eyes and eyelashes, black and long as the wings of a raven. I think she is prettier even than my niece Georgiana—yet I don't like to think so neither; and though older she is not so clever." Byron wrote this in 1813, when niece Georgey was five.

"I must get a toy for Eliza," he wrote in a note to himself. A few days later: "Have again forgot a plaything for *ma petite cousine* Eliza; but must send for it tomorrow. I hope Henry will bring her to me." The next day: "Henry has not brought *ma petite cousine*. I want us to go to the play together; she has been but once." Cousin Henry apparently caught on. Byron's attraction to children with eyelashes black and long as the wings of a raven was hardly innocent. His proclivities were there in the journal entries Moore thought he had no reason to disguise.

Moore's biography was not one of Lord Byron's satiric poems in which knowledge of specific references might fade with time. The world would believe Byron's bitter portrayal of his wife and Moore's account of her cold mediocrity. Lady Byron knew she was reading history.

She wrote to Frank Doyle, Dr. Lushington, Wilmot Horton, and Caro George of the predicament she faced. Characteristically, she could not access her own damaged heart and feelings in a way that would make her admit her own pain and attempt to right her own history. Instead, she wished only to defend her parents, right their reputation. Moore accused them of causing the breakup of the marriage. She wanted to clarify that it was she and she alone who made that decision. Her good friends told her this would not be a good idea. Doyle and Lushington were dead set against it, Caro George encouraged her, whereas Wilmot Horton asked her why she hadn't simply asked Moore for a retraction for printing Lord Byron's cutting and rather amusing comments about her talkative father and Byron's ferocious "mother-at-law." She answered she would not print her paper had Moore *offered* a retraction. As Lady Byron grew older, she became more and more incapable of asking for what she wanted (never her forte). She expected people to read the right thing to do directly from her high forehead. Not surprisingly it led her—and others—to many disappointments.

Against advice, Lady Byron wrote and printed a small number of pamphlets to defend the reputation of her dead parents, emphasizing that it was she and she alone who made the decision to leave Byron. She spoke of people being afraid he might harm himself should she stay, never mentioning they were more afraid Byron would harm her.

This "paper" was not to be published, but to be privately printed and circulated among those who knew her parents. Such private printings by the upper class were far from uncommon in her day. She hired two printers to work on separate sections, so nothing would be leaked. "My wish is to place the copy only in the hands of those who will make a discreet use of it, and prevent the *possibility* of its insertion in the Newspapers at present—I think I shall not send out more than a dozen at first. Moore's is dispatched." Over time she dispatched about sixty of them, meticulously ticking off names and number of copies in a notebook as she posted: Lushington, six copies; King George IV, one. Her world was a small circle of what had been the Regency elite. Of course a curious and larger world soon caught on, and she was chagrined to find a privately printed copy opened to relevant pages in a bookshop window.

Moore's response to Lady Byron's *Remarks on Mr Moore's Life of Byron* only added further insult. He tipped the privately circulated pamphlet into the first edition of the biography, and published it in the notes of subsequent editions of his *Life* without making a comment about what she had to say. Caro George said there were two ways to look at this. Either Moore agreed with Lady Byron or he considered her *Remarks* too inconsequential to be worth a comment. Caro George feared it might be the latter. She was right. As Byron once predicted, the world would love glorious "By."

Cousin Melbourne's death in 1848 had made Lady Byron think

of posterity once more. The next summer, Lady Byron herself was struck down after tending grandson Ralph, who had scarlet fever: "When I was lying between life and death . . . I felt a deep regret that I had not attempted to give someone capable of working it out, a portrait of that aspect of Lord Byron's mind which *related to the Invisible World.*" Again, she could not think of a memoir other than elevated beyond her own concerns.

She wrote this to the man who had become her second Byron. He was the Reverend Frederick W. Robertson. Three years previously, in August, 1847, at the age of thirty-one, Robertson had come to a ministry in Brighton reluctantly. He was from a military family and his passion had been to enter the military, fight bravely, and die heroically—to take his "Rest" in "A Soldier's Grave" just as his hero Lord Byron wrote on his thirty-sixth birthday. A series of small coincidences combined with the endless wait to be accepted by the Horse Guard in India convinced him to accept his concerned father's advice and enter Brasenose College, Oxford, instead and train for the ministry. Soon after Robertson entered Oxford, his acceptance to the Horse Guard arrived. What else could that missed opportunity be but the will of God?

Was Brighton the will of God as well? He had hoped for a military chaplaincy. His style of preaching—his speaking to man *as man*—hadn't gone over that well in "cold," cerebral Oxford. But move on to Brighton? Though the pay of 300 per annum at Trinity Chapel would be more than double his Oxford pay, he was leery of "a watering-place ministry." He took time out from his Oxford ministry and went trekking in the South Tyrol, away from his hectoring wife and only son to sort things out and come to a decision. Clear air and exercise always unclouded his thoughts and did him good. Resting after a day's trek, he met a well-dressed gentleman: impeccable lederhosen, short jacket, feather in his creased tweed hat. The man spoke a precise German. Robertson was surprised to find out the stranger was actually an Englishman married to a German baroness. Robertson had just met Dandy Bob. Pondering Brighton, was he? He was mistaken if he thought it all fashion. His cousin often resided there for her

*Robertson of Brighton, the young reverend
who championed the working men and was
Lady Byron's closest confidante in the years
in which she thought of writing
a memoir of her marriage.*

health and her love of the sea, and no one could be more interested
in the plight of the common person and less in hobnobbing with the
carriage trade. In fact, this cousin was "nearer perfection than any
he knows of all her sex." Bob Noel thought the two would get along
famously and he gave Robertson a letter of introduction to take with
him should he decide on Brighton. Robertson wrote this excitedly to
his father, at the same time cautioning him not to use Lady Byron's
name when speaking to others.

Lady Byron was fifty-five years old when thirty-one-year-old
Robertson appeared in her drawing room at Brighton with Bob
Noel's letter of introduction. Annabella had maintained her delicate looks, that faultless complexion hadn't failed her, and with her
slight frame as well, she still appeared younger than her years. Good-
looking Robertson with his manly airs and military posture, though
of medium height, was still much taller than she, and protective of her.

Whereas Byron's grey eyes often scorned the cant in the fashionable people he saw all about him, Robertson's empathetic deep blue eyes set off in his clean-shaven face reflected the down-to-earth concerns of ordinary men when he preached. Even with the twenty-four-year age difference, the attraction between Robertson and Lady Byron had an electricity that people noticed. They made a pair. Soon, she went from being "Byron's widow" to his "dear friend." She, on her part, was struck by Robertson's conversation and his convictions. Energetic, charismatic, and given to sharp changes in mood, he had a certain spiritual affinity with the Byron of her youth.

Robertson's marriage was an unhappy one. Up to the age of twenty-five he thought of women as belonging to a magical sphere of sensual beauty beyond his reach. Vacationing during an earlier trek to ponder his fate and to alleviate his recurring depressions, he met Helen Denys in Geneva in 1841. Helen was nothing if not direct. She most probably initiated Robertson. He felt it his duty to marry her soon after they met and before their son was born. It would be unmanly to complain, he would later write to Lady Byron, though there were hundreds of unhappy incidents concerning his wife that came to his mind. Lady Byron, on first meeting Helen Robertson, considered her "simple, not silly," the most favorable opinion she would form of Robertson's opinionated wife.

The relationship between Lady Byron and Robertson was so close that a recent writer thought she might be the "Sunshine" he referred to in his coded diary. This appeared to be a woman with whom, on scattered occasions, Robertson did find love and sexual bliss. Sunshine was actually an Irish aristocrat who lived in England. Lady Byron knew her "dear friend" considered himself entrapped by what he called one act of "chivalry" into a dismally unhappy marriage. Since there were no secrets between them, she knew about the "Irish Lady" as well. The love between Lady Byron and Robertson resembled one Jean-Jacques Rousseau once called "more than love," it was, for better or worse, the melding of two souls.

In 1848, the uprisings among the proletariat abroad caused such concern that when the workingmen of Brighton wanted a union of their own, with a place to meet and a small library, it was considered close to insurgency. The powers of the town wished to crush this idea of a union which could include up to 2,000 workers. However, preaching at Trinity Chapel, Robertson championed the union as did Lady Byron. Most of the carriage trade left his ministry, their places filled (to over capacity) by workers, servants, intellectuals, and important friends of Lady Byron. One Sunday "I was the cause, directly or indirectly, of his numbering among his hearers Ada, Lord Douro and the Rev'd G. Wellesley!"

Robertson spearheaded a peaceful revolution and was able to found the Working Men's Institute of Brighton, established in their own quarters and under their own rules. Trinity Chapel led the call. "I dare to be poor!" Lady Byron proclaimed in that year of revolution. If the social order was in upheaval, she said she'd give all she had if it were to be used for the common good—not for new greed. She supported the weavers' children weekly when their parents were out on strike. She stood with Robertson of Brighton, the name by which he would be known to future generations. She thanked cousin Bob for giving her the greatest gift one could make to another: "The means of intercourse with a great soul—Robertson's." To another she wrote simply, "I love him."

Before Lady Byron was forty, she read in Moore's biography how her husband twisted and turned the truth about her—even in his private journals. Before she was sixty, she read how the public turned against dear Melbourne at his death. After she herself almost died the next year, she wondered about her own legacy. She insisted what the public thought of her never mattered. But what about her grandchildren? Lord Ockham, young Ralph, whom she raised as a son, her darling Annabella, so often with her. What would *they* think? Should she write a memoir of the marriage? It would be a factual account as sympathetic to her husband as she could be. She did not want to disparage the memory of the great poet, but tell the truth dispassionately, as if she herself were a bystander. This idea was her nemesis, seen in her earlier defense of her parents. She believed she could recall the past not as a participant but as an impartial witness of her own life.

"Thirty Five years have not weakened my Memory, though they have enabled me to speak as a Witness merely,—and without any Self-reference," she wrote to Robertson.

"If it be in my power to assist you in the deeply interesting subject of which you speak," Robertson responded three days later, "it would be saying little to say that it would make me glad." Lady Byron was quite right, he continued, "in supposing that I had felt deep sympathy with that singular and fearfully gifted mind and heart in which your interest survives after so long a lapse of time, to an extent which is to me very touching, but perfectly expected." He could recite entire passages of *Don Juan* and *Childe Harold* by heart and knew Lord Byron expressed "a something which is in all of us, I suppose, in some of us acutely. I felt and feel that it is *in* human nature, but is not all of human nature." Nothing was more instructive to Roberston or "more mysteriously true to life than Byron's sudden sneers in the midst of sublimities of feeling—as if to say—'I know what all this means and how it ends—and yet how beautiful to feel!'"

So they collaborated. At first by mail, as Lady Byron had trouble expressing herself aloud, and she warned Robertson that she would reveal what she could, but that under one truth another deeper truth might be buried. She wrote to her daughter in a letter she allowed Robertson to read that "the very serious social disadvantages under which I have been placed," was "of less importance to me than the objects accomplished by my silence."

Worthy objects were best gained through truth, Robertson insisted. Nothing worthy came from silence. He urged his friend to voice her true feelings, not to "repress" them—his word. In astonishment, Lady Byron wrote to Mrs. Jameson that Robertson would have people pour out "all their feelings—all! . . . As if one *could*!—as if one *dared*!" As if such an opening up "would not become the channel of a Debacle!"

If she didn't repress her feelings, that "Debacle" would center on

Augusta, the sister-in-law she hadn't seen in decades. She had already admitted to Robertson that soon after her marriage she had become so jealous of her husband's attention to his sister that she was seized by murderous impulses, which she replaced with "romantic forgiveness" in order to keep sane. That was true as far as it went, she wrote, but there was a deeper truth below.

Did Robertson recall her saying there was "one whom I had not seen for years, but hoped before death to see again?" Well, that was the same person whose "*guilt* made a great part (*not* the whole) of my wretchedness" during the marriage. Since that *impulse* to plunge a dagger into her heart—"I have never had any feeling but one of—I can't get a right word." Could Robertson now sympathize with the "*objects*" gained by her silence "more completely"?

Robertson was astounded! "It appalled me, and I could not control an ejaculation of surprise and horror. Surely I have—I must have mistaken the implied meaning! And yet often as I read it I can find no new construction on your words. I shrink from suggesting the dreadful fancy that came across me, lest I should have mistaken, and should therefore shock you by having conceived it—" Did Byron's poem *Manfred* "shadow a truth?" he asked his friend, which was as close as he could come to asking if Lord Byron and his sister had an incestuous relationship. Lady Byron answered by not answering: "My silence has of course confirmed your supposition."

For Robertson this revelation about Byron and his sister was "almost as startling as a personal grief could have been." It made him a wiser and sadder man. To think of his friend's conduct, her "discipline, conscious and unconscious," in not exposing Augusta, of protecting her and allowing the world to judge Lady Byron a bad, unfeeling wife. Unconsciously, Robertson was comparing Lady Byron's silence with the lack of compassion he daily experienced from his own hectoring wife. Would Lady Byron forgive him, he wrote, for saying that he deeply honored her life. "To me it came opportunely, as a very precious lesson—I thank God that the best guardian a man has cannot be taken from me now—belief and trust in Womanliness."

Once he understood the "objects" of Lady Byron's silence, Robertson spread his cloak at his Lady's feet. In voiding his criticism of her silence, and turning it into eternal "Womanliness," he inadvertently appealed to Annabella's incipient narcissism in a way that opened her beyond it. Before January 1851, Lady Byron could only write to him of her life. Now she spoke. Robertson recorded their many "Conversations" and "Interviews" for the future memoir.

Their exploration of her marriage took a dramatic turn. In February 1851, Lady Byron received a letter from her godchild, Emily Leigh, Augusta's youngest child. Colonel Leigh had died the previous spring, and though his family no longer needed to provide the "many things that were necessary to his comfort," they were also left without his 300 pounds per annum, giving them so much less a year "to pay debts and to exist upon." Emily at the age of thirty-three remained her mother's constant and only support.

Her brothers were still "disasters," adept at selling Byron's letters for money against family wishes. Georgey and her three daughters were still living with and dependent on Augusta. The Seventh Lord Byron and his wife gave Lady Byron "a *frightful* description" of the hatred constantly raging between Augusta and Georgey. Emily said there were things her mother wished to tell Lady Byron that could not be put in a letter.

After decades of silences and with her memoir on her mind, Lady Byron responded: "We may not long have it in our power, Augusta, to meet again in this life." A meeting "might be the means of leaving both of us a remembrance of deep though sad thankfulness." It could take place only if they both concentrated on "entire and mutual truthfulness."

Augusta answered the same day, February 14, 1851. Though she was quite ill, she accepted the invitation thankfully and unhesitatingly: She wouldn't want to enter into any subject that would make an interview unpleasant (vintage Augusta), but "I shall be prepared if necessary to give and receive any explanations on any subject that concerns myself."

Lady Byron stipulated that though their meeting would be held in strict privacy, she would bring a friend to witness her own response to it. Out of the question, Augusta replied. Annabella insisted on "the presence of a friend of indisputable honor and character to attest what *I* may say." Protracted illness or fear delayed Augusta answering for two weeks, but when she wrote, she agreed, sacrificing her own feelings as proof of her sincerity. In case Augusta might have objections to the disinterested party who would accompany her, Lady Byron then named "The Rev. Frederick Robertson, of Trinity Chapel here," as if she was announcing the Second Coming.

Actually she was announcing her biographer, who found himself in the delicious position of witnessing Byron's sister and Byron's widow meeting after a hiatus lasting twenty years. Lady Byron had come to believe her marriage would not have failed if there had been *one* less person in the world, as she put it. All she wished from Augusta while they remained on the earth together was the truth. Letters to and from Byron had gone through Augusta after Byron left England, as he stipulated. Had Augusta withheld some of Annabella's or altered others in a way that kept Byron's hatred of his wife alive? Had Augusta helped to exacerbate Byron's bitterness that made its way into Moore's *Life* of the poet? Robertson expected the meeting to fill a lacuna in history.

Lady Byron selected a hotel close to a convenient railroad station to accommodate the frightened Augusta. At the age of sixty-three, Augusta had been on a train only *once*, five years previously, and was nervous of all such arrangements. She had to be sent specific directions on which train to take, where to stand to get it, what to avoid, etc.

Whereas Lady Byron was hoping for enlightenment, and had the means to pay not only for rooms at the White Hart, but for a "Fly" to pick up Augusta at the railroad station, Augusta, whom illness had turned into an old woman over night, was filled with family cares and money worries. Lady Byron's life had many disappointments, but Augusta's was one of many "disasters," as Theresa Villiers had seen through the years. "When mothers fail us, can we help ourselves?"

Barrett Browning wrote. But Augusta herself knew no mother. Could she help herself? If there was no compass to her morality outside of trying to keep people happy, that had been a pattern established early in her life, as we have seen. Orphaned early, Augusta was eternally needy, emotionally and financially. Weak-willed and goosey she was, twirling about during a lifetime of attempting to dance to the tune of others. Her waltz was about to end. How was she to provide for dear Emily, the one child who did not cause her heartache? She boarded a train for the second time in her life and attempted to hold steady.

Before arriving at the White Hart, Augusta wrote: "There are many things I may wish to say to you—indeed that you may wish to hear, which *could* not be communicated before ANY third party whatever." Lady Byron and her biographer arrived expecting the truth, the way one expects it at the end of a Greek tragedy in a burst of cathartic enlightenment.

On April 8, 1851, when Augusta entered the White Hart, Lady Byron immediately saw death on Augusta's face. Her former Sis was not secure on her feet, and her appearance was "shrunken," the word Lord George Byron's wife used to describe her. Robertson was introduced. Annabella expressed her "unaltered affection" and assured Augusta nothing would be divulged that was said in confidence. With that, Robertson left the two women to their private conversation, going to the second room Lady Byron had reserved for them at the White Hart. After twenty years the iron curtain of silence rose and the sisters-in-law faced one another on an empty stage.

Lady Byron, steady on her feet, had written a short list of what she wanted to say. First she wanted to admit her own culpability in terms of Medora. She wanted to confess to Guss that "I have wronged, by assisting self deception." She had led her adopted daughter to false expectations about her own position in society and she took responsibility for putting ideas into Medora's head that may have had the power to harm Augusta. However, Augusta spoke first, almost as if to make sure she remembered what she came to say. It was a very short and equivocal statement which Lady Byron thought had obviously been rehearsed, for it was delivered by rote, without any faltering at all, hardly Augusta's style.

Lady Byron had to wait till she could control herself enough to utter: "Is that all?"

Well, of course Augusta was extremely grateful for Lady Byron's many kindnesses to her and her family.

"It's all in vain!" Lady Byron cried out, for once in her life losing control. It was "utterly hopeless." Leave me alone! She called out to a shaken Augusta, who retreated, as fast as a feeble old woman could, to the room where Robertson waited.

Lady Byron joined them once she composed herself. She faced Augusta. The truth she sought pertained only to the years after Byron left England in 1816. She was asking nothing of what went on between sister and brother during the marriage. She was asking for Byron's sake more than hers (vintage Annabella), so "that he might not be blamed more than he deserved" for so misrepresenting his wife's love in his poetry, in his conversations, in his journals till the end of his life. For the husband who knew she loved him to have continued to be so bitter against her for so long, there must have been false representations made of her to him. She acknowledged Byron had mellowed toward the end. Still, she had come to believe Augusta must have done an injustice to her in her letters to her brother. Otherwise, how could Byron sustain such *hate*? The letters, the poems, the conversations with Medwin. . . . She was convinced that Byron must have been misled. Everything had to go through Augusta. She alone was "family." Had Augusta concealed letters or even altered others?

Augusta's weak voice gained in power. She had done her sister-in-law no injustice in her letters to Lord Byron. Byron's letters to her would prove it! He was very unjust, "poor soul," toward Annabella. He said "dreadful things" about her. But Augusta had never said anything to provoke his irritation. Lady Byron persisted. If he said terrible things in his letters that Augusta could show her, what had Augusta said in hers? She wasn't speaking as Augusta's judge, she emphasized. She just *had* to know the truth.

Augusta repeated that she had always defended Annabella to her brother. Fatigued by the journey and the emotional stress, her habitual nervousness was exacerbated by illness, debts, age. She had some hope looking at Robertson's kind face. Now she was happy he was there. Perhaps he would intervene. Suddenly she herself had a flash and brought the subject up again, with great relief. She remembered a substantial proof of fidelity to give her sister-in-law.

Hadn't Sir John Hobhouse witnessed Augusta's many attempts to calm her brother's rage against his wife? She quoted Hobhouse: "Lady Byron has every reason to be grateful to you." By defending Lady Byron, Augusta "not only risked the loss of property, but what was much dearer to you, his affection."

It was as if a descending deus ex machina missed stage left and crashed into Lady Byron's high forehead: "I was afraid of myself."

She couldn't remember what she answered, if she did answer. Her only desire was to be out of Augusta's presence, "lest I should be tempted beyond my strength." Hobhouse and Augusta speaking together of her husband's hate of her! Hadn't her mother warned her again and again that Augusta needed to stay on her brother's good side for the financial support he offered her monthly in life as well as in his will? Hadn't Judith warned her daughter that Augusta must "hate" her. Augusta had risked her *property* as well as her brother's love by not damning his wife.

Five days after the interview Annabella told Robertson her own "defective filial duty" had caused this "retribution." She wouldn't answer Augusta's letters. Her iron curtain of silence clanged shut. Augusta then wrote to Robertson personally—he had such a kind manner. She wanted to come to see him and bring proof that she was telling the truth. Robertson was at first open to Augusta's plea, but said he would do exactly what Lady Byron wished. Lady Byron wouldn't have it. "She will never consent to another meeting." If Augusta had a clear conscience, "the opinion of any human being is of no consequence." However, if there were a sorrowful acknowledgment Augusta could have made at the White Hart, it "must be heard very, very soon, when you meet God face to face." It was as if Robertson symbiotically channeled Lady Byron's pent-up rage. "I trust you will not look upon the plain words I have used as expressing harshness of feeling."

Augusta lay close to death the following autumn, and Lady Byron's conflicted feelings took a more humane turn. Early on, she had written to Robertson that she had loved Augusta from before they had ever met and still did. She wrote to Emily to offer any service that might be helpful. Not receiving an answer, she went often to Augusta's door in London that season to inquire after her. Finally she sent Augusta "some words of affection." Emily responded that her mother was worn out by dropsy and heart disease, each demanding a counterindicated medicine. Her bodily suffering was heaped on top of constant trouble and anxiety. She was in pain and slipping away. Emily whispered Lady Byron's message to her mother. They were two words from long ago. "Dearest Augusta."

On hearing them once more, Augusta cried tears of joy. She wanted Emily to tell Lady Byron they were "her greatest consolation." Augusta tried to say more, but her voice was so indistinct, though she spoke on and on, Emily could not make out the rest of what she said.

"*A second* message lost," Lady Byron wrote.

The Honorable Augusta Byron Leigh died on October 12, 1851, a week after receiving Lady Byron's message. "Thank God I sent it," she told Robertson.

ᘓᕲ 12 ᕲᘒ

ENDURING MOTHERHOOD

With the death of Augusta Leigh, Ada and her family wore mourning for the aunt and great-aunt who was a stranger in their lives. Ada admitted to Lady Byron that she had been very apprehensive about that meeting at the White Hart, fearing for her mother's health and peace of mind. "Filial propriety" had prevented her from daring to offer advice. "*That filial* relation is always hanging like a mill-stone round my neck."

Lady Byron hadn't been a millstone the previous decade when Ada returned to her scientific studies after giving birth to her youngest child: "I wished for *heirs*, certainly never should have desired a *child*," Ada wrote memorably to her mother. With that, Lady Byron suggested friend Louisa Mary Barwell to advise Ada in finding the proper help.

"The less I have *habitually* to do with children the better both for them and me," Ada wrote to Mrs. Barwell, throwing aside her "customary secrecy." Scientific pursuits rendered constant attention to children "absolutely intolerable." Her exceedingly delicate and irritable nervous system, added to this, so "you will not wonder that I begin to feel the children occasionally (to speak plainly but truly) a real nuisance."

In the Lovelace's London establishment the children were less annoying, she went on. The town house was so divided that the children could run riot on their side and not be heard on Ada's. Daughter

Anne remembered jumping up and down on beds, doing whatever she pleased, and greedily eyeing her adored older brother Byron's mutton chops. Lady Byron made the apt observation that she never experienced such unruly children.

Amid unheard chaos, Ada entered into her mathematical speculations with all the intensity and genius of her nature. She shared her mother's belief that "mathematical science" was not merely "a vast body of abstract and immutable truths," but "the language through which alone we can adequately express the great facts of the natural world," so that "the weak mind of man can most effectually read his Creator's works," and translate the principles behind them "into explicit practical forms."

This from the "Notes" Ada appended to her translation into English of Luigi Menabrea's twenty-four-page article on Charles Babbage's new conception, his Analytical Engine. These notes were three times as long as the article and established her posthumous fame. She wrote them to defend Babbage's abandoning the Difference Engine for which the government had already granted him more than 17,000 pounds. Never famous for finishing his projects, Babbage conceived of a more advanced steam-propelled engine. The Analytical Engine would calculate *information*, not just numbers, Ada wrote in her Notes. "It can do whatever we *know how to order it to perform*. It can *follow* analysis; but it has no power of *anticipating* any analytical relations or truths. Its province is to assist us in making *available* what we are already acquainted with."

She envisioned that "a vast, and a powerful language" would be developed for this Engine. To illustrate, she told Babbage that she wanted "to put something about Bernoulli's Numbers" into one of her "Notes." She asked him for "the necessary data and formulae" and with that she wrote a software language for Babbage's never-to-be actualized Analytical Engine. Her language would have to await the invention of the modern computer. A hundred and twenty-five years after she wrote her "Notes," a variation of the language Ada created was used by NASA, and named ADA, in honor of the woman regarded as the first computer programmer. Her brilliant foresight added gravitas to what she wrote euphorically to her mother in 1841: "Greatness of the very *highest* order is never appreciated here, to the fullest extent until after the great man's (or woman's) death. *My* ambition should be rather to *be* great than to be *thought* so."

Her fame has done nothing but grow in the twenty-first century. Students study her in computer classes as they do her father—and at times Ada—in English classes. For along with Ada's contribution in envisioning the information age, one can now find her as the heroine of much "steam punk" literature. She is presently an icon to the hip.

After her extraordinary "Notes" were published, Ada turned her genius back toward programming games with Babbage. They developed a mysterious "book" that passed between them once a week, most probably a program designed to predict horse-race results. For from the mid-1840s on, Ada gambled—in the compulsive manner of the grandfather she never knew, Mad Jack.

The Countess came to racing with a mathematical program, a childlike sense of her infallibility, and a focus that reminds one of when she was twelve and obsessed with flight. She was well aware of her mother's belief that moral traits could be inherited. Lady Byron became a millstone around Ada's neck as Ada attempted to keep the extent of her gaming from her mother, all the while requesting more and more money from her, ostensibly for fine books and Court dresses. At the same time, Ada being Ada, she bubbled over with racing news in her letters to her mother. On Lady Byron's fifty-eighth birthday, May 17, 1850, Ada wrote: "I am afraid you will take no interest in what interests *me* much just now,—viz: the winner of the Derby." That race was two weeks away and Ada was "in danger of becoming quite a sporting character."

Ada and Lovelace were guests of the aristocratic owners of the great horses of the day and went from country home to country home during racing season. As a result, they were often in proximity to Newstead Abbey, the medieval estate that her father had been forced to sell. In 1850, in the gap between meets, Ada visited

Newstead Abbey for the first time. It had been bought and was kept up by Colonel Thomas Wildman. For two days she wandered around the Abbey and the grounds without uttering a word to anyone, seeing nothing but death all around her. Newstead was like falling into a grave, she wrote to her mother. Her depression may have been heightened by the menstrual hemorrhage she had recently suffered, similar to the one she had had a few years previously while visiting friend Charles Dickens.

Yet, after this initial gloom, her spirits lifted and she became as enamored of the Abbey as she had previously been appalled. It is often said that Ada may have been bipolar. If she were, these terrible menstrual cycles, her Black Dwarf, contributed. Suddenly she was overjoyed: The tapestries, the skull's heads young Byron and his friends used to drink out of in nights of revelry, the ornate furniture, the medieval flavor of the estate—it was all kept as it once was. She went to the nearby church where Byron was entombed in the crowded vault with his ancestors and afterward wrote to her mother playfully: "I have had a *resurrection*. I do love the venerable old place and all my *wicked forefathers*."

Lady Byron, who was working with Robertson on the Memoir was appalled: For all Ada's secrecy, Lady Byron knew her daughter was lately living among "partizans" of Byron who "consider me as having taken a hostile position towards him. *You* must not be infected with an error resulting from *their* ignorance, and his mystification. I was his best friend, not only in feeling, but in fact." In her mind, Lady Byron considered she was writing about her marriage for her grandchildren, but Ada had no idea of what she meant when she wrote: "It often occurs to me that my attempts to influence your children favorably in their early years will be frustrated and turned to mischief,—so that it would be better for them not to have known me,—if they are allowed to adopt the unfounded popular notion of my having abandoned my husband from want of devotedness and entire sympathy— or if they suppose me to have been under the influence at any time, of cold, calculating and unforgiving feelings,—such having been his published description of me, whilst he wrote to me privately, (as will hereafter appear) 'I did—no do—and ever shall love you'—"

Ada was so astonished by her mother's outburst that she felt "some difficulty in replying." Her mother's letter seemed "addressed to a Phantom of something that don't exist.—No feeling or opinion respecting my father's *moral character*, or *your* relations toward him, could be altered by my visit to Newstead, or by any *tone* assumed by any parties whatever." As far as her "having a *mythical* veneration for my father, I cannot, (to adhere only to personal considerations) forget his conduct as regards to my *own* self, a conduct *unjust* and *vindictive*." A rift developed but was eventually resolved. Lady Byron made amends through her beloved son-in-law. Ada had told her of a prophecy that Newstead would one day return to the family. Should Lady Byron buy the estate for her daughter? She sent Lovelace to inspect Newstead and advise her as to its financial feasibility. It did not get as far as asking Colonel Wildman if he would sell, for as the Crow reported to his Hen, after careful inspection, Newstead was not a good investment.

Meanwhile, Ada kept gambling. On the recommendation of Babbage, she hired Mary Wilson, Babbage's deceased mother's lady's maid, as well as her husband. Each week as Babbage and Ada sent their mysterious "book" back and forth, Mary placed bets with the bookies, something a Countess did not do for herself. Protected as she had always been from the world below her station, Ada also trusted her lover—perhaps latest lover if the rumors were accurate—John Crosse.

John was a good-looking dark-haired man with a mysteriously marked jaw. Six years older than Ada, he was the eldest son of Andrew Crosse, a well-known amateur scientist whose eccentric experiments in electricity and electrocrystallization made him a prototype, people said, for Mary Shelley's Doctor Frankenstein. Ada met John while visiting his father's home laboratory. In these years before John inherited from his uncle Hamilton, took his name, and became the gentleman he pretended to be, John Crosse was a confidence man. It was he who brought Ada into a demiworld of gamblers and extortioners, and it was they who convinced her that her mother would never understand her gambling any more than she understood Lord Byron.

The one of them called only "Fleming" was most likely the Wilmington Fleming who had once attempted to blackmail Augusta Leigh with his copies of Caroline Lamb's explicit journals concerning Augusta and Byron's love affair. Caroline had foolishly let him borrow her journals while they were "good friends." Augusta had appealed to Lady Byron, who wrote to her cousin William Lamb about Fleming's demands. The future Lord Melbourne refused to be blackmailed over his wife's journals, and Lady Byron sought legal advice which she passed on to Augusta: No one in the family, particularly Augusta, should take any notice of Fleming's threats. Let him rave on if that was what he wished to do with his supposed "copies." To this, Augusta answered regretting that she had such unhelpful relatives and, against advice, had John Hanson go to Fleming. Lady Anne Wilmot-Horton would later wonder if Augusta had been blackmailed through her life, as she could find no other reason why a woman of her means—Augusta did, at first, have access to around 3,000 pounds per annum—was constantly in debt. Ada had no idea about any of this past history, shielded as she was from the underclass. It was no wonder that John Crosse, Fleming, and a bookie referred to as Malcolm wished to separate Ada from her mother, who knew much more about extortion—and specific extortionists—than did Ada. They impressed upon her that she, after all, was *Lord Byron's* daughter. They also told her all of her mother's friends hated her "like poison."

Except for one friend of her mother. Ada confided her gambling losses to Anna Jameson, swearing her to secrecy about that and about John Crosse. Hardworking Anna, who had a loan from Lady Byron, and who hardly made ends meet, lent a countess money and did keep Ada's floundering finances a secret from Lady Byron. Ada confided as well in her and her mother's mutual friend Woronzow Greig, sending him to Lady Byron to ask for an increase in Ada's allowance. Greig was the son, by her first marriage, of the famous woman scientist Mary Somerville, another friend of the family. Lady Byron trusted this amicable lawyer and amateur scientist. Greig was to impress on Lady Byron that Ada was in arrears because of the necessities of her station and her intellectual interests. "This is the *whole* my mother knows, she must not know more." If Lady Byron knew of "the *debt*," it would do immeasurable harm "in more ways than one."

Lovelace was doing a bit of gambling himself at the fashionable meets, but seemed to have no idea of what Ada was betting weekly. His passion was architecture, applied to constantly improving his properties, adding turrets and turns and even having a "Philosopher's Walk" for Charles Babbage at East Horsley, his estate, near Ockham in Surrey. At his summer residence at Ashley Combe, Lovelace did some superb landscaping. Though Ada suffered from increasingly horrific periods and hemorrhages, Lovelace never found enough money to make her a bathroom at any of his properties, even on the first floor as she requested. Nor did his interest extend to installing up-to-date water closets. He was an easy mark when it came to his wife's comings and goings, not when it came to advancing her money.

The Lovelaces' finances were indeed dwindling. The year after Lady Byron gave Ada the "hundreds" that she herself went and asked for, Ada and William moved from St. James's Square to a town house at 6 Great Cumberland Place. It needed many repairs and Lovelace took a loan from the Hen for 4,500 pounds secured by his life insurance policy. Money problems increased. In August after the Derby, Ada wrote to her fourteen-year-old animal-loving daughter that they were going to have to reduce their "family of dogs" at the Ockham estates. "They cost too much." Also "we must keep a horse or two less." Ostensibly, debts were attributed to William's passion for architectural improvements. He did win a prize the next year at the Great Exhibition of 1851 for improved brickmaking.

On her mother's fifty-ninth birthday, Ada wrote to Lady Byron under the heading "(*Doomsday*)." In it, Ada's peculiar mixture of naïve openness and deliberate fabrication appeared manic, like a back slapper who had too much to drink. She wished her mother would live as long as possible and that she herself would be "*as old* some day as you are." "Voltigeur's defeat distresses me less than your age." It was obvious she had staked her aristocratic friend's great horse, for she suggested another visit to her mother in that letter. A few days later, at the Epsom Derby a long shot came in and Ada lost 3,200 pounds. Mrs. Jameson wrote to Ottilie von Goethe that she heard the Countess of Lovelace had lost a fortune; she hoped it wasn't true.

It was. Ada was in debt with bookmakers, tipsters, merchants; she hadn't even paid the ten pounds or so outstanding to the chaperone on daughter Anne's first European trip. Her lover John Crosse had a partial solution. He convinced her to let him have paste replicas made of the Lovelace family jewels for a hundred pounds, and then he secretly pawned the Lovelace diamonds without Lord Lovelace knowing a thing. Paste and pawn came from a different world, one which now had its claws into Ada, and needed to be paid off. Dunned by bookmakers and, according to biographer Doris Langley Moore, also being blackmailed, an ill and depressed Ada was forced to enlighten her husband. Lovelace was stunned by the enormity of Ada's debts.

IT IS IMPOSSIBLE to impress upon the reader the extent of Lovelace's loving relationship with Lady Byron up until the middle of June 1851. This was the man Lady Byron told her daughter was *the comfort of my life.*" Lovelace's steadying arms had relieved Lady Byron of being the sole protector, the single mother, of an impressionable daughter. And as for Lovelace, he had never before experienced such motherly devotion. The Crow, however, was not an introspective man. Nor, would it seem, did he know much about women. On one hand, he frugally refused Ada a bathroom; on the other, there was John Crosse right under his nose having an affair with Ada and accepting expensive gifts. One shouldn't be derided for having faith in one's wife—or believing in the unconditional love of one's mother-in-law—but there you have it.

In the middle of June 1851, a despairing Lovelace arrived at Leamington, where his mother-in-law was resting. Lady Byron had just come from her estates at Kirkby with an aching face—a common problem in those days of primitive dentistry. She was taking a stop on her way to London, where dear Selina Doyle lay dying. Lovelace burst into his mother-in-law's quarters at eleven o'clock at night, intruding on the privacy, at times the *isolation*, so necessary to Lady Byron's stability. In panic, reaching out son to mother, he gave Lady Byron the shocking news of her daughter's enormous gambling debts.

"Genius is always a child!" Lady Byron cried out. Lovelace had allowed impressionable Ada to be exposed to low and unprincipled associates, the very people he should have protected her from. He sent her to the Doncaster meet *alone?* The moment he consented to Ada attending without him, he had *deserted* his wife! He knew what "overweening confidence" Ada had in her abilities. He was her husband, he had to be firm, not afraid of her violent eruptions! Ada's temper tantrums passed away and never did lasting harm. He knew that! Why hadn't Ada told her the truth last spring? Lady Byron moaned. "She might have had as many *thousands* as I gave her *hundreds*."

For fifteen years Lady Bryon believed her exceptional daughter had finally found the "protection" of a father's arms. That night at Leamington, she withdrew to her bedroom. When Lovelace asked to see her the next morning, she refused. Her affection for Lovelace, though strong, had been the conditional love of a mother who believed she had found a safe and fatherly haven for her Byronic genius of a daughter.

She wrote to Mrs. Jameson a few days later expressing her distress without revealing its cause, having no idea Jameson knew all about Ada's gaming and hadn't alerted her. She told her friend she had left her estates at Kirkby for Leamington on a rainy day, supposing she was "done with acting Queen upon a ludicrously small scale." However, on the road through the village, though the rain continued, "I was to pass lines (like Washerwomen's lines)" of suspended flowers.

"At last my carriage was stopped by a crowd of Women. They had assembled to offer me a hugh Garland, with a paper pinned to it expressive of their wish that I 'should live long and die happy.'—I got out of the Carriage to take the Garland, and demonstrate my gratification. Some of the elder school girls had come up to show me how well they had *worked* the Prodigal Son and Mount Vesuvius! You should have been there to admire." In her new bitterness, she made light of the gratitude of the girls for whom she had set up a school and of the women whom she had supported during the weavers' strike. Looking back at that scene, she told Jameson obliquely, "It seems to me now like a play—other and deeper interests even than those I have *told* you, have made the scenes unreal—so much loved by strangers—so little by the nearest!"

Selina Doyle died before her old friend could reach London, so Lady Byron returned to Brighton and sought out Robertson. Then she did something reminiscent of the dark days after her separation from Byron. She hired a small boat and "cradled" herself on the "rough" roll of waves. Once more she emptied her stomach into the foaming sea. "My whole frame seemed to be liberated."

Lovelace was stunned by the Hen's anger. Family friend Greig attempted to mediate. Using the approach that he and Dr. Lushington and other intimates knew worked best on the dowager Lady Byron, he first confessed his own error to Lady Byron—that of *not* considering her attitude toward Lovelace justified. He hoped she would forgive him. When he recently learned that Lovelace gave Ada an open-ended letter of credit to bring with her to the Doncaster races, he understood Lady Byron's position entirely. Lovelace was in the wrong to have done such a thing. "Remember that *he never had a Mother*, and let your heart pity while your judgement condemns him. He has lived a solitary and an isolated life, so far as parental ties and habits are concerned. I admit that he is to be blamed, but I think he is also to be pitied as . . . he *wishes* to act right."

The only problem with genial Greig's psychologically apt attempt to mediate with a woman who had an overriding faith in her own judgment was that Lady Byron had not known that Lovelace gave her daughter—this childlike genius with no sense of her own limitations—a *limitless* letter of credit! She only knew he had allowed her to go off to the races without his protection. Lady Byron became more

*The elderly Lushington, who attempted to reunite
Lady Byron and her daughter.*

convinced than ever that she was only loved by strangers stringing up paper flowers on rainy days.

Ada was outraged at her mother's treatment of Lovelace and took her husband's side. It also gave her a good excuse for not facing her mother after so many of her lies were exposed. That her daughter would not see her did not stop Lady Byron from settling Ada's debts. She sent Dr. Lushington to procure a complete list of what was owed. By that March 1851, Dr. Lushington was close to seventy, still as active as he was distinguished. As he traveled to Ada, Lushington remembered he had been the girl's champion almost since her birth. Arriving at 6 Cumberland Place, he was shocked. In the months since he had last seen the thirty-five-year-old, she had turned into an emaciated invalid who had to be rolled out into the London air in what he described to Lady Byron as a bath chair with rubber wheels. When

Lovelace had burst in on Lady Byron at Leamington, he brought along a worrisome doctor's report as well. Lady Byron had been so distraught that she seemed unimpressed by it. She may have thought he brought it to placate her. Ada always had bad periods. Her health was constantly up and down.

However, Ada was in decline. Her Black Dwarf was uterine cancer. As doctors gave hopeful and erroneous prognoses, it was already spreading into her intestinal tract. Not that anything could have saved her, but she was heading toward excruciating pain. There is a portrait of Ada at her piano at this time. One could easily mistake the woman in her mid-thirties for a frail innocent child of twelve. In a way, she was. As Ada's physical condition worsened, her gambling cohorts pointed their shark's teeth at her, and a frightened Ada agreed finally to see her mother.

"SUCH A DAY," Lady Byron wrote to Robertson of the reunion with her daughter in London that spring of 1852. "I believe I am now in possession of all that has been so studiously kept from me." She told Robertson these revelations did not come "from spontaneous confidence." They came from Ada's "fine capacity for arriving at a Truth"—through inductive reasoning. Ada had reached "the conclusion (in her own words) that the wisest course for her is to consider me as her *best friend*—that she should do so at this moment may save her life, and be of the greatest consequence in other ways—"

The "other ways" in which Lady Byron could save her daughter's life were daunting. For a short time in June, Lady Byron took Ada off pain medications, for which her later detractors demonized her, suggesting Ada was allowed to suffer through the course of her illness for the good of her soul. In fact, Ada was given opiates, belladonna; cannabis was discussed as a possibility; and finally it arrived—the water bed. In that unmedicated period Ada was able to unburden her conscience to her mother. It was then that she told her that she had given her lover John Crosse the Lovelace family diamonds to pawn and sub-

Ada in the last year of her life.

stituted paste. Ada hadn't dared include this on Dr. Lushington's list of her debts. What was going to happen when her husband found out? Lady Byron acted immediately. She sent Dr. Lushington with the 800 pounds plus interest to reclaim the diamonds from the pawnbroker, and gave them back to her relieved and suffering daughter.

Ada was in constant pain for all the cheerful prognoses she was offered. Her sickroom was moved to the drawing room floor, where she could be closer to whatever activity of life she could perform, at the same time as she was more easily attended to by her round-the-clock nurses and her chief physician, Dr. West. She was able to get to her piano occasionally, took meals at table at times, wrote a plethora of notes in these months, all in pencil. Pencil was a sign of decline. The person could no longer control inkpot and pen, and was usually writing in bed. Lady Byron lodged in London that summer to be with her daughter every day; Lovelace split time between Ockham and London.

When Ada could not get to her piano, daughter Anne played for her—not as well, but that no longer mattered. How could she have ever wished not to have a daughter? Ada asked her mother more than once. Anne came up to her grandmother one day after Lady Byron left the sickroom and asked, "Whatever will Daddy do?"

"Not another word would she utter. I burst into tears."

RECONCILED WITH ADA, her mother wrote to Robertson that Ada told her she could no longer go "24 hours" without prayer. Lady Byron hoped for a cure. The pain was such that Ada could not stay still. Her "strange contortions" were a cruel mirror image of her fidgeting childhood. Lady Byron heard of a successful cure of a case like Ada's by mesmerism. "I only want to mesmerize her once." Which she did in July, after dubious Ada agreed to it. The mesmerist stilled her for a short time, leaving her with a flushed face and hot hands. The experiment was not repeated.

What had the power to calm Ada was this renewed contact with her mother. When one reads in Lady Byron's unpublished papers of the two of them together, it is almost as if the past were rekindled—perhaps "redeemed" is a better word—and the child in Ada no longer had to search for her mother through the flight of birds and the invention of steam-run machines. When finally diagnosed properly, Ada told her mother, the thing she most dreaded was "the idea of your being far away." That same day, the actor Mrs. Sartoris, Lady Byron's friend, came and sang Handel. That evening, as her mother left the room, Ada said "the worst of dying was that 'it must be done *alone*.'"

By the middle of July, Lady Byron decided "to write a journal" and to make her friend Emily Fitzhugh, a minister's daughter, "the keeper of it." She wished "to write it like a *disembodied spirit*," setting down "pure fact," not personal feeling. This disembodied persona served her better in Ada's sickroom than it did when speaking with Robertson about her life with Byron. For she was now caregiver in the service of her daughter, her one object "to make myself the medium of Christian influences, everlasting cheering."

Twentieth-century critics of Lady Byron emphasize "Christian influences" as if mother spent her time sermonizing a dying daughter. Far from it. Ada wished to make her peace with her maker before she died, a common desire in the nineteenth century, and in doing so her mother was a help. However, neither was doctrinaire. Ada was a Unitarian, and Christianity to Lady Byron was following he who did good. Lady Byron's "everlasting cheering" did reflect Ada's hope of redemption. But it also meant that Lady Byron as mother rose beyond her own grief. When Ada's eyes opened, she had the comfort of her mother's loving face. When she spoke, she had the comfort of an honest response. In the unpublished journal one realizes the ongoing conversation between mother and daughter was the bridge that healed the rift between them and brought Ada peace. "I don't see my way out of this," Ada said, and felt "regrets" at not having done more while she lived.

"I pointed out few thinking minds ever felt their ends accomplished yet the survivors had been influenced by those lives in an *unforeseen* manner leading us to believe that the ends of our existence were hidden from us."

Ada said, "I suppose the process of dying is not so painful as some things we suffer in life." She told her mother it was very curious that "she had never felt discontented *for a moment*—that the constant nausea was the most difficult to contend against."

During the last week of July, Lovelace had been at East Horsley with friend Greig. They were speaking of Ada and her illness and of Lady Byron's coldness to her son-in-law when they were caught in a sudden summer shower. They ducked into a nearby shed to wait it out. As they continued their conversation there, Greig happened to mention John Crosse's wife and children. Whatever did he mean, Lovelace asked in astonishment. John Crosse was a bachelor.

"Is it possible that you do not know Mr. Crosse is married?"

"You must be mistaken."

Lovelace, unaware that Crosse was Ada's lover, would not believe his friend had purposely misrepresented himself. He called Crosse on it and within a few days received one conflicting story after another, which Lovelace tried to believe, at the same time sending each of these rather loony fabrications on for Greig's legal opinion. John Crosse, on his part, was tipped off by Lovelace's questioning him. He got to 6 Cumberland Place as fast as he could in the first days of August. Maid Mary Wilson made sure he could visit while Lady Byron was not present. Crosse once more left with the Lovelace diamonds to pawn. This time he obtained Lovelace's letter of open credit to Ada, as well, one that could be used against Lovelace in court. Later that month the shadowy "Fleming" found his way to Ada while she was alone. Not only did he gain access unobserved, but he brought a lawyer with him and Ada signed a life insurance policy and deed of appointment over to him at a time when it was obvious she could hardly hold a pencil.

Ada told her mother that through her life she would always "try experiments" but their outcome carried no weight with her. She would try again. Was Ada aware that she had once more "experimented" by giving Crosse the family jewels for a second time? She may have had a shadowy recollection, but soon it was erased. In the middle of August at two in the morning, Ada's screams woke up the household. Lady Byron was called from her lodgings. Lovelace was already by Ada's bedside when Lady Byron arrived and together they witnessed "Indescribable pain." On all fours, the only position that offered the slightest relief, Ada howled. Then after a series of epileptic seizures, Ada fell into a sort of coma. Lady Byron went over and touched Lovelace's arm "kindly" when she passed. "(Could not help it)," she wrote, "but no notice was taken."

Could God's love be proved? Ada asked her mother when she returned to her senses a few days later.

"Can you prove what I feel towards you, Ada? Yet can you disbelieve it?"

In the last week of August, Lady Byron moved in to what she called "Lord Lovelace's house" to be "in constant attendance upon Ada." She was put in charge of 6 Cumberland Place by her son-in-law's request. "I am not fond of power," Lady Byron wrote, "but I must *submit to rule*." She meant it. When a college for women was being founded a few years previously, she was willing "to be on the *committee* of the New College," but she refused to be a "Patroness" when asked: "I want to give advice *without* authority to enforce it." Her advice: Maria Edgeworth should be "*first* in the list of Patronesses" and "Miss Segewick should represent Educational America."

The day before Lady Byron moved in, on August 21, Charles Dickens came to visit. Though many artists had come, particularly to sing for her, Ada herself had asked for Dickens. He "amused" her, Lady Byron wrote. Dickens was a world-famous reader of his work; audiences thronged to hear him. His entrance caused a stir among the staff. One imagines the downstairs servants coming far enough upstairs and those maids above leaving their chores and peering down into the drawing room where Ada laid tended by her nurses. Dr. West was there, as well as the visitors who dropped by to inquire. Lady Byron and granddaughter Anne were in attendance. Ada had requested her friend read the death scene from *Dombey and Son*. Dickens's voice rang out through 6 Great Cumberland Place and there were plenty of tears when he ended with: "Now the boat was out at sea, but gliding smoothly on. And now there was a shore before him. The golden ripple on the wall came back again, and nothing else stirred in the room. The old old fashion! The fashion that came in with our first garments, and will last unchanged until our race has run its course, and the wide firmament is rolled up like a scroll. The old, old fashion—Death!"

If death had any art to it at all, Dickens's reading would have brought down Ada's curtain. She seemed prepared. She wished her husband "every earthly happiness." She begged her mother not to let her be buried alive. (That happened a lot in France.) Daughter Anne and son Byron, on leave from his ship, were allowed to sponge Ada's hands and face. It reminded her of rippling waters and she smiled. Her children did too. The next day, when Lady Byron moved in to be with Ada "day and night," Lord Lovelace took son Byron with him to Ockham to repair after that horrendous scene of his mother's seizures.

It had been Lovelace who insisted—actually forced—son Byron

to go to sea at the age of thirteen, against the boy's objections. The father wanted to make a man of him, and had been severe in his treatment of his firstborn since Byron's earliest years, ridiculing his sensitivities. When the Seventh Lord Byron thought of sending his son to sea at an early age, Lady Byron would write to him of the damage it had done to her grandson.

"Can nothing save me?" Ada asked her mother after her husband and Byron left.

"Nothing," Lady Byron replied, but there might still be ways for easing her suffering. Cheerfulness did not mean duplicity.

Ada told her mother that she had many regrets concerning her. "I have been thinking what a strange fate yours has been."

"I replied, 'So would the fate of most people appear if all were known.'"

So was Ada's: "I had been thinking how she might have some pleasing feeling associated with that last resting place," Lady Byron wrote in her journal letter, for Ada had told her she didn't want to be buried at Ockham. "I determined to propose Newstead." If this caused people to gossip, what could the opinions of the world "be to *me*?" She told her daughter she had an alternative to the Lovelace family vault to suggest.

Ada looked at her eagerly: "Well?"

"Newstead," I replied.

"Her face lighted up with pleasure and relief and she said 'We have settled it. I have written to Colonel Wildman about the spot situated by my Father.'" She hadn't told her mother because "I thought you would be angry with me."

"I dispelled that apprehension entirely." However: "I was secretly wounded by the *reserve*. My journal is not however to be feelings of my own—away with them."

Even in their new intimacy, Lady Byron was still Lady Byron, shooing away her feelings. Ada was still Ada, keeping a secret about wanting to be with her father that might displease her mother. When with her husband, she did not wish to displease him either. "Within a week of her seizure in August," Lovelace wrote to Lady Byron, "Ada told me that before her hour came she should speak strongly to you about your injustice to me." Ada never spoke up for her husband. She had long since lost whatever affection she once had for him. Instead, her guilty conscience was such that awakening from the seizure to find her mother and husband with her, she told them that after death she was sure she would have "a million years" of the pain she was suffering.

"Her terror and distress were great. At last she turned to me earnestly: 'May I ask God to forgive me from *you*?'

"My answer freed her from all fear. 'Have I lived in vain?'"

Then Ada turned to Lovelace: "'Will you forgive me?—'"

"This is the *best* moment she has had and for *that* she must have been kept alive," Lady Byron wrote.

Later that day, that "*best* moment" turned to fright. Ada saw the ghost of Lord Byron. Lady Byron's usually clear handwriting mirrored mounting stress. Ada had mistaken a dream for reality: "That her *father* had sent her this disease and doomed her to an early death!" Disturbed as Ada was, her mother finally made her laugh. Her handwriting deteriorating, Lady Byron then wrote: "She says she hopes to *live*. I said, 'You are dying—you may not have another day use this well.'"

Ada would have three more months.

"Have I lived to hear it?" Lady Byron wrote in September. "—She has just said 'There is but one reason why I could wish for life—*to live with you entirely*.'" With her mother's protection she might have lived "happily for herself and others." Lady Byron kept "saying to myself 'Wonderful God! There is something sublime in the redeemed heart. I have the feeling of looking up to it.'" The redeemed heart had hard truths to reveal to her husband, though she did not tell him about the pawning of the diamonds. Instead, in her penciled scrawl Ada "confided all my letters, property and affairs to my mother and informed her of *all* that had passed respective of the family jewels." Before Lord Lovelace went into Ada's room that third week of September, to listen to Ada's confession about her affair with John Crosse, Lady Byron demanded that "he must hear what she might wish to say, but reply as little as possible and as calmly." Instead, "I saw his angry countenance after he left her," and "he was unwilling to speak of the Interview to me, as he usually does. I inquired—he said 'It was very painful.'" Lovelace had found it "impossible *not* to contradict" Ada, though before he left his wife he did say, "'God be merciful to you!'"

"God be merciful to *him*! Pharisee as he is, from whom his poor penitent wife could draw no kinder expression by her complete submission and humbling. For such was her spirit—*I knew*."

Right after that painful interview, Lovelace put in writing that when he was out of London, "it is my wish that Lady Byron should be considered in every respect as mistress of my home and family and to possess all the authority of Lady Lovelace and myself." He also agreed with Ada and made Lady Byron guardian of the two younger children, Anne and Ralph, who had recently arrived. He must have expected, after Ada's confession, to be away from home more often.

Lovelace later complained to Lady Byron: "That I should forgive Ada the wrong she confessed appeared to you so simple as to elicit from you neither surprise nor approbation. And you who remain unforgiving to the end accuse me of rigidity!" Of course, what the poor man would never understand was that Lady Byron in those months had become every inch a mother—only not his. No longer was she the "Hen," she was the Lioness protecting her cub.

At the end of September, in one of her penciled notes, Ada confirmed that she wished to be buried "by my Father's side" with a "simple little marble monument," with a quote from St. James. She double-underscored "If he hath committed sins, they shall be forgiven him." She took a "fancy" for her mother's black muslin shawl to be wrapped around her shoulders. "All causes of mental disturbances have been averted and if the mind turns to the past, it is only for the relief of speaking to me." Ada "liked to be told little pleasing things." Lady Byron "made her smile, almost laugh, by saying to her (having read a bequest of hers to the neighboring Poor in the County) 'You mean to make the poor people rejoice in your death'—but I added 'it will be a tearful joy.'"

In a jagged, pain-ridden handwriting Lady Byron told her journal, "My fog thickens and my throat and chest too." She looked at her daughter as she wrote. "I see more deadly paleness and some drop of the jaw yet it is not yet the seal of Death." On October 1: "Yesterday evening I sat by her bed in Twilight, silently—then I said, 'I feel what I must call happiness—so calm and thankful!'" Ada answered, "'And I share it in a degree—at least I am *not unhappy*—only sometimes when in great pain.'"

A spent Lady Byron took her granddaughter to Westminster Abbey the following Sunday. The day before, young Anne had experienced her mother losing sight and hearing. She told her grandmother going to Westminster "'did her good.'" Music raised her above the painful things and "'made life appear only a dream and the reality beyond it.'" Always devoted to granddaughter Anne, Lady Byron wrote, "I had gone for *her* sake—for rest alone would have been better for me."

When her sight and hearing returned two days later, Ada pointed out to her mother a "'man all light, sitting at the foot of her bed and calling her to come with him.'" She was sure that "*I* must see him also." Since her attack in mid-August when her howls ripped through the house, Ada's memory of preceding events had fogged. Suddenly tranquility was shattered. In looking over her papers in October, Ada remembered. She had handed John Crosse the Lovelace diamonds a second time! Her panic was so severe that her mother thought it might kill her. Lady Byron tried to calm her, reassured Ada she would take care of everything. Which she did, retrieving the diamonds for under 900 pounds. This time Lady Byron kept the jewels and the paste replicas in her possession until she was able to deposit them at Drummonds. Lovelace still didn't know.

Ada expressed "bitterest regret that she had not earlier *trusted* me—that she *could not*." Lady Byron comforted her daughter, saying that all of us had at times trusted "shadows."

"The shadows are gone, are they not?" Ada asked fearfully. Her mother assured her "they would never again return."

Mary Wilson and her husband, who had facilitated her private meetings with her lover Crosse and with Fleming, had come to Ada through Babbage, whom Lady Byron respected. Lady Byron dismissed them in October, to Babbage's anger and to the dismay of later critics who saw it as another example of Lady Byron's implacability. Why wouldn't she dismiss them? They had colluded with John Crosse, yet Lady Byron did not yet know half of it—that the blackmailer Fleming had been allowed entrance with a lawyer at a time when Ada was hardly in her right mind. However, Ada begged her mother that "no consequences painful to them should be inflicted, unless absolutely necessary." So Lady Byron later paid the Wilsons the 100 pounds Ada had bequeathed each, sending with the money a letter clearly stating she had no use for them and that she honored the bequest only because she obeyed all her daughter's final wishes.

"The less serious topics" spoken of in October have been "amusing anecdotes of the Children, simple plans for the Poor, using her—power *to put things in order* (order now a word of hers)." Ada also expressed a *"passionate"* desire to see natural beauty, and was given prints of mountains, flowers, birds with bright plumage. Illness had also turned Ada less self-involved. She was quite aware she was comforted by competent doctors and an entire nursing staff. She wanted to leave something to help the poor who were ill. Though Lady Byron always preferred Florence Nightingale's older sister, when she conferred with Florence concerning Ada's bequest, she admired Nightingale's way of entering into the plan with her strong mind and managerial skills.

When Emily Fitzhugh blamed Ada for becoming "alienated" from her mother, Lady Byron would not have it. Once more she protected her cub. Emily must "remember the 'conspiracy' the uniform image of me that was reflected from all sides—the terrible, stern, unrelenting Lady B." With Ada having a guilty conscience, how "could she have sought *such* a Parent?" Alienation was not her daughter's fault, but the result of the "black treachery" of false friends. "She was a mere child—and became a *slave*." She told her mother, "There never was such a conspiracy as that against *you* on all sides."

There had been a concerted attempt "to enrage her towards me—*and prevent any renewal of intercourse.*" Who could love such a woman? Lady Byron told her friend to reread the ending stanzas of The Third Canto of *Childe Harold's Pilgrimage* to underscore the world's negative conception.

"She has mentioned as one of the causes of her loss of moral perceptions the Idolatry in which she was encouraged by all around her." They praised Lord Byron saying he was as good a man as he was a poet, and a "halo" was thrown around his aberrations. "Gradually *I* was then placed in an unfavorable light . . . as if I could not enter into the Byron nature and could sympathize as little with the Daughter as the Father—yet she says she never ceased when with me to feel differently, and to be drawn towards me—and *therefore* she kept out of the way of being influenced by me." Now however, "the voice of Nature and the Will of God together have given me my Child again." She corrected herself. "No not *again*—for she never was mine."

Ada's children surrounded her. Ralph, the youngest and meekest, knit cuffs for her, Anne, the middle child, played piano for her, Byron nursed her. When Byron was summoned back to his ship, Lady Byron was advised not to allow Ada a parting. "She would die they say under the emotion. I must take it on myself to deprive him of that Farewell."

On October 21 at seven in the evening, she watched her teenaged grandson look "through the half opened door at his Mother's wasted form and hands—her face he could not see—she was awake—but unconscious of that *last* look—more affecting to me than what was ever more effecting."

Soon after, Ada called for her mother "to talk cheerfully to her." When Lady Byron told her daughter Byron was gone "she said she could not have borne to know he was *going*."

"Poor Anne came to me for consolation last night." Her granddaughter told her "she never *hopes anything* here, only 'beyond,'" but "drawing is her great comfort." (Lady Byron hired John Ruskin as Anne's drawing master.)

"'O what a *good bargain* my Illness has been,'" Ada exclaimed at

the end of October. However, a few weeks later Ada's "renewed agonies have been mitigated by Bella Donna but Dr West says we must
not expect it to be effective long. I am no comfort to her now."

Ada had warned Lady Byron in August that her mother's good
influence would be wasted on Byron, just as it had been wasted on her
when she was young: "He has so many of my faults." It takes a Byron
to catch a Byron, she quipped. However, his grandmother had witnessed Byron "gliding" around his mother's room with the "gentle-
ness of an experienced Nurse." "I see his character—as fixed principle
to do what is Right." In November, Lady Byron only had "time for
facts." Byron had jumped ship and a warrant had been issued for him.
He made two attempts to get hired as a common sailor on an American
ship and "had been living and sleeping and drinking with the common
sailors." Byron, the titled Lord Ockham, called himself Johnny Okey
and escaped the police by living quietly. "I believe I will withdraw
now from the position of advisor," Lady Byron wrote.

"'Speak to me,'" Ada whispered a few days later, breaking a long
silence. "I spoke of the persons I had seen today and of their feelings
toward her—"

"'It seems to me interminable—I *may* get a little strength again to
look at a book or write.'" Just saying that exhausted Ada until "some
support was administered—Then she said that her great distress was
the inability to *utter* her thoughts, that she was *always* thinking when
awake."

It was "the last time she has spoken to me." In the stillness, Lady
Byron sketched Ada, who was perhaps still thinking. Hardly a consolation as her mother traced the outlines of her wasted face, as if to hold
on to what remained.

Two weeks later Ada was still alive. Only "*physical* relief" was of use.
Ada was at the stage which Robertson wrote so realistically about in one
of his most powerful sermons, "Victory over Death." She had moved
past her human life—only her wracked body remained. Lady Byron
listened to the groans of her daughter while outside a little bird sang and
in another room Lord Lovelace sat alone. She had bitter thoughts about

Byron, Viscount Ockham, sent to sea at thirteen.
Lady Byron suggested naming her first grandson after
her husband. He rebelled against the aristocracy and
became a railroad worker before his early death.

her lack of Christian charity toward him. She had bitter thoughts about foolish Anna Jameson, who could not have known the condition Lady Byron was in when she sent her last letter castigating Ada's veracity, erroneously thinking Ada had spoken against her. Then the mother put down her pen. The time had come to tell Ada she was about to die. She went over to her child's bed and said something about trusting in God, "or words of that kind for I can't recollect." What she said as she bid her daughter farewell moved both Dr. West and the nurses to tears, he later told her. Perhaps she had been "a *very little* Comfort," she wrote.

On Saturday night, November 27, after much agitation and torment Ada was tranquil. Lady Byron left the room to speak with Dr. Lushington, but Lovelace and Greig called her back in.

Lady Byron sketched her dying daughter.

"Ada lay so quiet and like herself I could not believe it tho all said she was gone."

Lady Byron took a candle and brought it to her daughter's mouth to try her breath, and then she brought it to her eyes. She must have kept repeating this motion, for the assembled men had trouble convincing the mother that her child was gone. No matter how often she tested, the candle did not flicker, nor did Ada blink. Finally she stopped.

"Then they wished me to go to my room." There "every thought turned into *one*." Hours later she crept downstairs, where she could be alone with her daughter. Laid out, Ada did not look like herself. She regretted her grandchildren viewing their mother the next day.

"I cannot yet banish the pictures of agonies I have witnessed day after day—and when I have fulfilled some remaining duties here I must seek change," she wrote. "How much I have learned in the last three months!—how ignorant one seems to have been and how much in need of pardon for that ignorance!"

"*If I had loved her less, she would have believed I loved her more.* If I had been anxious she should *appear* to advantage—that she should be the object of admiration for person and talents—all this would have been intelligible to her as the language of affection, but I could not express what I did not feel. A course consistent with truth might perhaps have been found had I known how little she cared for all that seemed to me the most convincing proof of my affection for her and yet these were not mainly abstract—watching her in illness—providing her with enjoyment that *she* asked, etc.

"What should I have done?"

"To see clearly *too late*," Lady Byron lamented, her "mental suffering" at times transcending her "body's power of endurance."

"How weak I have been, tortured and harassed as I was." She couldn't stop thinking of "what *Might have been*."

Lady Byron left Great Cumberland Place a few days later wishing to go abroad, "but *must not* I fear. These children bind me. I am *ALL* to them."

Ada died at thirty-six, the same age as her father. She had told her mother she would. She was transported to her father's lost estate, to be buried in the Byron vault in the church outside Newstead Abbey as she wished.

However, rather than the simplicity she requested, the Countess of Lovelace's coffin was "too ostentatious," according to Ada's dear Dandy Bob, who attended. It was massive; "escutcheons and coronets" were "everywhere." They and the handles were silver. "Lord Lovelace's taste, not Lady Byron's." With regal ceremony, Ada was placed in the chaotic vault of her wicked forefathers' bones. Some of their remains had been rearranged so that her coffin could touch her father's, as she wished and he had prophesied:

> My daughter! with thy name this song begun—
> My daughter! With thy name thus much shall end—
>   I see thee not,—I hear thee not,—but none
>   Can be so wrapt in thee; thou art the friend
>   To whom the shadows of far years extend:
>   Albeit my brow thou never should'st behold,
>   My voice shall with thy future visions blend
>   And reach into thy heart,—when mine is cold,—
> A token and a tone, even from thy father's mould.

Lady Byron did not attend. She had a flight of fancy though, that by Ada's being buried next to her father, Ada joined hands with him and with her mother, uniting all three through love. The fancy faded quickly, like early snow.

BOTH DR. LUSHINGTON and barrister Greig were kept busy during the winter after Ada's death. John Crosse expected to be paid off to return Ada's love letters and Lovelace's letter of credit. Fleming was expecting Ada's life insurance to be paid to him. Lady Byron would have none of it, not even "for *her.*" Mother and daughter "understood each other—She trusted me with the *whole* truth that I might make it of use, if possible, not make her appear better by proclaiming her virtues or concealing her transgressions." She likened John Crosse "to a ferocious bird of prey—I fancied him standing over his dying victim cruel and relentless."

The lawyers were insistent. Not paying these men off would do no good. If things went to court, they'd lose even as they won. "All would become public—nothing could be kept secret—." It would harm the living as well as the dead, and that included her grandchildren. As the winter progressed, Lady Byron relented, anger turning to acceptance. The life insurance was paid out to Fleming and Crosse received money before destroying Ada's letters to him as well as Lovelace's letter of credit.

These threats of suits, these paying off of extortioners after holding out, these many tangles sorted out by her lawyers, were a constant through Lady Byron's life, and again her critics blamed her exclusively. There was no understanding that being as wealthy as she was and being a Byron whose every action could be scandalous grist for the press made her quite vulnerable to blackmail.

Usually she cared nothing about public opinion, but she was perturbed when Charles Babbage threatened to take her to court. He had been Ada's executor until Ada replaced him with her mother. Babbage believed Lady Byron had forced her will on her daughter. He was furious that Lady Byron had taken over at 6 Cumberland and that the Wilsons had been summarily dismissed. Babbage also believed he was owed furniture and books. Lady Byron respected Babbage, never linked him with the extortioners who had circled her daughter. She considered him a gentleman and a man of honor and, stunned by his anger, thought they could reconcile. It was not to be.

Two months after Ada's death she wrote to Robertson: "When I am *forced* into a position of Antagonism, one of the greatest pains I suffer and the least understood, is the suppression of kind feelings. I am so sorry, even grieved, for those who are suffering from false visions of relative facts, or from internal warfare, that I long to express sympathy, & yet my own course (which I suppose to be that of truth) would be damaged, as people think, by my doing so. Is there no way of reconciling the want to be kind with the duty to be true?"

At first this response appears evidence of that narcissism of hers. She believed cutting off offenders with silence was the right thing to do and that she was forced to suffer isolation because of her rightful convictions. However, in this case the "people" who "think" she would be damaged by not repressing kindness were her lawyers. "I feel this very strongly about poor Babbage," she wrote to Robertson. "I know intuitively that his passions and his better nature are tearing him to pieces. Is there no voice to say to him—'Be still!' It is very hard to be represented by those who act for me, though I cannot say it is without my sanction, seeing no other course open. I do not believe that you or any friend of mine can enter fully into this part of my trouble."

"You know that she is very peculiar in her views, opinions and actions," Greig attempted to explain to Lovelace: "These you cannot expect to change. You must therefore take her as she is—and receive and cultivate the opportunity now." In January 1853 there was a hope of reconciliation, for Lady Byron "proposes that you should make the best of each other as your interests are identical—the children's welfare." Greig advised Lovelace not to throw away the opportunity presented and "accept her overture in her own terms, omitting entirely all notice of any other part of her letter which might lead to discussion."

Lovelace had received no sympathy for his tragedy from Lady

Byron. She had admonished him severely for keeping Ada's debts a secret from her. But what about her? Lovelace had kept Ada's gambling debts a secret from Lady Byron for *one* month after learning of them. Lady Byron had kept the pawning of his family jewels a secret from him for over *six* months, until after Ada's death, when he was apprised of it through Dr. Lushington. Perhaps in his own anger and grief he couldn't help himself, or perhaps a characteristic abstruseness added to his own isolated nature and aristocratic pride. Not heeding Greig's advice, Lovelace wrote to his mother-in-law in accusatory and stiff language, beginning: "No casuistry will convince me that after your unmitigated censure of my concealment from you [of Ada's debts], you were entitled to suppress the jewel transactions of 1852."

He had rung the death knell on their relationship.

A few months later Lovelace wrote Lady Byron the most supplicating letter, telling her how much she meant to him and how he hoped for a reconciliation. It might have melted someone else's heart. Years later son Ralph, who carried animosity toward his father, would wonder if his grandmother's forgiveness would have made some dent in his father's increasing severity. Perhaps in the long run nothing would have helped mend the breach. It is doubtful that Lady Byron could ever forgive her son-in-law for not protecting her genius of a daughter, any more than she forgave herself. On Ada's first birthday she had written:

> Thine is the smile and thine the bloom
>   Where hope might fancy ripened charms;
> But mine is dyed in Memory's gloom—
>   Thou art not in a Father's arms!

She realized too late that what Ada had needed from earliest days was to be in her Mother's arms.

Part Three

13

STRANGE HISTORY

*T*hree months after Ada's death, Frederick Robertson let Lady Byron know he had completed going through the many letters, journals, and statements she had placed in his keeping. While she had been caring for Ada, he had pondered over her "strange history" and ways in which it might be possible to tell all.

"I shall give pain to no one near and dear to me by speaking," Lady Byron wrote in a memo to herself. She could now judge Byron "without a bias—for certainly I have always had one—I had looked upon him as almost sanctified by being her Father. All that has ceased." Also, writing might solace her, for, with Ada gone, "I have to find out for what purposes I can live."

Robertson would have been her ideal collaborator, however a warning of his own strange history had occurred during the Christmas service two years previously. Right before his sermon, Robertson collapsed at the pulpit. "The hollies seemed to change to cypresses," Lady Byron wrote. The collapse, the sudden weaknesses that he hid as best he could, the terrible pain in his head—all ominous symptoms. He sought out the doctors of London. One medical man gave him a "hash" of medicine that did no good. Another told him to give up his ministry, his writings, do nothing. The third told him—eat lettuce.

Robertson returned to work. He wrote to Lady Byron that it would take the pen of Coleridge the "Opium Eater" that February

1853 to describe the miserable thoughts coming to him in the winter solitude: "I walked over that wild scene of glittering snow, unbroken plain, glaring sunshine, bleak and silent, all the waters locked in ice, and the sea booming in the distance."

Spring came, and with it Easter Sunday. Robertson gave a sermon filled with "melancholy views" concerning "the nothingness of all in this life, and the mortality of all our affections." His dour view of his own mortality did not correspond to the letters he wrote to Lady Byron during Ada's illness. They were full of clergyman-like consolation, a paean to suffering being more than worth it for the salvation of Ada's soul. "Welcome to your piece of the Cross," he wrote to Lady Byron. Some of the congregation found the Easter sermon "desolating" and Lady Byron thought Robertson should be made aware: "And I told him."

Hardly considering it a "Victory over Death" to die at the age of thirty-seven, Robertson fought his fate like the soldier he had hoped to be and remained resistant to his share of the Cross. He did not repress his anger and his despair. "My very dear friend," he wrote to Lady Byron in his last note at the beginning of August 1853. It was in pencil. He had scarcely the "manhood" to hold a pen. He told Lady Byron he could not come to her. He had fallen attempting to go downstairs: "If you can call here, would you kindly let me know the hour beforehand and will arrange so as not to be interrupted." She left her own sickbed to see him, he wrote proudly to a friend. With all that, he could only speak with her for three minutes. He died on August 15, 1853. Nine months after Lady Byron lost Ada: "He is gone." Ada dead at thirty-six, Robertson at thirty-seven.

Shops closed the day of his funeral, and the outpouring of grief was massive. Lady Byron did not assume her rightful place in the carriage with the family. When asked why, she said she was not worthy even to walk behind the hearse of such a man. It was from another vantage point that she witnessed. She climbed the hill off the Lewes Road from which one saw the churchyard: "I was there soon after Eleven on foot, wishing to mingle with the people," she wrote to close friend Caro

George. Many of the townsfolk were already "sitting on the banks overlooking the grave or watching for the Procession."

The bells tolled and Lady Byron saw the road below her "blackened" by the procession of over 2,000 mourners, those from the Atheneum, those from the Working Men's Institute. All classes of people. When the coffin was taken from the hearse and borne into the chapel, there was a slight shudder from the townspeople around her. The service completed, the coffin was brought from the church to the open grave. From the hill she could see the "Working Classes" most clearly grouped around it. The fine, clear voice of the minister rose up to those looking down.

Soon after his death, Robertson's family arranged for the publication of his sermons. His words had stirred his congregation. As an American newspaper put it, "Every sufferer found in him a neighbour, every weak one a helper, and every outcast a brother." Still, Robertson had refused to publish a collection of his sermons while he lived. He abhorred the idea of being mistaken for some sort of evangelist crying out to the masses. As he said, his heart was with the common man, but his tastes were with the aristocrats. The posthumous *Sermons Preached at Brighton* by Frederick William Robertson became an immediate bestseller with edition after edition printed through the rest of the century. Posthumously he became known as "Robertson of Brighton," his name forever interlinked with the genteel watering town for which he maintained mixed feelings. Talk of strange history: The Dowager Lady Byron was asked to write *his* life. She declined.

Lady Byron's papers—letters, her notes, his notes, the "Conversations," the "Interviews"—the entire bulk of material for her memoir—were sealed up and all those boxes returned to her. She was again confronted with the raw material of her life with Lord Byron.

She needed a collaborator if she were to write a memoir, a first-rate writer who could aid her in forming a narrative structure that would allow her access to her voice. Why not Anna Jameson? Mrs. Jameson had never been considered.

"I think you and Mrs Jameson will understand each other better," she once wrote to Robertson, "if I tell you some points in her character from twenty years knowledge of it. She is the very reverse of my presumptive Correspondent—neither sure of herself, nor of any one else." It made Lady Byron sad to see her friend so often "resting her heart upon something purely fictitious, because it has so little real to rest upon." She was alluding not only to Jameson's fluctuating faith, but to her romantic attraction to her female friends. Yet, when it came to taking care of her mother and "destitute" sisters, she was as "practical as if she were not Artistic. Of her married life I *know* nothing."

Of the many literary women who had been Lady Byron's friends, two had "the cloudless brightness of Faith" combined with "original minds." These were the playwright Joanna Baillie and the mathematician Mary Somerville. She had also known "minds of a secondary class however superior, but I have wandered from my object—Jameson." Had she? However superior in certain aspects, for Lady Byron, intellectually Jameson was "secondary class."

During Ada's last months, Jameson, with her adoration of the women she loved, and her flair for the dramatic, let Lady Byron know that Ada had confided her debts and her lover to her and that she could not tell Lady Byron as Ada had sworn her to secrecy. When Lady Byron did not respond to this admission, Jameson interpreted her silence to mean Ada was speaking against her and was spreading falsehoods. However, Ada had not maligned her. "*All* I have heard has been most favorable to Mrs J. most distinctly." Still, Jameson continued "to believe Ada her enemy!" When Mrs. Jameson was not allowed to visit the sickroom, she blamed Ada, not Lady Byron.

The day before Ada died, Lady Byron wrote in her journal: "I should be sorry for Mrs J.—if she knew under what circumstances she had just sent me a letter full of bitter resentment toward me and unmitigated severity toward Ada—whose character for veracity has been sacrificed by me to Mrs J.'s justification—was not this enough to have appeased her?—It is past reconciliation now."

However, her usual curtain of silence did not descend. "You say to be just," Lady Byron wrote in January 1854, a year and a half after the rupture, "as if I have been unjust! My justice toward you has been *Gratitude*—How could it be otherwise when you, who could so often command the first place in the regard of others were generously content, as you have told me, with the second in *mine*."

A month later: "In the close of the year 1852, when my whole being was so absorbed that I could not have borne any added excitement or agitation and whilst you were accusing me of being false to friendship, I maintained that I was 'as ever your friend.'" The next year at Dover Street "you drove me, by your persevering attacks, to say something about 'alienation'—but if you would look to *facts*, my subsequent intercourse with you, my visits in your society, would shew how far that *word* was from being verified—" Finally, "You tell me you have 'shielded the memory of Lady Lovelace from the cruel world.' If the world is cruel, let it alone!"

In *Memoirs of the Life of Anna Jameson*, niece Geddie would write that she had good reason to know that the loss of Lady Byron's friendship was a wound from which her aunt never recovered. Jameson added salt to that wound by denying herself the friendship of Dandy Bob: "You are in every way bound to Lady Byron; be to her all you can and ought to be—leave me alone—I will not see again any friend who reminds me of her."

Robert Browning was livid when it came to Lady Byron. He blamed Jameson's death a decade later to heartbreak. He wouldn't subscribe to a fund to help Jameson's remaining sisters. Worrying about them had "sucked her dry." If there were a surplus collected for the sisters: "I advise the administrators of the fund to expend it on a votive table to Lady Byron, whose share in the worrying quite deserves one."

Jameson, with the martyrdom of a spurned lover, felt compelled to destroy all of Lady Byron's letters to her, though a few remain through Lady Byron's copies. The letters Jameson wrote while Ada lay dying were also destroyed—not by Lady Byron. In her concise, clear last will of 1859, Lady Byron stipulated that her executors should exercise their discretion in dealing with her papers. They should act in accordance with "what they consider would be my wishes," especially in "regard to the welfare of my Grandchildren." Obviously, the executors did not think what Mrs. Jameson had to say about their mother as she lay dying would contribute to the welfare of Ada's children. *They* destroyed those letters. Lady Byron held fast to the documentation of her own strange history. Her papers were all intact and waiting when a third woman Lady Byron considered superior came her way.

THE LOST CHAPTER

It was in 1853 after the publication of *Uncle Tom's Cabin* had rocketed Harriet Beecher Stowe to international renown that Stowe traveled to Europe for the first time. She was forty years old and had become as famous as Lord Byron when he was twenty-four. Every important person of progressive sentiment wished to meet her. At a London gathering of notables: "All my attention was fixed principally on Lady Byron. She was at this time sixty-one years of age, but still had, to a remarkable degree, that personal attraction which is commonly considered to belong only to youth and beauty."

Stowe and Lady Byron were already in correspondence. Both abolitionists, they helped the fugitive slaves Ellen and William Craft escape to England, as the Crafts remembered in *Running a Thousand Miles to Freedom.*

The Crafts had first escaped from Macon, Georgia, in a most imaginative way. Ellen was white enough to pass, while husband William was dark-skinned. On a Christmas Day half holiday, William disguised his wife as a disabled and bandaged young white gentleman in a top hat who needed his slave's assistance in order to travel north. Since slaves were legally barred from learning to read and write, the gentleman's bandaged hand was given as reason for his asking other gentlemen to be kind enough to sign for him when necessary. The Crafts traveled openly, slave and master, by train and steamboat, and made it north to Philadelphia and then on to Boston, where William, a master craftsman, operated a shop and made furniture. However, the Fugitive Slave Act was passed in 1850, and it meant the Crafts could be picked up and sent back into slavery. Stowe had contacted Lady Byron, who opened her purse to aid in their escape to England. Once the Crafts debarked safely, Lady Byron sent them to her Co-Operative school at Ockham. There they followed the Hofwyl ideal: During part of the day they learned to read and write; during the second part, William taught carpentry, Ellen, homemaking. After the Civil War, the Crafts returned to Georgia and established the Woodville Co-operative Farm School for educating and training freedmen, which ran for about five years. The Crafts were referred to as "our friends" in letters between Stowe and Lady Byron.

Seeing Lady Byron for the first time at that London gathering, Stowe wrote:

> Her form was slight, giving an impression of fragility; her motions both graceful and decided; her eyes bright, and full of interest and quick observation. Her silvery-white hair seemed to lend a grace to the transparent purity of her complexion, and her small hands had a pearly whiteness. I recollect she wore a plain widow's cap of lavender, which harmonized well with her complexion. When introduced to her, I felt in a moment the words of her husband: "There was awe in the homage that she drew; Her spirit seemed as seated on a throne." Calm, self-poised, and thoughtful, she seemed to me rather to resemble an interested spectator of the world's affairs, than an actor involved in its trials, yet the sweetness of her smile, and a certain very delicate sense of humour in her remarks, made the way of acquaintance easy.

Lady Byron must have felt immediately comfortable with the younger woman, for almost everyone else—including Lady Byron—mentioned an instinctive reluctance when she first met a person.

*Lady Byron maintained her good looks as well as her
remarked-upon calm demeanor as she grew older.*

They were both "little women," by the way, each around five feet
tall. Within a few minutes the two "were speaking on what every
one in those days was talking to me about—the slavery question in
America." The American author of *Uncle Tom's Cabin* was generally
besieged at parties and dinners:

> When any one subject especially occupies the public
> mind, those known to be interested in it are compelled to lis-
> ten to many weary platitudes. Lady Byron's remarks, however,
> caught my ear and arrested my attention by their peculiar inci-
> sive quality, their originality. . . . I had no wearisome course
> to go over with her as to the difference between the General
> Government and State Governments, no explanation of the

United States Constitution; for she had the whole before her mind with a perfect clearness. Her morality upon the slavery question, too, impressed me as something far higher and deeper than the common sentimentalism of the day. Many of her words surprised me greatly, and gave me new material for thought.

(Lady Byron predicted emancipation would not come without bloodshed.) The women were interrupted as the conversation turned to religion and in a subsequent note Stowe wrote asking Lady Byron to finish giving her views "of the religious state of England."

"I look upon creeds of all kinds as chains," Lady Byron answered. Creeds caused "much hypocrisy and infidelity. I hold it to be a sin to make a child say, "I believe.' Lead it to utter that belief spontaneously. I also consider the institution of an exclusive priesthood as retarding the progress of Christianity at present." She desired a "lay ministry," she wrote to the wife of theologian and biblical scholar Calvin Stowe: "I ask you, my friend, whether there would not be more faith," if "a wider love" superseded "creed-bound" sects?

Stowe was more than impressed: It underscored for her "Lady Byron's habits of clear, searching analysis, her thoughtfulness, and, above all, that peculiar reverence for truth and sincerity which was a leading characteristic of her moral nature." She "parted from Lady Byron, feeling richer in that I had found one more pearl of great price on the shore of life." She returned three years later, in 1856, to establish international copyright for her latest novel *Dred*: "The hope of once more seeing Lady Byron was one of the brightest anticipations held out to me in this journey."

Sixty-four-year-old Lady Byron was ill but invited Stowe to her home in London. Decorum was not needed between them, Lady Byron wrote, and Stowe was ushered into her bedroom:

Her sick-room seemed only a telegraphic station whence her vivid mind was flashing out all over the world. By her bedside stood a table covered with books, pamphlets, and files of letters, all arranged with exquisite order, and each expressing some of her various interests. From that sick-bed she still directed, with systematic care, her various works of benevolence, and watched with intelligent attention the course of science, literature, and religion; and the versatility and activity of her mind, the flow of brilliant and penetrating thought on all the topices of the day, gave to the conversations of her retired room a peculiar charm. You forgot that she was an invalid.

After that visit Stowe sent her a copy of *Dred*, "saying that I had been reproved by some excellent people for representing too faithfully the profane language of some of the wicked characters." Lady Byron responded: "If there is truth in what I heard Lord Byron say, that works of fiction live only by the amount of truth which they contain, your story is sure of a long life."

Struck by her mention of Lord Byron, Stowe told Lady Byron she had since childhood been "powerfully influenced" by Byron and how the news of his death affected her, "giving up all my plays, and going off to a lonely hillside—."

"I know all that," Lady Byron said, cutting her off "with a quick, impulsive movement. 'I heard it all from Mrs. Jameson; and it was one of the things that made me wish to know you. I think you could understand him.'"

"With her pale face slightly flushed," she went on to talk of the best of Byron's works and the best of his traits. "She told me many pleasant little speeches made by him to herself; and, though there was running through all this a shade of melancholy, one could never have conjectured that there were under all any deeper recollections than the circumstances of an ordinary separation might bring."

Soon after, Lady Byron's health once more improving, she invited Stowe and her family to a private lunch in London, and impressed

Stowe by speaking with each of her children separately. At a subsequent evening at Lady Byron's home, Stowe's son Harry was introduced to Lady Byron's grandson, Ada's first-born, Byron, Lord Ockham: "eldest son and heir of the Earl of Lovelace."

"I had heard much of the eccentricities of this young nobleman, and was exceedingly struck with his personal appearance," Stowe wrote. "His bodily frame was of the order of the Farnese Hercules—a wonderful development of physical and muscular strength. His hands were those of a blacksmith. He was broadly and squarely made, with a finely-shaped head, and dark eyes of surpassing brilliancy. I have seldom seen a more interesting combination than his whole appearance presented." She expressed "wonder at the uncommon muscular development of his frame," to Lady Byron, who responded that it accounted for many of his eccentricities. "He had a body that required a more vigorous life than his station gave scope for, and this had often led him to seek it in what the world calls low society." At the time he was an iron worker on the railroad. He had laid aside his title, and thought of himself as one of the workmen. "The great difficulty with our nobility is apt to be, that they do not understand the working-classes, so as to feel for them properly; and Byron is now going through an experience which may yet fit him to do great good when he comes to the peerage." Lady Byron was "trying to influence him to do good among the workmen, and to interest himself in schools for their children."

She told Stowe she thought she had great influence over her grandson, "the greater, perhaps, that I never made any claim to authority." One pictures muscular Johnny Okey, as he called himself, looking down at his small grandmother with a smile or a nod as she spoke of the peerage he would never have claimed—even had he lived. A drinker and a workman, Ada's oldest and Lovelace's heir seemed to have contracted tuberculosis, unless it was alcoholism that would claim him when he was in his late twenties. Lady Anne, the little sister who had idolized him as she eyed his mutton chops when they were children, nursed him in his final days.

IN SEPTEMBER of 1856, Lady Byron was well enough to travel to her summer home near Richmond on Ham Common and to invite Stowe and her sister to a luncheon. After it, Lady Byron was anxious to speak with Stowe privately, and she excused the two of them from the other guests. When they were alone, Lady Byron appeared to be repressing strong emotions.

There were rumors of a penny edition of Byron's work that would include a biographical sketch once more casting Lady Byron as the cold, insensitive wife of genius. The introductory sketch would be needed in order to explain some of Lord Byron's references to these new readers, the working class who, through a cheap edition, would for the first time be exposed to *Don Juan*, *Childe Harold's Pilgrimage*, and short works such as "Lines on Hearing That Lady Byron Was Ill," written after Byron left England: "I had many foes, but none like thee," he wrote. He went on to call his wife "the moral Clytemnestra of thy lord," who had cut him down "with an unsuspected sword."

Lady Byron believed she was loved only by strangers. Now these strangers, the many generations of young people she had led through education to meaningful work, the girls she had saved from the streets and gotten into Mary Carpenter's Red Lodge, the striking workers and the needy whom she had helped to educate, would read that Lady Byron was a heartless, cold, unsuitable wife to a genius. The literary magazines and newspapers had cast her in that light for decades. What they did for the educated class, the penny edition would now do for the masses.

She had the idea of writing her memoirs before she died, she told Stowe. With a penny edition on the horizon, should she go forth as her surviving friends urged? If Harriet Beecher Stowe could read her older friend's broad forehead—Stowe did attend séances—she would have understood that Lady Byron was hoping she had found her second Robertson, a writer secure in "the cloudless brightness of faith" who had an "original," not a "secondary," intelligence. That day at

Ham Common, Lady Byron, sequestered with Stowe, went back a half century to when she and Byron first met. Two years after she refused him, Byron sent her "a very beautiful letter," offering himself again. "I thought that it was sincere, and that I might now show him all I felt. I wrote just what was in my heart." Stowe saw a moment of anger flash across her face. Lord Byron, she later read, had handed that letter to his sister saying, "A letter from Bell,—never rains but it pours."

"And did he not love you, then?"

She put her hand over Stowe's. "No, my dear: he did not love me."

"Why, then, did he wish to marry you?"

"You will see."

This was Lady Byron's youth. She did not rush it. When she experienced how erratic Byron acted at Seaham while they were engaged, she went to him and told him plainly that she understood his exceptional nature, and if, after so long an absence, he no longer wished to be engaged, she would never blame him. His reaction to her words? He fainted dead away!

Lady Byron paused. Her words took great effort, "Then I was sure he must love me."

"And did he not? What other cause could have led to this emotion?"

"Fear of detection." Lady Byron grew pale. "He was guilty of incest with his sister!"

"What?" She had heard such rumors, but did that cause really exist?

"Yes it did."

One had to understand his psychology, she told Stowe. Lord Byron had grown to manhood without a guide. "The manners of his day were corrupt," she went on, explaining the morals of the Regency to this child of the Victorian age. "What were now considered vices in society were then spoken of as matters of course among young noblemen: drinking, gaming, and licentiousness everywhere abounded and, up to a certain time, he was no worse than multitudes of other young men of his day—only that the vices of his day were worse for him. The excesses of passion, the disregard of physical laws in eating, drinking, and living, wrought effects on him that they did not on less sensitively organised frames."

Often he spoke of incest indirectly. It was no sin, he told his wife. It was the way the world was first peopled. Doesn't the Bible say "all the world descended from one pair; and how could that be unless brothers married their sisters?" If it wasn't a sin then, what makes it one now?

"Why, Lady Byron," Stowe interrupted, "those are the very arguments given in Byron's drama *Cain*!"

"The very same."

When his wife pressed him hard on the universal sentiment against incest, that it was considered a crime, he "took another turn." It was the very horror and the criminality of it all that was the very attraction for him!

But didn't he faint? Stowe asked. Hadn't Lady Byron just said he dreaded detection?

Her husband told her she could never be the means of detection: "'The world will believe me, and it will not believe you. The world has made up its mind that "By" is a glorious boy; and the world will go for "By," right or wrong.'"

Stowe couldn't contain curiosity: "Was Augusta Leigh a particularly beautiful woman?"

"No, my dear: she was plain."

"Was she, then, distinguished for genius or talent of any kind?"

"Oh, no! Poor woman! She was weak, relatively to him and wholly under his control."

"Was there a child?" Stowe asked. "I had been told by Mrs Jameson that there was a daughter."

There was.

On it went. Lady Byron recounting much, some of which Stowe had already heard from Jameson, all without a hint of Byron's homosexuality, which may have been a greater "remorse" than the love he felt for his sister. Finally Lady Byron came to the advice she was seeking. Should she herself make a full and clean disclosure "before she left the world"?

It was evening by then, and Stowe told Lady Byron she would let her know what she thought in a few days. Stowe and her sister stayed up all night: "I was powerfully impressed with the justice and propriety of an immediate disclosure." Her sister "on the contrary, represented the painful consequences that would probably come upon Lady Byron from taking such a step."

Before they left the next day, Stowe asked Lady Byron for some memoranda and outlines of "the general story, with dates as well." Lady Byron handed her a significant selection. After the visit, she followed up with a time line outlining the events in her marriage.

Stowe didn't take days, she took months to mull things over. It wasn't until the week before Christmas 1856 that Stowe wrote from France, letting Lady Byron know that she had changed from her first impressions. She now wished that "the sacred veil of silence, so bravely thrown over the past," should not be withdrawn during Lady Byron's lifetime.

"Leave all with some discreet friends," to decide after her death. She would not have the woman "I so much respect, love and revere" placed within reach of the world's "harpy claw" that pollutes what it touches. Truth will out, Stowe told her with confidence. "Such, my dear friend, are my thoughts; different from what they were since first I heard that strange, sad history. Meanwhile, I love you ever, whether we meet again on earth or not."

Lady Byron might, after years of struggle, be able to say "Incest!" aloud, but she still could not ask for what she wanted. She needed another of Robertson's caliber who could help her tell her story, to bring her many fragmented "Statements, " "Conversations," and "Interviews," not to mention a plethora of important letters, into narrative shape. Whether or not Stowe understood her silent plea to be her collaborator, Stowe returned the papers, and Lady Byron accepted her advice.

Stowe did meet Lady Byron again in 1859: "That interview was my last on earth with her, and is still beautiful in memory. It was a long, still summer afternoon, spent alone with her in a garden, where we walked together. She was enjoying one of those bright intervals of freedom from pain and langour, in which her spirits always rose so buoyant and youthful; and her eye brightened, and her step became elastic." When it came time to leave, Lady Byron took Stowe to the train station in her carriage. Stowe realized she had left her gloves behind and hadn't time to go back. "With one of those quick, impulsive motions which were so natural to her in doing a kindness, she drew off her own, and said, 'Take mine if they will serve you.'

"I hesitated a moment; and then the thought that I might never see her again, came over me, and I said, 'Oh yes! thanks,' and took them as a token of love." Stowe had been right to accept those gloves. Her older friend's days were numbered.

LADY BYRON's granddaughter and namesake was her constant comfort toward the end. Lady Byron wrote proudly to Stowe that Anne stayed in London, to be of use to her: "Not ostensibly, for I can neither go out, nor give parties; but I am the confidential friend to whom she likes to bring her social gatherings. Age and infirmity seem to be overlooked in what she calls the harmony between us,—not perfect agreement of opinion (which I should regret, with almost fifty years of difference), but the spirit-union: can you say what it is?"

One can: Love.

Her grandmother's constant affection was a counterbalance to Ada's early and ferocious dislike of her constantly hungry, and at that time, "fat" daughter, whom she would slap to Lady Byron's admonishment. One sees it so often as to wonder if it is a law of nature: an imperfect remote mother becoming a perfectly accessible and loving grandmother. Lady Byron complained of being loved only by strangers. She was loved unconditionally by her granddaughter, Anne Isabella Noel King.

The future Lady Anne Blunt would ride horseback, "the only

woman in the cavalcade" through the Arabian desert. The Byrons' granddaughter would cross "the Tigris, Euphrates and Kherkha rivers either on goatskin raft or clinging to swimming horses." She and her husband, the poet Wilfred Blunt, a womanizer far surpassing her grandfather, would "set up the stud of Arabian horses" at their estate at Crabbet, saving the breed. She could still mount a horse unassisted at the age of seventy-seven. She spoke and dreamed in Arabic and died in Eygpt in 1917 at the age of eighty. She was buried "under the Eastern sun she loved so well." Her drawings of exotic locales can still be purchased. However, in her early twenties, young Anne stayed put, the devoted companion of her grandmother.

"My darling suffered very much, except the few hours before the end," Anne wrote to Caro George. "The end was in sleep, which passed into the sleep of death—gently and calmly."

Lady Byron died the day before her sixty-eighth birthday, a few months after Anna Jameson passed. She lies buried at Kensal Green Cemetery in West London. Her stone reads:

> Ann Isabella Noel Byron
> Born at Seaham
> In the county of Durham
> 17th May 1792
> Died
> 16th May 1860

No forty-seven carriages in procession. No coffin weighed down by silver insignia. No regal burial ground or family plot. No "Lady Byron." Not even a correct spelling of her first name. She requested simple interment at the relatively new, park-like cemetery in which some of Dr. Lushington's family lay, and where she was consigned to dust. "Seaham" (she'd actually been born elsewhere in Durham) was cherished by her until the end. Not even her tombstone told her story.

"When I am speculating to little purpose," Lady Byron wrote to Harriet Beecher Stowe the year before her death, "perhaps you are

Harriet Beecher Stowe, who became the friend and champion of the older Lady Byron.

doing—what? Might not a biography from your pen bring forth again some great, half-obscured soul to act on the world?"

A DECADE later Stowe did pick up her pen, for Lord Byron's Italian mistress, Contessa Teresa Guiccioli, at the age of seventy, published her *Recollections of Lord Byron*. By then Guiccioli was the widow of her second husband, the Marquis de Boissy, who reportedly used to introduce his wife as "formerly the mistress to Lord Byron" (ah, the French). *Blackwood's Magazine*, an influential organ that had all through Lady Byron's life ruthlessly parodied her for separating from Byron, realized the memoirs were, as Harriet Beecher Stowe called them, "twaddle." Byron's Italian mistress told "us nothing but what had been told before over and over again." Still:

"There is something inexpressibly touching in the picture of the old lady calling up the phantoms of half a century ago," not faded by time, "but brilliant and gorgeous as they were when Byron, in his manly prime of genius and beauty, first flashed upon her enraptured sight, and she gave her whole soul up to an absorbing passion, the embers of which still glow in her heart." It would be absurd to criticize the book by the usual standards. As Stowe summed up the review: "A very stupid book" was praised by "one of the oldest and most classical periodicals of Great Britain," on the basis of its being written by Lord Byron's mistress.

In her bestseller of 1869, La Guiccioli had repeated every claim Byron ever made against his wife, but *Blackwood's* defamation went further. Byron had labeled his wife his moral Clytemnestra, however Byron's metaphor was too kind. Clytemnestra "only killed her husband's body; whereas Lady Byron's silence was destined to kill the soul." The reviewer suggested it would have been a truer metaphor had Byron called Lady Byron his "moral Brinvilliers." Stowe looked up "Brinvilliers" in a lexicon. In the eighteenth century, the Marchioness of Brinvilliers murdered her sister and two brothers, but it took her eight attempts to kill her father. Then she went to hospitals, poisoning the ill.

As Guiccioli phrased it, Byron's wife was "an absolute moral monstrosity, an anomaly in the history of types of female hideousness." Lord Byron, however, took care "to shield her from blame." The review insisted: "There is no proof whatever that Lord Byron was guilty of any act that need have caused a separation, or prevented a reunion," and concluded, "'She dies and makes no sigh. O God! Forgive her.'"

The "heaviest accusation against Lady Byron," Harriet Beecher Stowe realized, "is that she has not spoken at all. Her story has never been told." The advice Stowe had offered her friend, to remain silent in her lifetime, had proven disastrous. In a nervous state over the injustice and her part in it, Stowe waited for a rebuttal from Lady Byron's friends or family, or for the publication of Lady Byron's memoir itself. Stowe was sure Lady Byron had written one. No memoir appeared, nor was there one word of defense. Lady Byron's name was drawn through the mud again. The silence Stowe advised only abated the harpy claw.

"MEN OF AMERICA, men of England, what do you think of this?" Harriet Beecher Stowe cried out to her large audience as if the public were a trusted friend to whom she could confide. In the pages of the *Atlantic Monthly*, on her side of the pond, she wrote "The True Story of Lady Byron's Life." Lady Byron was being "branded with the names of the foulest ancient and foulest modern assassins," while "Lord Byron's mistress was publicly taken by the hand, and encouraged to go on and prosper in her slanders, by one of the oldest and most influential British reviews." The truth was, Lord Byron had not been content "as the husband of a noble woman," but instead "fell into the depths of a secret adulterous intrigue with a blood relation." This unnamed relative was "so near in consanguinity, that discovery must have been utter ruin and expulsion from civilised society."

"An adulterous intrigue with a blood relation?" This was a bombshell. How could a *woman* put such a thing in print. The media barrage was immediate and staggering. True or false—and some considered it true—it made no difference. To the public, Harriet Beecher Stowe had fallen from President Lincoln's revered "little woman who made the great war" to scarlet woman. Her stellar reputation was literarily obliterated in the blink of an eye. Stowe said she read none of the outcry, but she could not close her ears to its roar.

Lady Byron's two remaining grandchildren were furious. Ralph attempted to suppress the reprinting of Stowe's article in England by *MacMillan's Magazine*, but it could not be done. Instead, he wrote a letter to the *Times*, not under his own name, but signed by the law firm of Wharton & Ford. Lady Anne, recently married, thought it another of her baby brother's botches. The letter said Stowe should have hesitated "before giving to the World a statement which however it may affect the memories of the dead must inevitably inflict much pain on the living." However, Stowe's charge of a secret adulterous intrigue with a blood relation was not specifically denied and continued to produce media hysteria on both sides of the pond.

Ralph himself had had suspicions of his grandfather's relationship with his sister since reading Lord Byron's *Manfred* when he was twenty-three. *Manfred* was published the year after the separation and is a poignant—and unabashed—paean to the grieving hero's tragic, incestuous love of the dead Astarte:

> She was like me in lineaments—her eyes,
> Her hair, her features, all, the very tone
> Even of her voice, they said were like to mine;
> And soften'd all, and temper'd into beauty;
> . . . .
> Her faults were mine—her virtues were her own—
> I loved her, and destroy'd her!

In the early twentieth century Ralph would title his book documenting his grandparents' marriage *Astarte*, a reference to his grandfather's incest with Augusta Leigh. But thirty-five years previously, it was only Stowe who raised the terrible swift sword of her pen—twice. After she believed the uproar over her article had subsided—"I must say the storm exceeded my expectations"—she wished to explain her point of view more rationally and less obliquely in book form, *Lady Byron Vindicated*. She would "add to my true story such facts and incidents as I did not think proper at first to state." Apparently she clung to the belief that truth would go marching on and that righteous indignation concerning slavery could be transferred to the plight of maligned women.

Not only had *Blackwood's* castigated Lady Bryon by believing Guiccioli's twaddle. The press had been unfair to Lady Byron through the years.

"Here is what John Stuart Mill calls the literature of slavery for women," Stowe wrote. As far back as 1830, when Lady Byron defended her parents against what was said of them in Thomas Moore's biography of Byron, *Blackwood's* countered there were other widows "whom brutal, profligate, and savage husbands have brought to the brink of the grave,—as good, as bright, as innocent as, and far more forgiving than Lady Bryon." Such a decent widow goes weekly to her husband's grave. "He was a brute, a ruffian, a monster. When drunk, how he raged and cursed and swore! Often did she dread that, in his fits of inhuman passion, he would have murdered the baby at her breast; for she had seen him dash their only little boy on the floor, till the blood gushed from his ears. Often he struck her; and once when she was pregnant with that very orphan now smiling on her breast." Still this widow "tries to smile among neighbours, and speaks of her boy's likeness to his father." "Her eyes brighten with tears" when she remembers how strong and beautiful he was on their wedding day. "That, I say, sir, whether right or wrong was—forgiveness."

Stowe concluded: "It is because of such transgressors as Byron, such supporters as Moore, that there are so many helpless, cowering, brokenhearted, abject women, given over to the animal love which they share alike with the poor dog,—the dog, who, beaten, kicked, starved, and cuffed, still lies by his drunken master with great anxious eyes of love and sorrow, and with sweet, brute forgiveness nestles upon his bosom, as he lies in his filth in the snowy ditch, to keep the warmth of life in him. Great is the mystery of this fidelity in the poor loving brute,—most mournful and most sacred."

If the best periodical in England's best advice to Lord Byron's widow, a "peeress of England," whose husband they admit might have committed crimes "foul, monstrous, unforgivable," was to accept marital abuse with humility, well, then what of women who hadn't title or wealth? To put it in a nutshell, "If the peeress as a wife has no rights, what is the state of the cotter's wife?" Lady Byron's married life? "Alas! it is lived over in many a cottage and tenement-house, with no understanding on either side of the cause of the woeful misery."

Stowe was no longer pulling her punches. She quoted Lady Byron directly. He "was guilty of incest with his sister!"

"Was there a child?" Stowe had then asked her friend. "Was there a daughter?"

Yes, Lady Bryon had answered, there was.

A second bombshell. A daughter, a child of incest? The newspapers ignited with the "Byron Mystery." Broadsheets featured drawings of Augusta and Byron and Medora on their covers. Did he or didn't he? It was as if what happened fifty-five years previously had happened yesterday.

Both Ada and Medora would have been in their mid-fifties had they lived, and both were more or less forgotten in 1870 before Stowe's book came out. The publication of *Lady Byron Vindicated* fulfilled a wish Medora had had in her wild days back in London with her adoptive mother. Then she wished to bring her real mother to court to prove, through Lady Byron's auspices, that she was Lord Byron's daughter. Now the literary world and the public buzzed with that scandalous suspicion. Medora's name was in the papers and on everyone's lips. She had had "Byron" engraved on her tombstone in a remote village in France. Less than twenty years later, there was Medora Byron in print. Her half sister Ada rested undisturbed in the elaborate coffin that touched her father's. It would take more than a century after *Lady Byron Vindicated* before Ada, Countess of Lovelace would emerge from the obscurity to which Medora returned.

Stowe's book had its own strange fate. It reverberated "powerfully within the political culture of the American woman's movement," biographer Joan D. Hedrick observed astutely. For the public outrage unleashed by her defense of Lady Bryon in the *Atlantic Monthly* had caused Stowe "for the first time to think systematically about the issue of women's rights." Her subsequent book was particularly relevant to those feminists "led by Elizabeth Cady Stanton and Susan B. Anthony, who had made marriage, divorce and sexuality prominent topics of debate." True as this was, *Lady Byron Vindicated* never reverberated outside of that circle: "The world may finally forgive the man of genius anything; but for a woman there is no mercy and no redemption," Stowe wrote from experience.

"We have heard much mourning over the burned Autobiography of Lord Byron, and seen it treated of in a magazine as 'the lost chapter in history,'" Stowe cried out. "The lost chapter in history is Lady Byron's Autobiography." Not having her life and letters open to the public is "the root of this whole mischief." With that "I claim for my countrymen and women, our right to true history."

15

LADY BYRON AND
HER GRANDSON

*I*t would take the boy Lady Byron raised as a son a great portion of his later life to bring that lost chapter of history to light. "She was both father and mother to me," Ralph, by then Baron Wentworth, wrote of his grandmother, whose name and title he had taken. He had been a bookish, timid lad, with whom his own father Lord Lovelace had little rapport. Ada had wanted heirs, not children, so her shy spare had little to recommend him in the years when mathematics was king and the children a nuisance. His parents were more than happy for his grandmother's love and care of the little boy with the big brain.

Because of Lady Byron's progressive educational ideas and her dread of the morals and the bullying encouraged in the fashionable public schools, Ralph became considered an odd boy out by others of his social class: "I have lost I think by the 'education' she substituted for a public school. I should not have lamented any loss if I could have been entirely formed and instructed by her—but alas!" he had a succession of dreary tutors. "I was supposed to possess such a vigorous genius as to need a very serious, solitary and depressing education." All of this was partly his fault, he realized, for he had "the want of power to communicate what was innermost in my heart." It would appear the apple hadn't fallen far from the tree.

In chaotic, revolutionary 1848, Ralph's time at Hofwyl School had been cut short because of safety concerns. Still, experiencing the

Alps had a permanent effect. As timid as Ralph was, he had found his enduring passion. "His first recorded climb was the ascent of the Rigi at the age of eight." When he reached maturity, he returned to the Alps yearly, always preferring rock climbing to "snow work," and put his flag atop and named more than a few previously unconquered peaks. It was in the solitude of nature that he was most at home and, perhaps like his grandfather Lord Byron, considered he was most himself.

As Lady Byron's heir, Ralph sought out his grandmother's sealed papers. Not until 1868, the year before Stowe published in the *Atlantic*, was he able to obtain "the principal bulk" of them. It had not been easy. He had to wrestle these documents out of the arthritic grasp of an older generation who more or less followed the dictates of the octogenarian Dr. Lushington, who still advised silence as he had through Lady Byron's life.

Until he obtained these papers, Ralph had been entertaining the idea of writing of his grandmother's life, "leaving aside as far as possible the story of her marriage and separation." It would be "the sober narrative of a virtuous life," the philanthropic life of the older woman he knew. He hardly knew there *was* an Augusta Leigh. He had asked his grandmother if his grandfather was an only child. "She replied quickly, 'No, there is his sister, Mrs. Leigh.' The subject was then dropped; she had spoken without emotion or interest perceptive to me." This great-aunt of Ralph seemed to him more or less "a stranger to my grandmother, and perhaps my grandfather." He knew nothing of his mother Ada's half sister, Medora, until Stowe's book appeared.

"My grandmother often spoke of my grandfather's greatness as a poet; she said they had been parted by events which made a separation inevitable, which could not be disclosed." With his access to the papers, even before Stowe's article, Ralph had, in his second wife's words, "to reconcile his own mental picture of the tender guardian of his childhood, the loving mother, the steadfast friend, the living embodiment of generosity and liberal ideas, with the hateful portrait traced of her by her own husband and with his cruel accusation of her as 'the moral Clytemnestra of her lord.' And the interest of her character was made more poignant to him by the knowledge that the prejudices born of her bitter experience had been all-powerful in shaping his own youthful life."

By November 1868, Ralph appeared to have a grasp on the situation and a firm hold on his grandmother's psychology. An unnamed friend said he knew Augusta to be the cause of the separation, and that it was Dr. Lushington's influence that helped prevent a reconciliation. This angered Ralph and he wrote to his sister:

"I myself do not believe Augusta was the cause of her leaving B., but that she thought it her duty to shun the moral temptation with which she herself was beset, and she felt horror at the idea B. might become answerable for her moral destruction." With that, Ralph came as close to the truth as one can. He understood the complexities of his grandmother's motivation, not only through her letters and "Statements," but through his blood.

By the time Harriet Beecher Stowe's article was published in the *Atlantic*, Ralph had other duties that claimed his time. At thirty he had married a "minor," Fanny Herriot, her father, a clergyman, consenting. No age of the bride is recorded on the marriage certificate—she was at least fourteen years younger than Ralph. Ralph, given his education, was not wise in the ways of the world; in fact, with women his immaturity appeared endless. Being Baron Wentworth was a major attraction to the fair sex and their parents.

The couple had a daughter, Ada Mary. Fanny bolted soon after, leaving her daughter, taking a lot of jewelry. Everything was hushed up, but Ralph would spend years in financial arrears. Sister Anne was made Ada Mary's legal guardian and given her to raise. Ralph spent much of his time in the Alps. Lady Byron had made a stipulation in her will that he was to return to England once a year to maintain his inheritance. She knew him well and in a sense that stipulation gave him a modicum of grounding. When Fanny died of tuberculosis a decade later, his sister Anne, but not Ralph, rejoiced.

Lady Byron's loving granddaughter, Lady Anne Blunt, by one of her Arab mares.

A free man by the end of the 1870s, his next romance was with a cosmopolitan novelist known to the expatriate artistic community in Rome. Julia Constance Fletcher, an American apparently born in Brazil, was the author of the novels *Kismet* and *Mirage*, part of the No Name Series. At the time of her engagement to the Baron, a bawdy joke was circulated that Julia had taken a tumble in the Alps that allowed her to spread her legs in front of clueless Ralph. An anonymous observer called Ralph "the most timid hearted of mortals" and Julia an ugly woman who wore "her meretriciously yellow hair racked up to the top of her head into the latest aesthetical style." This time sister Anne did not leave her younger brother to his own devices. She hired a detective. There seems to have been no birth certificate, Julia's parents might not have been married, her mother might have been Jewish! How bad could it get? Lady Anne was adamant.

"Either we must prove your parentage," Ralph wrote to Julia, or the two of them would have to abandon the idea of being accepted by others. "The worst of this latter alternative would be that if we were married under these circumstances, we should be put to a kind of election and have either to renounce my sister (and probably others) or your mother."

On January 9, 1880, the *Globe* had some "Roman Gossip" to report. It appeared "American society in Rome is just now much exercised by the abrupt termination to the matrimonial engagement announced between Miss Fletcher, authoress of "Kismet" and Lord Wentworth. In this transaction no blame is attached to the lady, but the gentleman is highly censured. The Americans love a title, and feel aggrieved that their fair compatriot has been deprived of a coronet."

Julia wrote to lawyer Ford, whom she knew to be "quite as much Ralph's personal friend as his family advisor": "Lord Wentworth is not a boy. He assured me repeatedly that those family considerations which have now betrayed him into so unworthy a position, were for himself, almost non extant. If Lady Byron were still living I should send this letter to her: I should not be afraid of her misunderstanding me." Lady Byron might very well have understood her, especially when in other letters to Ford pressuring him to intervene, Julia made veiled yet ominous threats of exposing what may have been a lapse in Ford's fidelity toward his wife. The matter was resolved out of court.

Julia returned jewels and Ralph offered a "sum." Soon after, Ralph fell in love with Mary Stuart-Wortley. He wrote to her from the Alps, and his letters reveal a sensitivity to her feelings and a sense of his own unworthiness. "I could not write all I do to you to any one else, for with you I feel secure from ridicule."

He was quite aware he had botched much in his life; he had not lived up to the genius of his youth. There was pathos in his regrets, kindness in his heart, and stirring descriptions of the Alps, the country people, the local guides, the dangers of the invigorating climbs, the scaling to heights not reached before. He pressed lone mountain flowers to Mary in his letters.

Their marriage in 1880 was perhaps the best thing Ralph had accomplished in his life. He was baptized into the Church of England beforehand: "My grandmother told me I had never been baptised,

Ralph Milbanke, the intellectually promising grandson and heir of Lady Byron who spent much of his life securing Lady Byron's immense archives and agonizing over whether he should tell the truth of his grandfather's incest, which he did in Astarte, *1905.*

as when I was born my father and mother were Unitarians, who, I believe do not use those words that are necessary for validity. My grandmother disapproved of what they did, or rather of what they did *not* do, though she did not herself consider any form of words essential. But she thought it was the worst way of attaching importance to words to omit the recognised forms intentionally." Widower Robert Browning, who never forgave Lady Byron her treatment of Anna Jameson, was a guest at the wedding.

Though Ralph had not spoken to his father in years, this second marriage to a woman of good family and both aristocratic and literary connections brought Lord Lovelace, who had remarried and had other children, back into Ralph's life. Ralph's uneasy reconciliation with his stern father was necessary. He had earlier realized that there were many more of his grandmother's and mother's papers in his father's hands and that he could not tell his grandmother's story without them. Medora, too, had left papers with his father when she returned to France. "But nothing could be got from Lord Lovelace about the missing papers," wife Mary wrote.

"Always unapproachable, Lovelace had become doubly so from age and extreme deafness, and he was always particularly hard of hearing on subjects that he disliked. The danger that, if provoked, he might put the papers out of his son's reach in the future could not be ignored. There was nothing for it but patience."

The American writer Henry James, a good friend of Mary, had become a good friend of Ralph as well. He visited the couple in their Chelsea home often in the 1880s and witnessed Ralph's preoccupation with his grandmother's letters and his need to somehow answer the inaccuracies of Harriet Beecher Stowe. He observed Ralph's anxiety over the possibility that his unforgiving and ancient father might burn important letters and documents in his possession before he died. If he did so, Ralph would never be able to reconstruct his grandmother's true story.

What James witnessed became the immediate inspiration for his masterpiece of a novella, *The Aspern Papers*. It concerned a green trunk of letters from a great American poet, considered the American Byron, to his lover, Juliana Bordereau. The poet was long dead and his love had turned into an ancient, quasi-blind and imperious old woman who guarded her trunk of letters zealously. In James's tale, the obsessed narrator is not Ralph, but an American scholar who has come as a boarder to Juliana's run-down Venetian villa in hopes of somehow getting access to the letters: "I had perfectly considered the possibility of Juliana destroying her papers on the day she should feel her end really approach."

In 1888 when *The Aspern Papers* was serialized in the *Atlantic* and then published in book form, Henry James with some justification might have felt that Ralph's effort to secure the rest of his grandmother's effects was a lost cause and that the revealing Byron papers held tight by remote, implacable, deaf Lord Lovelace might never reach the light of day. That's what happens in James's novella. The blind old woman destroyed the papers of the great Byronic American poet before she died, burning them slowly one by one.

If James thought intractable Lovelace would burn documents before he died, he was wrong. Five years after *The Aspern Papers* was published, in 1893, old Lord Lovelace passed at the age of eighty-nine. The metaphoric green trunk of letters had survived, and the precious documents were inherited by Ralph. Though for a while Ralph debated accepting his father's title, he did become the second Lord Lovelace. The estates at Ockham and Ashley Combe devolved to him and for the first time in his adulthood he was free of financial stress.

Friend Henry James might not have been free from stress, however, for the title of James's novella, *The Aspern Papers*, was suddenly uncomfortably close to the entire scope of Lady Byron's enormous archives, called the Lovelace Papers. James had witnessed living history. He had been able to read from the plethora of documents at Ralph's disposal. He witnessed as well his friend's conflict: "How to hide the faults of one ancestor without doing black injustice to another, how to suppress truth without adding to a mountain of lies." Ralph knew by then that Harriet Beecher Stowe had been right concerning the incest and the birth of Medora, but the truth caused her to turn his grandfather into a one-sided villain and his grandmother who raised him into an all-suffering saint. For Stowe the sexual relationship between the siblings had been the reason Lady Byron had left her husband. How could Ralph rectify this false position and still somehow *not* deal with the incest?

Wife Mary remembered "listening for the hundredth time with indescribable weariness, and in secret revolt at the sacrifice of *his* life, at the constant waste of his talents and energy in the effort to solve an insoluble problem and at the hateful atmosphere of the miserable story which he was compelled to have constantly in his thoughts." Pacing the room, Ralph called out: "Oh! if I could have peace!"

"There never will be peace till the truth has once for all been acknowledged!" Mary exclaimed, thinking out loud.

Ralph "wheeled round" and faced her: "Ah! You think so, do you?"

"And I realized that my words had confirmed the thought that was already formed in his mind."

From then on, the only question was how the truth of the Byron marriage would be told. Ralph had spent years, decades actually, reading and annotating his grandmother's archive. As much a scholar— pedant?—as Henry James's character in *The Aspern Papers*, Ralph tended toward too much overly erudite information. "He remembered too well how the public had seized on every detail of Guiccioli's *Recollections*, as well as on Harriet Beecher Stowe's *Lady Byron Vindicated*, and dreaded a similar succès de scandale," his wife wrote. His only desire was "to put the truth beyond question." In order to avoid "newspaper notoriety, and above all the possibility of making money," from his grandparents' lives, "he decided to print the book privately and to circulate it as a gift among friends and prominent persons in the literary world."

Here too he was like his grandmother. He wanted in effect to tell without telling. Ralph was forced to print 200 copies to claim copyright, otherwise he would have printed fewer. Many remained with the family, a few sent to select libraries. Presentation copies went to intimates and literati such as Anne Thackeray, Vernon Lushington, Lady Gregory, William De Morgan, Sydney Cockerell, Algernon Swinburne, and to Henry James. The truth is in *Astarte*, albeit in a convoluted fashion. Little public notice was taken of his book, as Ralph had wished, though many of his literary friends responded, the longest letter coming from Henry James:

> Let me tell you at once that I am greatly touched by your friendly remembrance of my possible feeling for the whole matter, and of your own good act, perhaps, of a few years ago—the to me ever memorable evening when at Wentworth

House, you allowed me to look at some of the documents you have made use of in "Astarte." Ineffaceably has remained with me the poignant, the in fact very romantic interest of that occasion. And now you have done the thing which I then felt a dim foreshadowing that you would do—but the determination of which must have cost you.

James saw his friend's book as "an incantation out of which strange tragic ghosts arise." But just as Ralph evoked "ghosts," he sent them back into their shade never to rise again. "Great is the virtue of History—when it has waited so long, and so consciously to be written, and to be enabled to proceed to its clearing of the air."

Ralph's justice to his grandmother had "the same final and conclusive character." Ralph had not "yielded to any insidious but considerable temptation to dress her in any graces, in any shape of colour, whatever, not absolutely her own. To have spoken for her so sincerely and with such effect, and yet with such an absence of special pleading—I mean with so perfectly leaving her as she was can't have been an easy thing, and remains, I think, a distinguished one. Clear she was, and you have kept her clear; and amid the all too heavy fumes one puts out one's hand to her in absolute confidence. I think her spirit somewhere in the universe, must by putting out its hand to *you*!"

James even understood Lady Byron's at times convoluted prose style, beyond what Anna Jameson called its "strangulation." The subtleties involved in its mixture of psychological penetration, empathy for others, narcissism, and strong self-will spoke to him. Lady Byron, when dealing with complex issues of the heart, particularly when it came to her sister-in-law Augusta, wrote in what could be called the patois of the cultured aristocrat. Thomas Carlyle who had little good to say of anyone or anything—though he did like Lady Byron—was overwhelmed by what he called the perfection of the manners of the English aristocrat. In that tradition, Lady Byron was able to say without saying, but her meaning both literarily and psychologically spoke out to Henry James.

Henry James saw a beauty in the complexity of motives that might have seemed to others a failure to communicate. He did not reduce this complex woman. Influenced by Lady Byron's magical papers, including many letters to and about Augusta Leigh, James incorporated in his late style a method of arriving at both emotional and moral truth reminiscent of Lady Byron's aristocratic indirection. He could look under the piety of Lady Byron's expression to the submerged "ghosts," to the darkness in her heart.

MARY BELIEVED the five years her husband spent writing *Astarte*, published in 1905, "were the happiest of Lovelace's life." The doubts that plagued him for thirty years were cast away: "When I think of those who paced the garden at Ockham with him on those happy summer afternoons, I see the well beloved figures of W. H. Lecky, Henry James, William de Morgan, Lord Courtney." When he saw his book in print in 1905, Ralph sighed with relief and told Mary he hoped never to think or speak of it again.

In the late summer of 1906 the couple hadn't sought out the cool pines of Ashley Combe but remained at Ockham. One very hot August morning, "the head-woodman came to report damage done by mischievous boys in Lovelace's favourite plantation." Extremely angry, Ralph rushed into the hot sun to see the destruction caused. That afternoon he and his wife had a delightful visit from a friend who sat with them on the terrace and was amused as usual by the goings-on in their aviary: "The love-drama between Pierrot, the green Amazon parrot, and Rosy Talbot, the pink cockatoo." As the guest left, Ralph made a joke about Pierrot's ardent courtship. An hour later Ralph was found out on that terrace, facedown in the twilight. "He had passed away without fear or pain."

The newspapers took more account of *Astarte* after Ralph's sudden death, but, of course, that soon became yesterday's news.

For all of Ralph's own eccentricities of style and documentation, he had presented an extraordinary balanced portrait. He regretted hearing his grandmother often say "Happiness no longer enters into my views." He considered it a shame that she fell from "the world of intellect and fashion to the world of Methodists, Quakers, Unitarians," to "reformers" who distrusted "the pleasures of this world." His grandmother herself joked that one day she might revolt from the dismal company of good works. But she never did. Instead, Ralph wrote, "She renounced the world of enjoyment, like the founder of a severe monastic order," and would have forced everyone under her power "to live a life of Spartan self-denial, and devotion to a somewhat despotic philanthropy."

She often told her grandson that she considered "Be Yourself" a better precept than "Know thyself." She *was* herself, at the same time as she consciously splintered off from the dark part of herself.

At twenty-two, she had married a great poet. When that marriage ended, she had a daughter by him and a deep, complex relationship with his sister. She had sworn to Byron that she would "be kind to Augusta still," and she turned the darkness of her jealousy into a determined effort to keep sister and brother apart. However, it wasn't jealousy alone; she also believed she was saving brother and sister through her silence, and that she protected her husband's reputation through her long life. During that life, she raised a daughter, Ada, Countess of Lovelace, who would become world-famous more than a century after her tragic early death. She attempted to influence the tortured life of Lord Byron and Augusta's daughter Medora Leigh, who bore a striking resemblance to Byron. She raised as well her grandson Ralph and just about raised and certainly loved her granddaughter Anne and her grandson Byron, Lord Ockham, who went his own Byronic way and died two years after his grandmother.

Lady Byron expressed love the way she knew how, through deeds. She advanced the working poor through the Infant Schools and Co-Operative Schools she founded on her shores. She was also the silent benefactor of more unfortunate girls and women in England than we will ever know. Through her friendship with Harriet Beecher Stowe she aided runaway slaves to escape to England after the Fugitive

Slave Act was passed. She spent all her money on others, and the reason she remained wealthy in spite of this was that she understood the future of the railroads grandson Byron was helping to build and had, in managing her estates, the business acumen of her mother and her aunt, Lady Melbourne. She reaped as she sowed.

Two hundred years have passed since that fateful one-year marriage that has entered literature and social history in so many ways. Two hundred years since the birth of Ada, Countess of Lovelace. And almost two hundred since Byron died at Missolonghi. Lady Byron lamented, put on widow's weeds, and was haunted that her husband's last words to her were garbled by fever and could not be discerned. What he wanted to tell her was lost. Twenty-five years later she would lament that Augusta Leigh's last words to her were too feeble to be heard. A second message lost, she wrote.

Who was this woman? We can see parts of her through Augusta Leigh, Anna Jameson, Walter Scott, Joanna Baillie, the Brownings, Robertson of Brighton, Harriet Beecher Stowe, Henry James, Ralph Lovelace; other parts through Byron's searing poetry. Through her eventful life we can see her struggle with the complexity of her motives in her letters, her poetry, her "Statements," her "Conversations," all of which come down to us. So do some delightful personal letters that shine with that "attic wit" Lord Byron satirized. Speaking of her granddaughter: "Anne said one day with some truth as well as humour, 'This world seems to me one great Dining-room.'! She could not see all the philosophy of what she was saying."

We can experience Lady Byron's humanity most fully in her complex relationship with her "two daughters," one born to every advantage, the other raped as a child and betrayed by her own mother. She wasn't a perfect mother; neither was Ada or Medora. Ironically, like Medora, she was a single mother. She raised Ada the best she could and not only learned but accepted her failures at the end, at the same time that her unconditional love shone through in unsentimental yet constantly "cheerful" caregiving to her dying daughter. She raised grandchildren who loved her, a grandson who devoted his life to reclaiming her papers, and a granddaughter who stayed with her till death.

Anna Isabella Noel Byron sealed up, did not destroy or alter, those papers Ralph saved. They tell her truth both in darkness and in light. Though she was ill adept at facing the darkness in her own soul, she did not shield herself from posterity. "If the world is cruel, let it alone," she snapped at Anna Jameson. Lady Byron took her own advice. She made no attempt to censure records and never attempted to shape her life in order to find favor with the world. She was herself. She remained herself. Perhaps the time has come to realize that history is also her story.

NOTES

ꙮ ꙮ

Foreword

xvi "does touch me": Ralph Milbanke Lovelace, *Astarte*, 140–141.

PART ONE

For the majority of quotations in this section, the reader is referred to Ethel Colburn Mayne, *The Life and Letters of Anne Isabella Lady Noel Byron*; Malcolm Elwin, *Lord Byron's Wife*; and Joan Pierson, *The Real Lady Byron*. These authors had access to and rely on the Lovelace-Byron Papers, from which they quote—and duplicate quotes with slight variations. I have checked their sources against the original documents at the Bodleian and refer to published sources to accommodate the reader. Of the three, Malcolm Elwin is the most accurate, but the variations are too slight to be of more than psychological interest. For example, in Lady Byron's "Dearest Duck" letter to Byron after she leaves London, she describes the elegance of her parents' new home. Mayne uses ellipses rather than allowing Annabella to lure her husband to the country via a state-of-the-art "w.c." I reprint the unexpurgated letter as it appears in Elwin.

The reader is also referred to *Byron's "Corbeau Blanc": The Life and Letters of Lady Melbourne*, skillfully edited by Jonathan David Gross, and to Leslie Marchand's *Byron's Letters and Journals*.

References are accessed by page number and the last words in the quotation or relevant passage. The Lovelace-Byron Papers are referred to as Lovelace Papers in the Notes.

Chapter 1: On Her Own

3 "when it began": Malcolm Elwin, *Lord Byron's Wife*, 56 (see the note in Chapter 5 notes for the phrase "cannot be sucked!").

7 throughout her life: Ethel Colburn Mayne, *The Life and Letters of Anne Isabella Lady Noel Byron*, 8; and Elwin, 67.

8 "kindness last night": Joan Pierson, *The Real Lady Byron*, 24.

8 "this year," she wrote: See Pierson, 25; Elwin, 108; and Mayne, 24.

9 For Annabella's dinner party, first impressions of Byron, and thoughts of Caroline Lamb, see Elwin, 108–114; for Annabella's sympathy for his "friendlessness," Mayne, 39.

21 "I left thee Seaham" and "Degraded genius!": Mayne, 12.

22 "habit of deceiving": Gross, ed., *Byron's "Corbeau Blanc,"* 47.

26 "I wish to propose to her": Leslie A. Marchand, *Byron's Letters and Journals*, 1: 73–79. For Annabella's first impression of Byron, also see Elwin, 105–106. For Byron's reaction to rejection by Miss Milbanke, *Byron's Letters and Journals*, 1: 90–95.

29 "I speak from experience": Elwin, 156–157.

Chapter 2: Letters in Love

33 "leave me in peace": Paul Douglass, *Lady Caroline Lamb*, 136.

37 "form your happiness": Pierson, 63–64.

39 "About ten": Mayne, 122.

41 "in his cup": Pierson, 68. Lady Byron would describe this scene to Harriet Beecher Stowe. See Part Three of this biography.

42 "shall be Annabella's": Mayne, 154–156.

Chapter 3: The Underside of the Moon

44 "surely in hell!!": Pierson, 76; and Mayne, 161, widely quoted from the "Statements" about her marriage that Lady Byron wrote, particularly for a proposed memoir of her marriage, during her deep friendship and collaboration with the Reverend Frederick W. Robertson. See my Chapter 11, on. Original "Statements" in Lovelace Papers.

46 "as very troublesome": Elwin, *Lord Byron's Wife*, 254–256.

46 "anguish and horror": Mayne, 164–165.

47 "heart is already mine": Lady Caroline Lamb, *Glenarvon*, 188.

48 "more *malleable*": Mayne, 168–169, taken from Lady Byron's "Statements."

52 "suggested to my mind": Elwin, 256–258; and Mayne, 157–173, for further accounting of the *Moon* constructed from Lady Byron's "Statements" in *Astarte* and the Lovelace Papers.

53 "mischief in private": Elwin, 275.

54 "better even than Thyrza": Pierson, 79.

54 "it takes away. . . .": He had already written *Lara*, which described disillusionment in extended terms. In it, the chieftain Lara resembled Byron in his rage and in his calling on "Nature's self to share the shame" of marking his "fleshly form." That shame of a physical defect "clogged" Lara's soul. Lara is served by a young graceful page from the East with whom he speaks a secret language; no one else can understand them. At the end of the poem, Lara dies and the young page reels and falls, "Scarce breathing more than that he loved so well." Then the beautiful boy discards his robes, lays bare his breasts, revealing that *he* is a *she*. Very convenient given the depth of their love.

54 "spoil him but me": Mayne, 171.

55 Aunt Melbourne had been busy: See letter from Lady Melbourne to Lady Byron, Gross, *Byron's "Corbeau Blanc,"* 288–289.

56 "yours or mine," she responded: Pierson, 77–78.

56 "going to be married" to "To my own room": See Elwin, 292–298.

57 "throbs and yearns": "Memories of Memory," written when Lady Byron was nearing the age of fifty.

58 "on my feelings": A few days later a package arrived from Byron's London jeweler. Two gold broaches. One engraved "A" and the other "B." The "A" broach was for Augusta, not Annabella. Both were inscribed "XXX." "She does not know what these mean," he told Guss with contempt in his voice. XXX was their secret language for their love of each other.

62 "not be 'affronted'" : Elwin, 300.

62 "Reason can hardly balance": Mayne, 189.

63 *"in all ways!"*: Mayne, 181.

Chapter 4: 13 Piccadilly Terrace

73 "from this source": Elwin, *Lord Byron's Wife*, 323.

73 "She listens yet to hear his voice—": Lovelace Papers.

75 "change for me?" through "I feel all your kindness": See Elwin, 325–326.

77 "I acquired in you!": Pierson, 89.

77 "She pinches me": Mayne, 200.

77 "hated by my husband": Elwin, 344–345.

78 "if I can impose it?": Elwin, 346.

79 "In heaven, I hope": Though all three biographers—Mayne, Elwin, and Pierson—who had access to the Lovelace Papers quote this line, they

quote it without its literary significance, leading the reader to a false sense of Annabella's piousness at an emotionally crucial moment. Actually, Annabella immediately recognized Byron's ironic reference to the opening of *Macbeth* and answered him in kind. As unhappy as she was, she was up to a retort—and an exit line—worthy both of her intelligence and her insight into the way her husband's mind worked.

Chapter 5: Dearest Duck

81 The reference to Byron being a "jealous man" and to Annabella's own "strong sense of virtue" come from Frank Doyle's response to Annabella's situation as transmitted in a letter to Annabella from his sister Selina. Elwin quotes it on p. 359 of *Lord Byron's Wife*. Byron's "jealousy," the way he attempted to keep Annabella from her friends, for example, the way he didn't want her to have any contact with Hobhouse, even to write a thank you note, was a form of control not unusual in a mentally abusive relationship.

83 "The temperate are always believed": Elwin, 365.

83 "every day people": *Astarte*, 55–56. Condensed by Mayne, 222.

84 "cannot be sucked!": See Mayne, 199–200 and Malcolm Elwin, *Lord Byron's Family*, 16, for Annabella's state of mind at the time. Elwin's *Lord Byron's Family* will be referenced by title to distinguish it from *Lord Byron's Wife*, referred to throughout by the biographer's name.

84 "married women's rights" was an oxymoron: The author is indebted to S. M. Waddams, *Law, Politics, and the Church of England: The Career of Stephen Lushington, 1782–1873*, for an understanding of what legal steps were necessary to allow an Englishwoman to be granted a Separation of Bed and Board in 1816 (and through most of the century). Without such understanding of the prevailing laws, Lady Byron's refusal to see or talk with Byron after she left 13 Piccadilly by Byron's directive could be—and certainly was—considered "cold." Lady Byron was well aware of this opinion and that it was encouraged by not understanding the laws of her times.

87 "Augusta very uneasy": Annabella had begun a long and intimate correspondence with one of Augusta's friends from childhood days, the Honorable Theresa Villiers, which is documented in the privately published *Lady Byron and the Leighs*, compiled by Lady Byron's grandson Ralph Milbanke, eventually the Second Lord Lovelace, after his grandmother's death.

88   "her own heart!": Elwin, 467.

91   *"now despise her"*: See Elwin, 380–391. In my opinion, Annabella would never have revealed Byron's sexual relationship with her aunt Melbourne, forty years his senior, to her mother, had she not been under severe stress. Not only had she been the cause of her father's letter requesting separation being returned by trusting Augusta; Augusta had compounded Annabella's anger by constantly mentioning Lady Melbourne as the person who could bring about a reconciliation as well as the person who could do harm, through her powerful influence on Byron. Later in her life, in her annotation of *Medwin's Conversations of Lord Byron* that she passed on to Robertson, Annabella named Lady Melbourne as one of the three women who visited the newlywed couple and with whom Byron told Medwin he had former sexual relationships. The sexual relationship seemed known in Lady Melbourne's circle, but has not been acknowledged since.

91   "for his return": Elwin, 404.

94   "both from hence": The Dearest Duck letter can be found in Mayne, 203, and in its full form in Elwin, 351.

94   "ever met with": January 24, 1816, Elwin, 375.

97   "forget it––never!": *Astarte*, 57.

103 such a "villain": See Elwin, 455–458.

107 "Answer to Lord Byron's 'Fare Thee Well'" : Unpublished poem by Lady Byron in the Lovelace Papers.

PART TWO

*Chapter 6: Denial and Isolation—Anger? Bargaining—
Depression—Acceptance? Great Scott!*

111 "One bitter thought": Lady Byron's poem to her daughter, Lovelace Papers.

112 the Honorable Theresa Villiers: *Lady Noel Byron and the Leighs*, 41–42.

115 "near a Father's heart": "On Ada's First Birthday," Lovelace Papers.

115 "On a Mother Being Told She Was an Unnatural One": by Lady Byron, Lovelace Papers.

117 "be of service": *Lady Byron and the Leighs*, 64.

118 "I cannot send you Ada's smile": Poem to her mother, by Lady Byron, Lovelace Papers.

122 his positive review: *Familiar Letters of Sir Walter Scott*, 414–419.

123 "On Seaham—1817": by Lady Byron, Lovelace papers.

124 "the warmest welcome": Mayne, 273.

125 "at the same time": Mayne, 273–274.

126 "she seemed destined": Pierson, 141–142.

127 "me these sensations": Pierson, 142.

127 "saved me from myself": *Astarte*, 152.

130 "under her direction": Elwin, *Lord Byron's Family*, 178.

Chapter 7: Educating Ada

132 "I cannot say": *Lady Byron and the Leighs*, 67.

134 "be happy together": Elwin, *Lord Byron's Family*, 215–216.

135 "Ada will hers": Thomas Medwin, *Medwin's Conversations with Lord Byron*, 58.

136 "welcome to laugh": Mayne, 283.

140 "good to others": See Mayne, "Money Matters, Appendix II," 474–476.

141 "as a brother": Toole, 23–25.

146 "rivers, lakes, etc, etc, etc.": Toole, 32.

146 "like the waltz": Toole, 43.

148 "making of pins": James Gleick, *The Information*, 79–80.

149 "compared with numbers": Gleick, 80–81.

150 "to stultify oneself": Langley Moore, *Ada*, 50–51.

151 "of my own heart": Toole, 58–59.

152 "birds less—shall I?": Langley Moore, *Ada*, 73.

156 "mind of Augustus": Douglass, 270.

156 "he was gone": Douglass, 290.

157 "not for the public": Lovelace Papers.

159 "you and Ada": January 8, 1838, Lovelace Papers.

159 "little bird at all": Toole, 109.

Chapter 8: Educating England

162 "price 4d" to "as sympathising friends": See "History of Industrial Schools," by Lady Noel Byron, Appendix IV, Mayne, 479–492.

165 Lady Byron's plans for Ealing Grove, in Lovelace Papers.

Chapter 9: The Half Sisters

174 The information gleaned from Medora Leigh's "Autobiography" from *Medora Leigh: A History and an Autobiography*, ed. Charles Mackay; and Catherine Turney, *Byron's Daughter*. The manuscript exists at the Morgan Library and Museum. I thank the staff for access to it.

178 "I will to be but clay": unpublished poem sent in letter to Anna Jameson, Lovelace Papers.

179 "on deck at night": From shipboard letter to Anna Jameson, Lovelace Papers.

179 "was doing wrong": Medora Leigh, *Autobiography*.

180 "die away from him": Medora Leigh, *Autobiography*.

183 These letters of Augusta Leigh to Trevanion and to her daughter exist today in the Lovelace Papers and can be read in Mayne, 341–346.

185 "my adopted child": Letter from Paris, October 16, 1840, in Lovelace Papers.

187 what was going on: Augusta's letter, in Mayne, 349–350.

187 "Leave her in peace!": Paris, January 20, 1841, Pierson, 219.

188 "misrepresented to you": Pierson, 220.

190 "too imaginative": Toole, 118–119. Ada wrote this seven years before George Boole formed "the foundation for our being able to program games on our modern computer," in 1847, Toole wrote.

191 "going to Paris": Letters of October 28 and November 26, 1840, in Toole, 125–126.

191 "and my own": February 6, 1841, in Toole, 144–145.

191 "the Great Future": Toole, 146.

193 "come for that": February 27, 1841, in Toole, 153–154.

193 "*without reserve*": March 3, 1841, in Toole, 156.

193 "without foundation": Langley Moore, *Ada*, 373.

194 "on the Avis": April 8, 1841, in Toole, 161.

195 "Your personified Bon-bon": Mayne, 353–354.

Chapter 10: Intermezzo:
Lady Byron Time-Travels on the Brownings' Moon

196 See my biography *Dared and Done: The Marriage of Elizabeth Barrett and Robert Browning* for a full explication of both the Brownings' racial heritage and of their rush to Italy after their secret marriage. The quotations from these pages not noted below are from *Dared and Done*, "Riding an Enchanted Horse," 75–84.

197 "my dear Byron": Langley Moore, *The Late Lord Byron*, 506–507.

202 and some hens: Medwin, 9–10.

203 "much that is absurd": Jameson, *Winter Studies*, iBook, 310.

204 "its feverish glow": *Letters of Anna Jameson to Ottilie von Goethe*, edited by G. H. Needler, and referred to as Needler, Letter 7.

205 "shame overpowers me": *Anna Jameson: Letters and Friendships, 1812–1860*, ed. Mrs. Steuart Erskine, 128.

205 "if we were more together": Needler, Letter 14.

206 "I *may* not speak": Unpublished poem of Lady Byron, Lovelace Papers.

206 according to Joan Pierson: Pierson, 205–207.

207 of marriage: The love life of Charlotte Cushman and Harriet Hosmer and other women who loved women is explored in Julia Markus, *Across an Untried Sea.*

208 duty as a wife: Thomas, *Love and Work Enough*, 100.

210 would eventually regret: See Pierson, 224.

212 "a comfort to her": August 20, 1840, Lovelace Papers.

215 "in the expression": Thomas, 158–159.

215 "sympathies were with Satan": Lovelace Papers.

216 "*yours* to command": Thomas, 153. Also see Thomas, 157, for a letter in which Jameson speaks of the education of "girls" and asks Lady Byron, "Is not the Hofwyl system applicable . . . for their especial duties?"

217 "mischief and misery": See Thomas, 152–159, for a concise and always intelligent view of Jameson's relationship with Medora and of her feminism.

218 Medora's impressions of Anna Jameson are revealed in undated letters to Lady Byron in the Lovelace Papers.

223 "never exacted anything in return": July 4, 1842, Lovelace Papers.

224 "*because it was proper*": *Invisible Friends: The Correspondence of Elizabeth Barrett Barrett and Benjamin Robert Haydon*, ed. Williard Bissell Pope, 74. With thanks to Jack Wasserman for pointing out EBB and Haydon's mutual dislike of Lady Byron found in this correspondence.

227 "of them—Lord Byron": Thomas Moore, *Letters and Journals of Lord Byron*, 271.

231 "to be forgiven": Turney, *Byron's Daughter*, 274.

Chapter 11: Attempting Amends at the White Hart

233 "at some future day": See Mayne, 395. She leaves out "etc."

236 "so good a peeress": Thomas Moore, 250.

238 a notebook as she posted: The notebook exists at the New York Public Library.

242 "Rev'd G. Wellesley!": March 9, n.d., Lovelace Papers.

242 "I love him": Mayne, 398–399.

243 "'how beautiful to feel!'" : July 18, 1850, in *Astarte*, 346.

243 "by my silence": Langley Moore, *Ada*, 271.

243 "channel of a Debacle!": Lovelace Papers.

244 "confirmed your supposition": See Langley Moore, *Ada*, 263–265, and Mayne, 404.

245 "mutual truthfulness": Mayne, 406.

248 hardly Augusta's style: See Pierson, 225; and Turney, 252.

249 "afraid of myself": See Bakewell, 268–270.

250 "harshness of feeling": Bakewell, 372, and Langley Moore, 336–337.

250 she told Robertson: "Twenty-six moneylenders presented their claims after Augusta's death" (Pierson, 258). For the next three years Lady Byron contributed more than Augusta's half siblings toward niece Emily's keep.

Chapter 12: Enduring Motherhood

252 "already acquainted with": Toole, 257–258.

253 "be *thought* so": To her mother, from Ockham, February 1841, Lovelace Papers.

253 "winner of the Derby": Toole, 357.

254 "all my *wicked forefathers*": Langley Moore, *Ada*, 270.

255 "'ever shall love you'—": [September, 1850], Lovelace Papers.

255 "*unjust* and *vindictive*": September 23, 1850, Lovelace Papers.

257 "in more ways than one": Toole, 346.

259 "as I gave her *hundreds*": July 1, 1852, in letter to Lushington, Lovelace Papers.

260 "so little by the nearest!": To Anna Jameson, Summer 1852, Lovelace Papers.

260 "he *wishes* to act right": February 9, 1852, Lovelace Papers.

262 up and down: Langley Moore, *Ada*, 288.

262 "in other ways—": Lovelace Papers.

265 "difficult to contend against": On July 18, 1853, Lady Byron began her "Journal Letter," an extraordinary account of her day-to-day relationship with her dying daughter, which she sent to Emily Fitzhugh. (The letter just quoted was written on July 23.) The journal letters in the Lovelace Papers extend to November 29, 1852, when, after Ada's death, she writes "To see clearly too late . . ." They are quoted by date throughout as the drama unfolds, and all quotes are from the Lovelace Papers.

265 "You must be mistaken": See Langley Moore, *Ada*, 307–310. These letters of Greig and Lord Lovelace are from the Lovelace Papers.

267 "should represent Educational America": April 21, 1849, Lovelace Papers.

269 "your injustice to me": December 17, 1852, Lovelace Papers.

270 "her spirit—*I knew*": To Lushington, quoted in Langley Moore, *Ada*, 326–327.

278 "concealing her transgressions": January 7, 1853, Lovelace Papers.

279 "of my trouble": February 1853, Lovelace Papers.

280 "jewel transactions of 1852": January 12, 1853, Lovelace Papers.

PART THREE
Chapter 13: Strange History

283 "change to cypresses": Mayne, 422.

284 "He is gone": Letters to Mrs. George Lamb (Caro George), Brighton, August 15 [1853], Lovelace Papers.

284 "I was there" through the minister's voice rising, from a letter to Mrs. Lamb on August 22, the day of the funeral, Lovelace Papers.

286 Jameson's audacity: Robertson, *Life and Letters*, 2: 38–39.

287 "second in *mine*" through Anna Jameson's letter to "Dearest Noel" (with my addition of phrases via Lovelace Papers) can be found in Mayne, 380–383.

287 "quite deserves one": Thomas, 216–217.

Chapter 14: The Lost Chapter

299 "as a token of love": All quotations from Harriet Beecher Stowe, *Lady Byron Vindicated*.

301 "act on the world?": February 6, 1859.

302 Byron's wife: *Lady Byron Vindicated*, 113–114.

303 "Stowe's Article": A handwritten copy of the text for the *Times* dated September 1, 1869, by grandson Ralph is in the Lovelace Papers.

306 "prominent topics of debate": Joan D. Hedrick, *Harriet Beecher Stowe: A Life*, 354. See her fine discussion continuing in the next pages.

Chapter 15: Lady Byron and Her Grandson

308 he had taken: Ralph took his grandmother's family name, "Milbanke." The title Baroness Wentworth devolved to her. Though she rarely used it, Ralph did use it when it devolved to him.

308 "depressing education": Lovelace, *Ralph Earl of Lovelace*, 5.

309 "at the age of eight": Mary Countess of Lovelace, *Ralph Earl of Lovelace: A Memoir* [1920], 117.

310 "moral destruction": Lovelace, *Ralph Earl of Lovelace*, 18–19.

312 "or your mother": Lovelace Papers.

312 "secure from ridicule": Lovelace, *Ralph Earl of Lovelace*, 91.

314 "nothing for it but patience": Lovelace, *Ralph Earl of Lovelace*, 128.

314 an American Byron: In James's introduction to the 1903 New York edition of the novella, he discusses this possibility.

316 "already formed in his mind": Lovelace, *Ralph Earl of Lovelace*, 142–143.

317 "hand to *you!*": Lovelace, *Ralph Earl of Lovelace*, 150–152.

318 "happiest of Lovelace's life": Lovelace, *Ralph Earl of Lovelace*, 156.

318 "without fear or pain": Lovelace, *Ralph Earl of Lovelace*, 164.

SELECTED PRINTED SOURCES

Anna Jameson: Letters and Friendships, 1812–1860. Edited by Mrs. Steurat Erskine. New York: E. P. Dutton & Co., n.d.

Babbage, Charles. *Memoir of the Life and Labours of the Late Charles Babbage, Esq.* Edited by H. W. Buston. Cambridge, Mass.: MIT Press, 1988.

———. *Passages from the Life of a Philosopher.* Edited by Martin Campbell-Kelly. New Brunswick, NJ: Rutgers University Press, 1994.

Bakewell, Michael, and Melissa Bakewell, *Augusta Leigh, Byron's Half-Sister: A Biography.* London: Pimlico, 2002.

Barber, Thomas Gerrard. *Byron—and Where He Is Buried.* Hucknall, UK: Henry Morley & Sons, 1939.

Browning, Elizabeth Barrett. *Aurora Leigh.* Chicago: Cassandra Editions, 1979.

Byron's Poetry and Prose. A Norton Critical Edition. Edited by Alice Levine. New York and London: W. W. Norton & Co., 2010.

Byron and Women [and Men]. Edited by Peter Cochran. Newcastle upon Tyne, UK: Cambridge Scholars Publishing, 2010.

Cecil, Lord David. *Melbourne.* 2nd ed. New York: Bob-Merrill Co., 1954.

Chapman, John. S. *Byron and the Honourable Augusta Leigh.* New Haven and London: Yale University Press. 1975.

Daiches, David. *Sir Walter Scott and His World.* Thames & Hudson: London, 1971.

Douglass, Paul. *Lady Caroline Lamb.* New York: Palgrave Macmillan, 2004.

Doyle, Sir Francis H. *Reminiscences and Opinions of Sir Francis Hastings Doyle, 1815–1885.* New York: D. Appleton & Co., 1887.

Elwin, Malcolm. *Lord Byron's Family.* Southhampton, UK: Camelot Press, 1975.

———. *Lord Byron's Wife.* New York: Harcourt, Brace & World, 1963.

Familiar Letters of Sir Walter Scott. Edited by David Douglas. Vol. 1. Boston: Houghton Mifflin & Co., 1894.

Fox, John C. *Byron Mystery*. London: Grant Richards, 1924.

Gleick, James. *The Information*. New York: Pantheon Books, 2011.

Godwin, William. *Caleb Williams*. London: Penguin Books, 1987.

Gross, Jonathan David, ed. *Byron's "Corbeau Blanc": The Life and Letters of Lady Melbourne*. Houston: Rice University Press, 1997.

Guiccioli, Contessa Teresa. *My Recollections of Lord Byron*. London: Richard Bentley, 1869.

Gunn, Peter. *My Dearest Augusta: A Biography of Augusta Leigh, Lord Byron's Half-Sister*. New York: Atheneum, 1968.

Hedrick, Joan D. *Harriet Beecher Stowe: A Life*. New York and Oxford: Oxford University Press, 1994.

Hobhouse's Diary. Edited by Peter Cochran. Online, "Peter Cochran's Website." Also a fund of information on Byron matters.

Invisible Friends: The Correspondence of Elizabeth Barrett Barrett and Benjamin Robert Haydon, 1842–1845. Edited by Willard Bissell Pope. Cambridge, MA: Harvard University Press, 1972.

Jameson, Anna. *Winter Studies and Summer Rambles in Canada*. Edited and with an afterword by Clara Thomas. [Original title restored.] Kindle Edition.

Johnston, Judith. *Anna Jameson: Victorian, Feminist, Woman of Letters*. Aldershot, UK, and Brookfield, VT: Scolar Press, 1997.

Lady Blessington's Conversations of Lord Byron. Edited by Ernest J. Lovell, Jr., Princeton, NJ: Princeton University Press, 1969.

Lady Noel Byron and the Leighs. Strictly Private. Printed for the Descendants of Lord and Lady Byron. London, 1887.

Lamb, Lady Caroline. *Glenarvon*. Kansas City, MO: Valancourt Books, 2007.

Langley Moore, Doris. *Ada, Countess of Lovelace*. New York: Harper & Row, 1977.

———. *The Late Lord Byron*. Philadelphia and New York: J. B. Lippincott Co., 1961.

———. *Lord Byron: Accounts Rendered*. New York: Harper & Row, 1974.

Letters of Anna Jameson to Ottilie von Goethe. Edited by G. H. Needler. London, New York, and Toronto: Oxford University Press, 1939.

Lovelace, Mary Countess of. *Ralph Earl of Lovelace: A Memoir*. London: Christophers, 1920.

[Lovelace] Milbanke, Ralph Gordon Noel. *Astarte*. Edited by Mary, Countess of Lovelace, New York: Charles Scribner's Sons, 1921.

Macpherson, Gerardine. *Memoirs of the Life of Anna Jameson*. Boston: Roberts Bros., 1878.

Marchand, Leslie A. *Byron: A Biography*. 3 vols. New York: Alfred A. Knopf, 1957.

———. *Byron's Letters and Journals*. Vols. 1, 3, 4, 7, 8. Cambridge, MA: Harvard University Press, 1974–.

Markus, Julia. *Across an Untried Sea*. New York: Alfred A. Knopf, 2000.

———. *Dared and Done: The Marriage of Elizabeth Barrett and Robert Browning*. New York: Alfred A. Knopf, 1995.

Martineau, Harriet. *Biographical Sketches*. New York: Leypoldt & Holt, 1869.

Maurois, André. *Byron*. New York: D. Appleton & Co., 1930.

Mayne, Ethel Colburn. *The Life and Letters of Anne Isabella Lady Noel Byron*. New York: Charles Scribner's Sons, 1929.

Medora Leigh: A History and an Autobiography. Edited by Charles Mackay. London: Richard Bentley, 1869 and New York: Harper & Brothers, 1870.

Medwin, Thomas. *Medwin's Conversations of Lord Byron*. Edited by Ernest J. Lovell, Jr. Princeton, NJ: Princeton University Press, 1966.

Moore, Thomas. *Letters and Journals of Lord Byron with Notices of his Life*. London: John Murray, 1920.

Pierson, Joan. *The Real Lady Byron*. London: Robert Hale, 1992.

Robertson, Frederick William. *Life and Letters of Fred. W. Robertson, M.A.; Incumbent of Trinity Chapel, Brighton, 1847–53*. Elibron Classics, 2006; facsimile of London: Henry S. King & Co., 1872.

———. *Life and Letters . . .* Vol. 2. Edited by S. A. Brooke. General Books reprint, 2009.

———. *Sermons Preached at Brighton*. Third Series. London: Kegan Paul, Trench & Co., 1884.

Stowe, Harriet Beecher. *Lady Byron Vindicated*. Boston: Fields, Osgood & Co., 1870.

Thomas, Clara. *Love and Work Enough: The Life of Anna Jameson*. Toronto: University of Toronto Press, 1967.

Toole, Betty A. *Ada, the Enchantress of Numbers*. Mill Valley, CA: Strawberry Press, 1992.

Turney, Catherine. *Byron's Daughter*. New York: Charles Scribner's Sons, 1972.

Waddams, S. M. *Law, Politics, and the Church of England: The Career of Stephen Lushington, 1782–1873*. Cambridge: Cambridge University Press, 1992.

Winstone, H. V. F. *Lady Anne Blunt*. Manchester: Barzan Publishing, 2008.

ILLUSTRATION CREDITS

Page 6: Portrait of Lady Milbanke. Reprinted with the permission of Pollinger Ltd.

Page 6: Portrait of Sir Ralph Milbanke. Reprinted with the permission of Pollinger Ltd.

Page 6: Portrait of Annabella Milbanke after a portrait by John Hoppner at Ockham Park, 1802. Reprinted with the permission of Pollinger Ltd.

Page 17: Portrait of Lady Caroline Lamb by Thomas Phillips, 1813.

Page 18: Lady Byron, after a portrait by Charles Hayter, 1811.

Page 23: Duchess of Devonshire, Lady Melbourne, and Mrs. Dawson Damer as the Three Witches from *Macbeth* by Daniel Gardner, 1775.

Page 24: George Gordon Byron, 6th Baron Byron, by Richard Westall, 1813.

Page 28: Portrait of Elizabeth Lamb (née Milbanke), Viscountess Melbourne, by Braun, Clement & Co, after John Hoppner. Late nineteenth to early twentieth century.

Page 30: Princess Charlotte and Prince Leopold at the opera by William Thomas Fry after George Dawe, 1816.

Page 51: Portrait of Catherine Gordon by Thomas Stewardson, ca. 1765–1811.

Page 68: Drawing of the Hon. Augusta Leigh by Sir George Hayter, ca. 1812.

Page 69: Engraving of Lady Byron, Anne Isabella Milbanke, after portrait by W. J. Newton, ca. 1840.

Page 95: Portrait of Stephen Lushington by W. Holl, 1824.

Page 101: *The Separation* by Isaac Robert Cruikshank, 1816.

Page 104: Portrait of Caroline St. Jules.

Page 105: Portrait of William Lamb, 2nd Viscount Melbourne, by Sir Thomas Lawrence, ca. 1805.

Page 119: Lord Byron in Albanian Dress by Thomas Phillips, 1835.

Page 126: Sir Walter Scott in the Rhymer's Glen by Edwin Landseer, 1833.

Page 145: Portrait of Ada Byron by Count D'Orsay.

Page 145: Detail of engraving of Henson's "Aerial Steam Carriage," 1843.

Page 153: Detail of portrait of Ada, Countess of Lovelace, after the portrait by Margaret Sarah Carpenter at Ockham Park, 1836.

Page 158: Portrait of William Lamb, 2nd Viscount Melbourne, by John Partridge, 1844.

Page 161: Engraving of Lady Byron in her prime.

Page 190: Sketch of Charles Babbage by William Brockedon, 1840.

Page 192: Sketch of William, Earl of Lovelace. Reprinted with the permission of Pollinger Limited.

Page 204: Portrait of Ottilie von Goethe, 1859.

Page 211: Portrait of Ada, Countess of Lovelace by A. E. Chalon, ca. 1838.

Page 212: Portrait of Medora Leigh in Spanish costume.

Page 214: Anna Brownell Jameson (née Murphy) by Henry Adlard, after Denis Brownell Murphy, 1810.

Page 220: Engraving of Anna Brownell Jameson, 1873.

Page 225: Daguerrotype of Medora leaving England. Reprinted with the permission of Pollinger Ltd.

Page 240: Portrait of the Reverend Frederick W. Robertson from a daguerreotype by William Edward Kilburn, 1850.

Page 261: Portrait of Stephen Lushington, age eighty, by Holman Hunt, 1862.

Page 263: Ada at the piano by Henry Phillips, 1852. Reprinted with the permission of Pollinger Ltd.

Page 275: Photograph of Byron, Viscount Ockham.

Page 276: Sketch of Ada on her deathbed by Lady Byron, 1852. Reprinted with the permission of Pollinger Ltd.

Page 291: Photograph of Lady Byron in old age.

Page 301: Photograph of Harriet Beecher Stowe, 1852.

Page 311: Photograph of Lady Anne Blunt with her Arabian Mare, ca. 1900.

Page 313: Portrait of Ralph Milbanke, 2nd Earl of Lovelace, 1905.

ACKNOWLEDGMENTS

I am deeply grateful to Colin Harris, Superintendent of Reading Rooms, for his invaluable help as I read from the Lovelace-Byron deposit held by the Bodleian Libraries, University of Oxford. He and his staff offered the most speedy and gracious service at a time when they were in their temporary quarters. The experience at Oxford was made memorable, as well, by my Visiting Fellowship at Harris Manchester College and to the warm welcome of Principal Dr. Ralph Waller and his wife Carol. Many thanks to them, and to librarian Sue Killoran for always being an invaluable source and help in gathering information there. Thanks as well to the entire staff at Harris Manchester, who made me feel at home. Burns Night shall never be forgotten.

The Lovelace Byron Papers remain the main source for the life of Lady Byron, and it is through her enormous archive at the Bodleian that a well-rounded narrative of her later life can be reconstructed. The papers come down through Lady Byron's maternal line, and I thank the present Earl of Lytton for fascinating conversations about his ancestors and for my access to the papers.

Various poems and texts by Lovelace Byron are reproduced by permission of Pollinger Limited (www.pollingerltd.com) on behalf of the Estate of Lovelace Byron. I thank Sharon Rubin, Permissions Manager, for her help in this matter.

Thanks as well to Elizabeth Denlinger, Curator, and Charles Carter, Assistant Curator of the Pforzheimer Collection, New York Public Library, and to the librarian and the staff at the Morgan Library & Museum on the occasions when I consulted primary sources at those institutions. My fellow board members of the Bryon Society of America have always been supportive, and I thank Marsha Manns for all she has done for the Society and for including me as a member of the library committee advising Drew University in regard to the Byron Society Papers that have found such an inviting home there. I thank Andrew D. Scrimgeour, Dean of Libraries Emeritus, at Drew and his staff, as well as Lisa Napolitan for her generosity and talent in putting up my website, juliamarkuswrites.com.

Hofstra University has been a constant source of encouragement and support, offering me special leaves to pursue my research, travel, and research grants, as well as financial contributions toward the illustrations that enhance this biography. I thank the administration of Hofstra and my colleagues for their encouragement and good will.

To my friend and colleague Dr. Alice Levine, Byron scholar and intellectual light, I offer thanks for those lively dinner conversations about Lord and Lady Bryon that were the inspiration for my writing this book. I previously had no idea of how deep the prejudice against Lady Byron remained through the centuries. Alice also generously read the biography while it was in manuscript form and offered her insights and advice, which were a great help, though she is in no way to be blamed for any of its failings. I claim them; they are mine.

Many thanks to my editor, Jill Bialosky, whose brilliant editing strengthened my text in so many ways. I am also grateful for her faith in this work from its earliest stages. It was and is greatly appreciated. I am also happily indebted to the constant and kind support of her assistant, Angie Shih. To my wonderful literary representative, Charlotte Sheedy, who has been there for me in every way, and for those encouraging breakfasts and conversations—mille grazie.

The yearly conferences of the International Association of Byron Societies have been a constant inspiration. I thank all the friends I have made during them—including Professor Innes Merabishvili, President of the Byron Society of Georgia, and Rosa Florou, President of the Messolonghi Byron Society. To Lord Lytton and the present Lord Byron, whose interest and encouragement inspire us—much gratitude for all you do.

INDEX

&c &c

Page numbers in *italics* refer to illustrations.
Page numbers beginning with 323 refer to endnotes.